ECONOMIC HISTORY

THE COMMERCIAL RELATIONS OF ENGLAND AND PORTUGAL

INTERNATIONAL TRADE

THE COMMERCIAL RELATIONS OF ENGLAND AND PORTUGAL

V.M. SHILLINTON AND A.B. WALLIS CHAPMAN

Routledge
Taylor & Francis Group
LONDON AND NEW YORK

First published in 1928

Published in 2006 by
Routledge
2 Park Square, Milton Park, Abingdon, Oxfordshire OX14 4RN
711 Third Avenue, New York, NY 10017

First issued in paperback 2014

Routledge is an imprint of the Taylor and Francis Group, an informa business

British Library Cataloguing in Publication Data
A CIP catalogue record for this book
is available from the British Library

The Commercial Relations of England and Portugal
ISBN 0-415-38301-3 (volume)
ISBN 0-415-37978-4 (subset)
ISBN 0-415-28619-0 (set)

ISBN 13: 978-1-138-86539-6 (pbk)
ISBN 13: 978-0-415-38301-1 (hbk)

Routledge Library Editions: Economic History

THE COMMERCIAL RELATIONS OF ENGLAND AND PORTUGAL

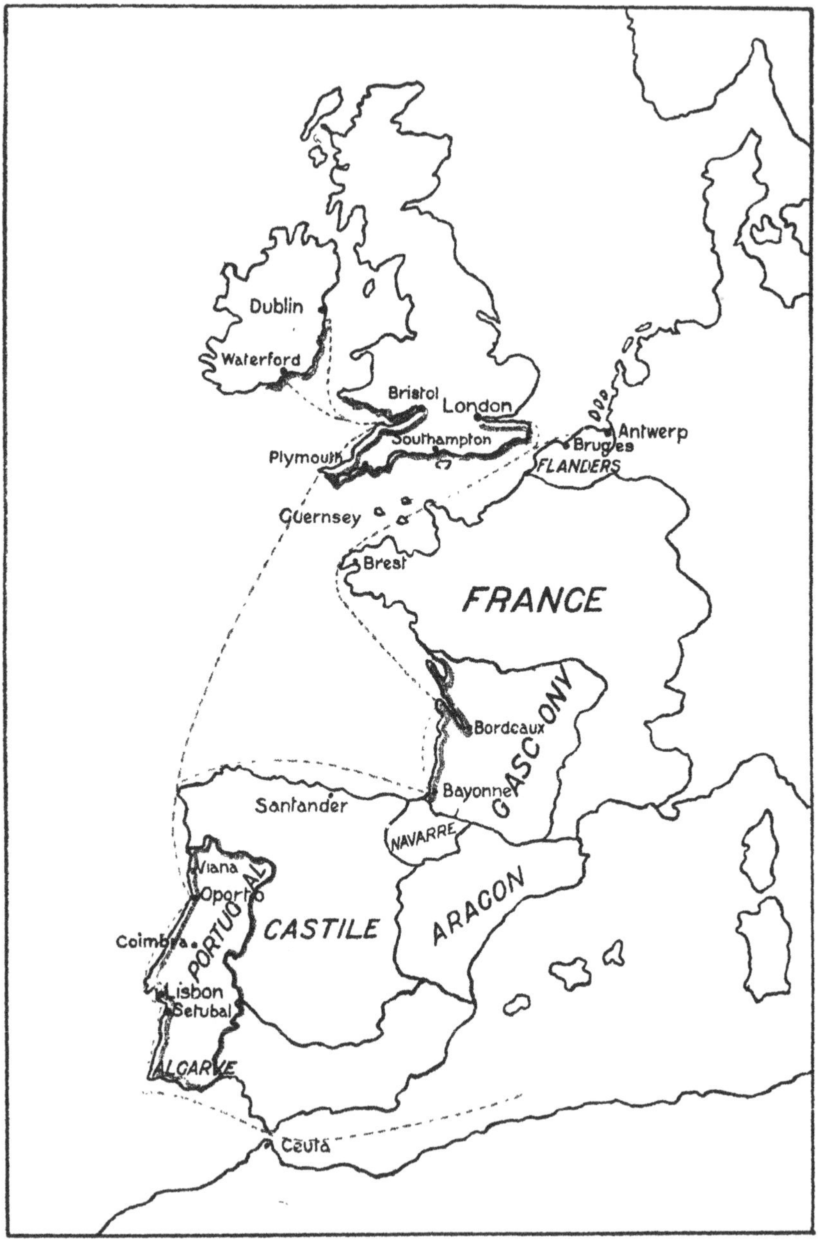

Dublin
Waterford
Bristol
London
Southampton
Plymouth
Antwerp
Bruges
FLANDERS
Guernsey
Brest
FRANCE
Bordeaux
GASCONY
Bayonne
Santander
NAVARRE
ARAGON
Viana
Oporto
PORTUGAL
CASTILE
Coimbra
Lisbon
Setubal
ALGARVE
Ceuta

THE COMMERCIAL RELATIONS OF ENGLAND AND PORTUGAL

BY

V. M. SHILLINGTON

(CAIRNES RESEARCH STUDENT OF GIRTON COLLEGE, CAMBRIDGE)

AND

A. B. WALLIS CHAPMAN

(HONOURS SCHOOL OF MODERN HISTORY, OXFORD)

LONDON

GEORGE ROUTLEDGE & SONS, LIMITED

NEW YORK: E. P. DUTTON & CO.

AUTHORS' PREFACE

THE authors desire to express their sincere thanks to Mr H. P. BIGGAR, for his kindness in making enquiries about the archives at Lisbon; to Mr C. R. BEAZLEY, for many valuable suggestions, and in particular to Mr HUBERT HALL; of H.M. Public Record Office, for the untiring help and encouragement which they received from him during the preparation of this book.

Inadvertently omitted from Title-page:

Theses approved for the degree of Doctor of Science (Economics) in the University of London.

INTRODUCTION

AMONGST the most important chapters in the commercial history of a nation, during any given period of time, must necessarily be those dealing with the commercial relations maintained during that time with the various foreign nations, through whose co-operation or rivalry its own trade has advanced towards the attainment of fuller limits. With regard to England, a good deal is already known respecting the commercial transactions carried on during the Middle Ages with Flanders, the Italian cities, or the Hanse towns; but, on the other hand, the trade relations of the English of this period with other important countries still remain more or less obscure, and this is especially noticeable in the case of Portugal. Possibly this obscurity is due to the small part played by the Portuguese in the political history of Europe. More probably, however, it may be attributed to the want of those monetary dealings with the English kings, which made the Italians, for instance, so famous in English commercial history. Be this as it may, the fact remains that the Portuguese have received comparatively very little notice in connection with England's foreign trade in the Middle Ages.

Yet, as the present writer has attempted to show in the following chapters, the mediæval commercial relations between England and Portugal were not without their importance. In the absence of sufficiently detailed statistics as to exports and imports, it is, of course, impossible to compare the bulk or value of the trade carried on during this period between England and Lisbon with that carried on for instance, between England and Genoa or Bruges; but it is clear that from a very early period the English and Portuguese merchants were well known to each other, and that as the prosperity of their respective countries increased, the extent and importance of the commerce carried on between them increased also.

Apart from the actual importance to mediæval England of her trade with Portugal, the commercial relations of the two countries during this period have an interest entirely their own. This is due partly to the close political alliance that existed during the same time between England and Portugal, and partly to the romance attaching to the commercial history of the latter country on account of the brilliant achievements of her illustrious sons, Prince Henry the Navigator, and Vasco da Gama.

The Anglo-Portuguese alliance, of which the origins can be traced back to the time of the crusades, and which lasted practically during the whole mediæval period, is almost unique in the history of the Middle Ages for the care with which it was maintained, for its popularity in both countries, and for its beneficial results to both parties. Though the present essay is not directly concerned with the subject of the early Portuguese navigators and their successes, yet these had also an important effect in furthering the growth of trade between England and

Portugal. It was a fortunate coincidence for the English that the country, which by virtue of having discovered the long-sought sea route to India, emerged at the end of the fifteenth century into the foremost rank of the commercial nations of the world, was one with which their government was so firmly in alliance, and in which they had already received valuable royal grants of trading privileges and exemptions from taxes.

Besides the interest bestowed on the subject by the nature of the political relations between England and Portugal, and by the important part played by the latter in the world's commercial history, the amount and character of the original material obtainable for the purpose seemed on the whole to warrant a study of the mediæval commercial relations of these two countries. Disappointing though it is in many respects, as, for instance, with regard to the environment of the Portuguese merchants living in England, for trading or other purposes, on which subject information is almost entirely wanting[1], yet on some points, notably the conditions of life and trade for the English merchants in Portugal in the fifteenth century, it affords much valuable information[2].

The study of the later commercial relations of England and Portugal is chiefly interesting as an

[1] See fol. 14 below note (5). See, however, *Ancient Petition*, 10810, transcribed in Appendix II. No. 8, which contains an account of a Portuguese merchant and his belongings at Sandwich.

[2] Two series of petitions, presented to the King of Portugal by the English merchants in Lisbon, in 1454 and 1458 respectively, still preserved among the Portuguese archives, and frequently referred to below, are specially valuable in this connection.

illustration of the immense development of England's foreign and colonial trade during that period.

As in the *earlier* period, it is difficult to obtain direct evidence as to the total value of the trade. Not till the eighteenth century are there any details available to show its volume, or the proportion it bore to the rest of England's foreign commerce; and even the figures given in the Board of Trade returns, which then began to appear, must be received with considerable caution. On the other hand, if accuracy of detail is unattainable, much general information of great interest may be gathered from the various *State Papers.* Roughly speaking, the *Domestic and Foreign State Papers* supply the bulk of what is known for the sixteenth and seventeenth centuries; while the *Board of Trade Commercial MSS.* are the chief source of information for the eighteenth.

In addition to these sources valuable supplementary information can be obtained from the various collections of MSS. in the British Museum—especially the *Cotton and Lansdowne Collections.* Further details can also be found in the numerous pamphlets put forward by the manufacturers, who looked to the government for the protection of their trade. These pamphlets are especially useful for the period 1690 to 1710. On the other hand, the opinions of persons trading from Portugal to England appear not only in communications from the Portuguese government, but in the reports from the consuls of the English factories at Lisbon and Oporto.

These factories, from the beginning of the seventeenth century onward, play a very important part in the commerce of the two nations[1]. The gradual monopoly of Portuguese commerce, and the Portuguese revolt against them, forms the main thread in the story of the trade between England and Portugal from 1654 to 1756, or even later. The growth of the factories, however, as well as other commercial phenomena, was deeply affected by the manner in which political and economic motives reacted upon each other at this time.

In the sixteenth century, colonial rivalry had added another element of such importance that it nearly drove the old allies to war; but by 1640 this had ceased to be a pressing question in Anglo-Portuguese relations. England had established her foothold in the east, while Portugal was still under the yoke of Spain, and henceforth disturbances in India only indirectly affected European policy; while, so far as America was concerned, a direct trade between England and Brazil was never seriously demanded by the English government as England's share in that commerce was absorbed by her merchants in Portugal.

Thus, commercial beliefs and political necessities could work unchecked. Both worked in the same direction. England valued her commerce with Portugal, because it was a trade in which she imported little and exported much, while Portugal's political necessities rendered the support of England vital to her; and this situation lasted till near the end of the eighteenth century.

In dealing with the earlier part of the subject, it has seemed desirable to begin with a brief sketch of the political relations of the two countries, tracing

[1] Part II., see especially chaps. iii., v., and vi.

the progress of the friendship which finally ripened into a close alliance. In the two following chapters an account is given of the growth of the trade between England and Portugal, noticing the measure of protection and encouragement enjoyed at various times by the merchants engaged in this traffic, with such other circumstances as from time to time affected the development of the trade. The two remaining chapters of Part I. are occupied with details omitted from the foregoing account. The first of these chapters [chap. iv.] deals with certain risks attending the trade, and the last chapter, among other conditions of the trade, attempts a description of the life of the English cloth merchants in Lisbon in the fifteenth century.

The later relations of England and Portugal, on the other hand, appear to fall into four parts. From 1487 to 1580 the dominating motive is mainly colonial, and England is at once the inferior and the aggressive power. From 1580 to 1640 Portugal had no independent existence, and though Anglo-Portuguese trade continued, the English government could not, of course, adopt a definite and separate policy towards a Spanish province. Thirdly, from 1640 to almost the middle of the eighteenth century, commercial and political motives alike combine to secure the predominance of England over her old ally. Finally, from about 1756 onwards, the development of Portuguese resources, the growth of the Brazil cotton industry, the change in England's commercial policy due to Pitt's adoption of the views of Adam Smith, all tended to effect a not undesirable change. A more equitable adjustment of the Anglo-Portuguese relations seemed to be almost in sight, when Portugal was suddenly overwhelmed by the flood of the French invasion.

Part II. of this book is an attempt to explain and support these views of the relations of England with Portugal between the years 1487 and 1807. A list of sources will be found below, and the Appendix contains text of some hitherto unpublished documents, which, however, are mere selections from a vast mass of inedited sources.

BIBLIOGRAPHY AND LIST OF MANUSCRIPT SOURCES

PART I

MEDIÆVAL HISTORY

A.—PRINTED SOURCES

(I.) *Bibliographies, Indexes, etc.*

CALENDARIUM ROTULORUM PATENTIUM. Record Com. 1802.

CARTE, THOMAS. Catalogue des rolles gascons, normans et françois. 2 vols. London, 1743.

FIGANIÈRE, F. F. DE LA. Catalogo dos Manuscriptos Portuguezes existentes no Museu Britannico. Lisbon, 1853.

FIGANIÈRE, J. C. DE. Bibliographia Historica Portugueza. Lisbon, 1850.

GROSS, CHARLES. Sources and Literature of English History. 1900.

HARDY, T. D. Syllabus of Documents in Rymer's Fœdera. London, 1869-85.

PUBLIC RECORD OFFICE. Lists and Indexes :—

i. List of ancient petitions of the Chancery and Exchequer. 1892.

xv. List of correspondence of the Chancery and Exchequer. 1902.

REPORTS OF THE DEPUTY KEEPER OF THE PUBLIC RECORDS. Appendices.

REPORTS OF THE ROYAL COMMISSION ON HISTORICAL MSS.

(II.) *Fœdera, Records, etc.*

CALENDAR OF THE CLOSE ROLLS, 1227-31, 1272-88, etc. Roll Series. 1892.

CALENDAR OF LETTER-BOOKS OF THE CITY OF LONDON. Ed. R. R. Sharpe. Letter-Books A, C, G. London, 1899-1905.

CALENDAR OF THE PATENT ROLLS, 1272-1348, 1377-96, etc. Rolls Series. 1891.

HISTORIC AND MUNICIPAL DOCUMENTS OF IRELAND, 1172-1320. Ed. J. T. Gilbert. Rolls Series. London, 1870.

ISSUES OF THE EXCHEQUER. Translated by Frederick Devon. London, 1837.

LITTLE RED BOOK OF BRISTOL. Ed. F. B. Bickley.

MONUMENTA JURIDICA: THE BLACK BOOK OF THE ADMIRALTY. Ed. Travers Twiss. Rolls Series. 4 vols. London, 1871-76.

MUNIMENTA GILDHALLÆ LONDONIENSIS. Ed. T. H. Riley. Rolls Series. Liber albus, Liber custumarum.

NICOLAS, N. HARRIS. Proceedings and Ordinances of the Privy Council of England, 1386-1542. Record Com. 1834-37.

PALGRAVE, FRANCIS. The Antient Kalendars and Inventories of the Treasury of His Majesty's Exchequer. Record Com. 1836.

ROTULI LITTERARUM CLAUSARUM, 1204-27. Ed. T. D. Hardy. Record Com. 2 vols. 1833-44.

ROTULI LITTERARUM PATENTIUM, 1201-16, Ed. T. D. Hardy. Record Com. 1835.

ROTULI PARLIAMENTORUM, 1278-1503. 6 vols, n.p.n.d.

RYMER, THOMAS. Fœdera, conventiones, litteræ, etc., 1101-1654. 3rd ed., 10 vols. The Hague, 1739-45.

——— New ed. 1069-1383. 4 vols. in 7 parts. Record Com. 1816-69[1].

RIBEIRO, J. P. Dissertaçoes chronologicas e criticas sobre a historia e jurisprudencia de Portugal. 5 vols.

SANTAREM, VISCOUNT OF. (Barros e Sousa de Mesquita, etc.) Quadro Elementar das relações politicas e diplomaticas de Portugal. Lisbon, 1876, etc.

[1] In the references to Rymer's *Fœdera* given below, the Record Edition has been followed up to the year 1383; beyond that date the Hague Edition has been used. References to the Record Edition are given thus, Rymer, III. 3; to the Hague Edition, Rymer, IV. ii. 97.

(III.) *Chronicles and other Contemporary Sources.*

(In Chronological Order.)

English.

ITINERARIUM REGIS RICARDI, 1187-99. Ed. William Stubbs' Memorials of the Reign of Richard I. Vol. I. Rolls Series. 1864.
WALSINGHAM, THOMAS. Historia Anglicana, 1272-1422. Ed. H. T. Riley. Rolls Series. 1863-64.
MONUMENTA FRANCISCANA. Ed. J. S. Brewer. Rolls Series. 1858-82.
WAURIN, JEHAN DE. Recueil des croniques et anciennes istories de la Grant Bretaigne. Rolls Series. 5 vols. London, 1864-91.
OFFICIAL CORRESPONDENCE OF THOMAS BEKYNTON, Secretary to Henry VI. Rolls Series. 2 vols. 1872.
LIBELLE OF ENGLISH POLYCYE, in Wright's Political Songs. Rolls Series. Vol. II. 157-205.
MACHADO'S JOURNAL OF A VOYAGE TO SPAIN AND PORTUGAL, in Bernard André's Vita Henrici VII. Ed. J. Gairdner. Rolls Series.
BACON, FRANCIS. Life of Henry VII. Pitt Press Cambridge. 1892.

Portuguese.

COLLECÇÃO DE LIVROS INEDITOS DE HISTORIA PORTUGUEZA. Ed. Correa da Serra. Lisbon, 1790, etc. 1824. 5 vols.:
LOPES, FERNÃO. Chron. delrey Don Pedro I. Vol. IV.
Chron. delrey Don Fernando. Vol. IV.
PISANO, MATHIEU DE. Guerra da Ceuta. Vol. I.
PINA, RUY DE. Chron. delrey Don Alfonso V. Vol. I.
Chron. delrey Don João II. Vol. II.
SANTOS, FR. MAN. DOS. Monarchia Lusitana. Vol. VIII.
LOPES, FERNÃO. Chronica del Rey Joam I. Lisbon, 1644.
AZURARA. Discovery and Conquest of Guinea. Ed. C. R. Beazley and E. Prestage. Hakluyt Society. 2 vols. London, 1895-99.
RESENDE, GARCIA DE. Chron. del Rey Don João II.

(IV.) *Modern Works.*

1. *Commercial History, etc.*

ANDERSON, ADAM. Historical Deduction of the Origin of Commerce. 2 vols. London, 1764.
BUSH, HENRY. Bristol Town Duties. Bristol, 1828.
CUNNINGHAM, WILLIAM. Growth of English Industry and Commerce. Vol. I. Cambridge, 1905. 4th ed.
GIUSEPPI, M. S. Alien merchants in England in the fifteenth century. Roy. Hist. Soc. Trans., N. S. IX.
HALL, HUBERT. History of the Custom Revenue in England. 2 vols. London, 1885.
MARSDEN, R. G. Select Pleas in the Court of Admiralty, 1390-1602. Selden Soc. London, 1894-97
M'KECHNIE, W. S. Magna Carta. 1905.
MICHEL, FRANCISQUE. Histoire du commerce et de la navigation à Bordeaux. 2 vols. Bordeaux, 1867-70.
MITCHELL, W. Essay on the Early History of the Law Merchant. Cambridge, 1904.
POSTLETHWAYT. Dictionary of Trade and Commerce. London, 1774.
SCHANZ, G. Englische Handelspolitik. 2 vols. Leipzig, 1881.

2. *English History.*

BELTZ, G. F. Memorials of the Order of the Garter. London, 1841.
SMITH, SYDNEY ARMITAGE. John of Gaunt. London, 1904.
WYLIE, J. H. History of England under Henry IV. 4 vols. London, etc., 1884-98.

3. *Portuguese History.*

BEAZLEY, C. R. Henry the Navigator. London, 1901.
FONSECA BENEVIDES, F. DA. Rainhas de Portugal. Lisbon, 1878-79.
HERCULANO DE CARVALHO, A. Historia de Portugal. Lisbon, 1846, etc.
MORSE STEPHENS, H. Story of Portugal. London, 1891.
SCHÄFER, HEINRICH. Geschichte von Portugal. 1836-54.
VILLA FRANCA, COUNT. Don João I. e a Alliança Ingleza. Lisbon, 1884.

B.—MANUSCRIPTS.

1. *At the Public Record Office.*

PATENT ROLLS, 42 Hen. III.; 20 Ric. II., etc.
GASCON ROLLS, 17 Ed. III.; 20 Ed. III., etc.
FRENCH ROLLS, 48 Ed. III.; 17 Ric. II.; 7 Hen. IV.; 1 Hen. V.; 5 Hen. VI., etc.
MISCELLANEOUS ROLLS (Chancery), Bundle 14, No. 8.
ANCIENT CORRESPONDENCE. Vols. XX., XXX., XXXIV., XXXVIII., XLIII.
ANCIENT PETITIONS. Files 32, 188, 217, 218, etc.
K. R. CUSTOMS ACCOUNTS. (Bristol, Sandwich, etc.).
TRANSCRIPTS FROM FOREIGN RECORDS. Series II. Nos. 153, 154, 155. Portugal.

2. *At the British Museum.*

BIBL. COTT. Nero, B. I.
Vespasian, C. XII.
BIBL. HARL. 6702.
LANSDOWNE. 190.

PART II

MODERN HISTORY

A.—PRINTED SOURCES

(1.) *Bibliographies.*

RIBEIRO, J. P. Memorias Authenticas para Historia do Real Archivo. Lisbon.
ADAMSON, J. Bibliotheca Lusitana. 1835.
FIGANIÈRE, F. F. DE LA. Catalogo dos Manuscriptos Portuguezes existentes no Museu Britannico. 1853.
FIGANIÈRE, J. C. DO. Bibliographa Historica Portugueza. 1850.
PINTO DE SOUSA, J. C. Bibliotheca de Portugal, etc. 1801.
D'AZEREDO, P., and BAIÃO, A. O. Archivio da Torre do Tombo. 1905.

(ii.) *Calendars, Indexes, etc.*

CALENDARS—
Calendar of Clarendon State Papers.
Calendar of Colonial State Papers.
Calendar of Domestic State Papers.
Calendar of Foreign State Papers.
Calendar of State Papers of Henry VIII.
Calendar of Home Office Papers.
Calendar of Simancas Transcripts.
Calendar of Treasury Papers.
HARDY, T. D. Syllabus of Rymer's Fœdera. 1869.

(iii.) *Collections of Treaties.*

CHALMERS, G. Collection of Treaties between Great Britain and other Powers. 1790.
DUMONT. Corps Universal Diplomatique. 1726 to 1731.
KOCH, C. G. DE and SCHOELL, F. Histoire Abrégée des Traités de Paix entre les Puissances de l'Europe depuis la Paix de Westphalie. 1837.
RYMER, J. Fœdera (Record edition and Old edition).

(iv.) *Collections of Laws.*

Collecção de Legislaçao antiga e moderna do reino de Portugal. 1816-32.
Os Privilegios do Inglez nos reynos e dominio de Portugal. 1736.
Privilegios de Naçao Britannica em Portugal. 1814.
Statutes of the Realm.

(v.) *Contemporary Authorities.*

(*Economic.*)

BERNARDO, JESUS MARIA DE. Arte e Diccionario do Commercio. 1777.
GUICCIARDINI, L. Descrittione di Lutti in Paesi Bassi. Edited by P. A. M. B. Van Hensbroek. 1880.
HALYBURTON, A. Ledger. Edited by Cosmo Innes. 1867.
MALYNES, G. DE. Lex Mercatoria. 1622.
MISSELDEN, E. Circle of Commerce. 1623.
WHEELER, J. Treatise of Commerce. 1661.

(*Historical.*)

Account of Portugal under Pedro II. 1701.
BLOUNT, E. Historie of the Uniting of the Kingdom of Portugall to the Crowne of Castille. 1600.
CHAMBERLAYNE, E. Rise and Fall of Olivares. 1652.
FRÉMONT D'ABLANCOURT. Mémoires contenant l'histoire de Portugal. 1701.
HALL, E. Chronicle. 1809.
LUTTRELL, N. A Brief Historical Relation of State Affairs. 1851.
PEPYS, S. Portugal History: or a Relation of the Troubles that happened at the Court of Portugal, etc. 1677.

(*Letters, Memoirs, Papers, etc.*)

CAMDEN SOCIETY, OLD SERIES. Lists of Foreign Protestants in England 1618-88. Ed. W. D. Cooper. 1862.
CAMDEN SOCIETY, NEW SERIES. Prince Rupert at Lisbon. Ed. S. R. Gardiner. 1890.
CAMDEN SOCIETY THIRD SERIES. Acts and Ordinances of the Eastland Company. Ed. M. Sellars. 1906.
FANSHAWE'S LETTERS. Editions of 1702 and 1724.
GAIRDNER, J. Letters and Papers illustrative of the Reigns of Richard II. and Henry VII. 1861-63.
HAKLUYT SOCIETY. The Hawkins' Voyages. Ed. Sir C. R. Markham. 1878.
The Discovery and Conquest of Guinea. Ed. C. R. BEAZLEY, and E. PRESTAGE. Vols I. and II. 1899.
ROYAL HISTORICAL SOCIETY, TRANSACTIONS OF:
Industry and Commerce in Mediæval Wales. By E. A. Lewis. N. S., Vol. XVII.
The English Occupation of Tangiers, 1661-83. By E. Routh. N. S., Vol. XIX. 1905.
THURLOE. State Papers. 1742.
WINWOOD, Sir R. Memorials. 1725.

(*Pamphlets.*)

Brief Examination into the Increase of Commerce. (581 h 22 [7]).
Case of the British Merchants Trading to Portugal. 1690. (816 m. 11 [109].)
Case of Their Majesties' Sugar Plantations. 1691. (816 m. $\frac{13}{157}$.)
Case of the English Sugar Refiners. 1690 (?). (816 m. $\frac{13}{166}$.)

DEFOE, F. Trade with France, Italy, Spain, and Portugal. 1713.
Interest of the Nation as it respects all Sugar Plantations. 1691. (1391 d. 4.)
Novas Instrucçoens de Feitoria Ingleza. 1754. (705 h. 12 [1].)
Occasional Thoughts on the Portuguese Trade. 1767. (113 n. 19.)
Reasons offered by Portugal Merchants against importing French Wines. 1709. (1890 b. 4.)
State of the English Sugar Plantations. 1670. (816 m. 13 [156].)
Whereas the Portugal Trade is very Advantageous. 1695. (816 m. 11 [9110].)

(VI.) *Modern Works.*

(*Economic.*)

ANDERSON, A. Historical and Chronological Deductions of the Origin of Commerce. Combe's edition. 1786.
BONNASSIEUX, P. Les Grandes Compagnies de Commerce. 1892.
CHALMERS, R. History of Colonial Currency. 1893.
CUNNINGHAM, W. The Growth of English Industry and Commerce. 1892.
DEPPING, G. B. Histoire du Commerce entre le Levant et l'Europe. 1830.
DOWELL, S. History of Taxation. 1884.
HEWINS, W. A. S. Trade and Finance in the Seventeenth Century. 1892.
KEAN, A. H., and CAWSTON, G. Early Chartered Companies. 1896.

(*Historical and General.*)

BARROS E SOUSA, VISCOUNT DE SANTAREM. Statement of Facts, proving the right of the Crown of Portugal to the territories situated on the Western Coast of Africa, etc. 1877.
——— Quadro Elementar das relações politicos e diplomaticos de Portugal com as diversas potencias do mundo. 1842.
BRUCE, J. A. Annals of the East India Company. 1810.
BUSCH, W. England under the Tudors. Translated by A. M. Todd. 1895.
DYER, W. History of Europe. Ed. Hassall.
FREIRE DE OLIVEIRA, E. Elemento para a historia do Municipia de Lisboa. 1882-91.

GARDINER, S. R. History of England. 1603-42.
——— History of the Civil War.
——— History of the Commonwealth and the Protectorate.
HARDY, W. J. History of the Rolls Chapel. 1896.
HUME, M. A. S. Life of Sir Walter Raleigh. 1897.
——— Year after the Armada. 1896.
LATIMER, J. Annals of Bristol in the Seventeenth Century. 1900.
——— Annals of Bristol in the Eighteenth Century. 1893.
LINDE, J. VAN DER. Institute of the Laws of Holland. Translated by Jabez Henry. 1828.
OMAN, C. W. C. History of the Peninsular War. 1902.
REBELLO DA SILVA, S. A. Historia de Portugal nos seculos. XVI. e XVII. 1860-71.
SELLERS, C. Oporto Old and New. 1899.
SMITH, J. A. Memoirs of the Marquis de Pombal. 1843.
STEPHENS, H. M. Portugal. 1891.
THEAL, G. M. Portuguese in South Africa. 1896.

B.—MANUSCRIPT SOURCES.

At the Public Record Office.

AUDIT OFFICE, DECLARED ACCOUNTS. (Customs.)
BOARD OF TRADE, COMMERCIAL MSS. Series I. Vols. A, XVII. ; B, XIX., L., LV., LXX., LXXIII. ; D, LXXII. ; E, XXXI. ; F, LXII. ; J, XXIV. ; K, XI. ; L, V., LXXXIX ; M, XIII., XIV., XV. ; N, XV., XVI. ; O, XVII., XVIII., XXI., LV., CXXVII. ; Q, XXI. ; T, XXVII. ; X, XXXII. ; Y, XCV. ; BB, VII., VIII., etc.
Series II. Vols. CDXXIV., DVI., DXIV., DLXII., DLXIII., DCXLII., DCXLIII., DCXLIV., DCXLVI., DCXLVIII., DCXLIX., DCL., DCLI., etc.
K. R. CUSTOMS ACCOUNTS. London, Bristol, etc.
PATENT ROLLS. El, XIX. ; pt. VIII. ; G.I, I. ; pt. XII., etc.
ST P. COLONIAL. America and the West Indies.
ST P. DOMESTIC. Elizabeth, Vols. XXXV., XLVII., LI., LXXXII., LXXXIII., XCIX., CXXII., CXXIX., CXLI., CXLVI., CXLVI., CCI., CCXXXV., CCLIII., CCLV. etc.
Jas. I. Vols. VIII., XI., XIV., XVI., XX., XXI., LXXII., CXVI., CLXXXIX., etc.
Chas. I. Vols. CLXXXIII., CCXLV., CCLXXII., CCCIII., etc.
STATE PAPERS, FOREIGN. Mary and Elizabeth.
STATE PAPERS, FOREIGN, PORTUGAL. Nos. 3, 4, 5, 15, 16, 17, 18, 46, 64, 89, etc.

At the British Museum.

BIBL. COTTON. (Especially Nero B. I.; B. XI.; and Vespasian C, 13, 19.)
LANSDOWNE. 41, 44, 53, 81, 152, etc.
BIRCH. 4155, 4192, etc.
EGERTON. 921, etc.
ADDITIONAL. 11682, etc.
BIBL. HARLEIAN MSS. 36.

CONTENTS

PART I: MEDIÆVAL

By V. M. SHILLINGTON

CHAPTER III

THE LISBON FACTORY AND THE TREATY OF 1654

(1640-1654)

CHAPTER IV

THE METHUEN TREATY

(1654-1703)

CHAPTER V

THE ENGLISH FACTORIES IN PORTUGAL AND THE BRAZIL TRADE

(1660-1756)

CHAPTER VI

THE COMPANY OF THE WINES OF THE ALTO DOURO

(1756-1787)

APPENDIX I

APPENDIX II

PART I: MEDIÆVAL

By V. M. Shillington.

CHAPTER I

THE ALLIANCE BETWEEN ENGLAND AND PORTUGAL IN THE MIDDLE AGES

Help given to early Portuguese kings by English crusaders—The beginnings of the Anglo-Portuguese alliance—Correspondence of Diniz of Portugal with Edward I. and Edward II.—Proposed marriages between the English and Portuguese royal houses—Political alliance between Edward III. and Fernando, 1373—John of Gaunt and King John I. of Portugal—The Treaty of Windsor, 1386—Commercial clauses of the treaty—The Anglo-Portuguese alliance in the fifteenth century.

THE friendly relations between England and Portugal date almost from the beginning of the latter's history as an independent kingdom, for, through the crusading energy of England in the twelfth century, and the convenient position of Portugal as a stopping-place for ships on the way to the Holy Land, it came about that English subjects were of great help on several occasions to early Portuguese kings in their long struggle with the Moors. Thus, for instance, in 1147 a company of English crusaders helped Alfonso I. to take the city of Lisbon[1], and the Portuguese king appointed an Englishman as the first bishop of the See, which was founded there when the Moors had been driven out. In 1189, again, Alfonso's son,

[1] Osbernus de Baldre (ton). *De Expugnatione Lixbonensi.* Ed. Stubbs. *Itin. Regis Ricardi* (Rolls), CXLII. sq. Ed. Liebermann. *Mon. Germ.*, XXVII. 3-10. See also my paper in *Trans. Roy. Hist. Soc.*, N.S. Vol. XX. on "The Beginnings of the Anglo-Portuguese Alliance."

Sancho I., received valuable assistance from a body of Londoners in his attack on Silves, in the kingdom of Algarve, and in 1217 yet another contingent of English crusaders helped to subdue the district south of the Tagus. Before this time Portugal had been recognised as a new and enterprising kingdom by her European neighbours, and among others King John of England sent an embassy in 1199 to ask for the hand of one of the Portuguese princesses. The request was refused, but already in an English despatch of the same year the King of Portugal appears as "dearest brother and friend[1]" of the English king, and one of Sancho II.'s sons, who married Joanna, Countess of Flanders, led the Flemish troops in alliance with England at the Battle of Bouvines, 1214.

The friendship between England and Portugal, which began thus at the time of the crusades, received a great impulse on the accession of Diniz to the Portuguese throne in 1279. During the thirteenth century, as will be seen[2], the merchants of Portugal were securing a foothold in England; and in their trade with this country they had already begun to show signs of growing prosperity. The long reign of Diniz was accompanied by a great increase of the wealth and prosperity of Portugal, and led to the progress of the Portuguese nation in almost every branch of seafaring and commerce. For the sake of his merchants, Diniz tried to maintain friendly relations with the rulers of the countries whose trade was of the most importance to them, and thus, during his whole reign, he carried on an amicable correspondence, chiefly on commercial matters, with Edward I. of England, or his son Edward II.

In one of his letters dated January, 1295[3], Diniz pointed out that the petty warfare carried on between

[1] Rymer, I. 76. [2] See below, fol. 21, 22, etc.
[3] Rymer, I. 815.

Edward's subjects and those of Castile entailed much suffering on innocent traders, and begged the English king to take steps towards the re-establishment of peace. Another contains an appeal to Edward on behalf of the Portuguese merchants[1], many of whom were complaining of having been forced by royal officials to sell in English ports goods intended for Flanders. Diniz represented that Edward must see the injustice of this, especially in the case of merchants of a friendly king; he requested that henceforth his subjects might come and go freely in England, promising that Edward's subjects should be equally favoured in Portugal. Just before his death, Edward I. received a last proof of the Portuguese king's friendship in a letter stating that, through his great affection for Edward and his people, Diniz had taken charge of a ship rescued by his subjects from certain pirates, hearing that it belonged to England, and was now waiting for its English owners to come and claim it[2]. This letter was accompanied by a friendly note[3] to Edward II., then Prince of Wales, who soon after his accession replied courteously to both missives[4].

The death of Edward I. made no difference in the relations between the two countries, and in July 1308 Diniz wrote Edward II. a long and important letter[5], in which he drew attention to the warm friendship which had already existed so long between the subjects of their realms. He informed Edward that he was sending herewith new letters of safe-conduct for English subjects in Portugal, in the hope of similar letters for his own merchants in England, and took the opportunity to mention the infamous behaviour of certain Castilians, who had been guilty

[1] *Anc. Corr.*, Vol. XX. No. 18. For a transcript of a letter from K. Diniz to Edward II., dated Nov. 1308, see Appendix I. below, No. 3.

[2] *Anc. Corr.*, XX. 19.

[3] *Ibid.* XXX. 183.

[4] Rymer, II. 7.

[5] *Anc. Corr.*, XXXIV. 160.

of piracy under cover of the Portuguese flag and insignia, thus provoking Edward's unsuspecting subjects against his own—a fact which Diniz deeply deplored.

Edward's answer to this letter[1], with the safe-conduct that accompanied it, has been described as the first commercial treaty between England and Portugal, but important as it was, it can hardly lay claim to this distinction, being in form simply a reply to the letter received from Diniz. The English king expressed his delight at the mention of the bond of affection existing between the merchants of the two countries, which, he trusted, would ever remain indissoluble. He promised, that so far as he was concerned, the duplicity of the Castilians should have no prejudicial effect on this friendship, and he declared that it gave him much pleasure to issue the required safe-conduct for the Portuguese merchants. A year or two later, Edward took advantage of the friendship of Diniz to send one of his own agents, a certain Peter Barde, on a special trading voyage to Spain and Portugal[2].

In the history of the relations between England and Portugal it is an important point that during the years when Portugal was rising so greatly in her own estimation, and in that of the world, she should have been governed by a man as anxious as Diniz was to improve the friendship with England. Alfonso IV., who became king in 1325, went further than Diniz, and sent envoys to England to arrange a marriage between his daughter and the Prince of Wales. The proposal did not succeed however; the first Portuguese envoys were sent back with a message that they were not of sufficiently high rank to treat of such important matters, and though Alfonso then sent the admiral himself, Emanuel Pessanha, he obtained no more substantial results[3].

[1] Rymer, II. 58. [2] *Cal. Pat. Rolls*, 1307-13, 375.
[3] Rymer, II. 603, 625, 626.

But although he thus missed the chance of a Portuguese wife, Edward III., who came to the throne almost immediately afterwards, showed from the beginning a strong desire to keep up the connection already established, and during his reign England for the first time entered into formal alliance with Portugal.

It will be seen[1] that the merchants of Portugal found in Edward III. a staunch friend and protector, and in this the English king was no doubt partly influenced by the value to England of the Portuguese commerce. But important as were purely commercial considerations in Edward III.'s eyes, he had another reason for keeping on good terms with Portugal. He was embarking on a hard struggle with France, and it behoved him, therefore, to attach as many as possible of the smaller rulers to his interests, not only to prevent their allying with the enemy, but also to allow of his borrowing from them, if need arose, ships and men to fight in his battles. The fact that Portugal was, passively, at any rate, on the English side, appears from an incident of the year 1342; a Portuguese ship, which had been arrested in the port of St Davids in Wales, as belonging to the king's enemies, was ordered to be set free at once, "because the inhabitants of the land of Portugal are in the king's friendship and in the enmity of Philip de Valois his enemy[2]." But after the first few years of the war with France, Edward seems to have made up his mind that circumstances required something more than an indefinite friendship with Portugal. In 1344 envoys were sent to treat of an alliance with this country, as also with Castile and Aragon, and in the following year ambassadors were again sent with a letter to Alfonso IV., in which Edward expressed himself most desirous of an alliance with Portugal. He therefore proposed a

[1] See below, pp. 39, 40, and chap. iv.
[2] *Cal. Close Rolls*, 1341-43, 613.

marriage between his son Edward or any of his other sons, and one of the daughters of Alfonso, promising to agree to whatever should be settled as to the dowry and other necessary matters[1]. At the same time fresh orders were issued to prevent the molestation of Portuguese merchants by English subjects.

After much debate the marriage was agreed upon, in 1347, and English ambassadors arrived in Portugal to fix the day for the ceremony, and superintend the departure of the Infanta, when to their amazement they were informed that the wedding was not to take place[2]. For some unknown reason Alfonso at the last minute fought shy of the English alliance, and married his daughter instead to Pedro, King of Aragon; while the discomfited English king could only protest that the failure of the scheme was in no way his doing. A few years after this Edward III. concluded a treaty with the merchants of Portugal[3], but it was not till 1373 that the Kings of England and Portugal entered at last into formal alliance with each other. This time it was the Portuguese king, Ferdinand, who proposed it as a means of escape from the difficult position in which he then found himself.

Alfonso IV. was succeeded in 1357 by his son Pedro, in whose reign a civil war broke out in Castile, where the opposition to the rule of Pedro the Cruel found a leader in his half-brother, Henry of Trastamare. The latter won the support of France, whereupon the Black Prince, fearful for his duchy of Acquitaine, led his English adherents to the assistance of Pedro the Cruel. Pedro of Portugal wisely kept out of the dispute, but in 1367 he was succeeded by his son Ferdinand, under whose capricious rule Portugal soon became hopelessly involved in the Castilian struggle. On the

[1] Rymer, III. 8, 62, 63. [2] Ibid. 129.
[3] See p. 42 below.

death of Pedro the Cruel in 1369, leaving only daughters, Ferdinand claimed the crown through his grandmother, but Castilian pride revolted at the idea of a Portuguese king, and the majority in Castile went over to the side of Henry of Trastamare, who was proclaimed king as Henry II. Ferdinand set himself to oppose him in alliance with the King of Aragon, but his treacherous character soon lost him his ally, and having thus endangered his own safety, Ferdinand, at his wits' end, and remembering the help given by the Black Prince to Pedro the Cruel, turned to the English for assistance. The Black Prince had lately returned to England in broken health, but it happened that his brother John of Gaunt, Duke of Lancaster, had claims of his own to Castile through his wife[1], so he willingly sent ambassadors to adjust an alliance[2] with the King of Portugal; and having made sure of this friend at court, Ferdinand then sent ambassadors to Edward III., with full powers to treat of an alliance and confederation between England and Portugal[3].

The proposal came at a fortunate moment for Ferdinand. The war between England and France had lately gone very much against England; and as the French were still supporting Castile an alliance with Portugal against the King of Castile seemed an effectual way of embarrassing them. Moreover, Edward had already been glad to hire the assistance of Portuguese men and ships, and he no doubt foresaw future occasions when Portuguese help might prove useful. Thus he was easily persuaded to listen to the advice of John of Gaunt and sign this first political alliance between England and Portugal, 16th June 1373[4]. Both kings undertook in the most solemn terms to assist each other against all enemies whatso-

[1] Constance, daughter of Pedro the Cruel.
[2] At Braga, July 1372. [3] Rymer, III. 966.
[4] Ibid. 983.

ever, and to make no alliance without the other's knowledge. But inconstant as ever, Ferdinand in the following year was hand and glove with the King of Castile, to whom he even lent ships to help France against England; and from the behaviour of the Portuguese king it might have seemed as though the first treaty between England and Portugal was also to be the last.

Nevertheless Edward III. did not allow his commercial policy to be disturbed by the caprices of the King of Portugal; as in 1353, after Alfonso's sudden withdrawal from the marriage scheme, Edward had still been glad to treat with the merchants of Lisbon and Oporto, so now, in spite of Ferdinand's lack of faith, he continued his favours to the Portuguese merchants in England[1]. Moreover, in 1379, on the death of Henry of Castile, Ferdinand took steps to renew the alliance with England, in the hope of a successful invasion of Castile, promising that if the Earl of Cambridge, son of Edward III., would come to Portugal with 1,000 men-at-arms and 1,000 archers, he would help him to wage war on Castile in favour of John of Gaunt; also if the earl would bring with him his eldest son, Ferdinand would marry him to his daughter and heiress[2].

Ferdinand had already given proofs of his uncertain character, and such fair promises should have roused the suspicions of the English, but Richard II., who had succeeded his grandfather in 1377, was young, and inclined to listen to the advice of his uncle, John of Gaunt, who had already set his heart on the crown of Castile. The result was the preliminary departure in 1381 of an expedition under the Earl of Cambridge, while John of Gaunt used his utmost powers of persuasion with the English Parliament to induce them to supply him with men and money for his own departure to Portugal. But by the time they had reluctantly consented Ferdinand had already come to

[1] See chap. iv. below. [2] Rymer, IV. 93, 94.

terms with the new King of Castile, whereupon the amazed English troops were sent home again without striking a blow, Castile even supplying the necessary transport ships to hasten their going[1]. John of Gaunt bore his disappointment as best he could, and waited for a new opportunity to make good his claim to Castile. In 1383 Ferdinand died, and his widow Leonora assumed the regency for her daughter Beatrice, and Juan, King of Castile, whom the Portuguese princess had married as soon as the English returned home. But, at the idea of a Castilian king, fearful disorder arose in Lisbon and other important cities, while the people began to seek a national leader to rally them against Juan, when he should bring his army into Portugal.

Their choice fell upon John, Master of the Order of Aviz, and half-brother of Ferdinand, who had won their respect and incurred the bitter hatred of Leonora by his determined opposition to her schemes. He was on the point of leaving for England, where he meant to serve as a knight in the king's army[2], but after much persuasion he consented to remain in Portugal, and assumed the regency instead of Leonora. But the Nationalist party, however ardent, were few in number compared with Juan's advancing army, and the new regent debated anxiously with his council as to means for increasing his strength by help from abroad[3]. England was obviously the first country to which appeal should be made, as the traditional friend of Portugal and the enemy of Castile and France; but an alliance with England was more than John could allow himself to hope for, after Ferdinand's behaviour, and under the present

[1] Rymer, IV. 156. A full account of the events leading up to the Treaty of Windsor will be found in S. Armitage Smith, *John of Gaunt*, chap. xiii; Villa Franca, *João I e a Alliança Ingleza*; Morse Stephens, *Portugal*, etc. See also Walsingham, *Historia Anglicana*, 83.

[2] F. Lopes, *Chron. Delrey João I.*, cap. 18, 23, etc.

[3] Ibid. cap. 48. Many other graphic details are given by this writer.

circumstances, so the result was that envoys[1] were sent to Richard II. to ask only for permission for his subjects to come as hired volunteers to help the regent against Castile.

Arrived in England, after a preliminary interview with the Duke of Lancaster[2], the envoys produced their powers before the king, from the regent, John of Avis, and also from the cities of Lisbon and Oporto. They promised that when, with English assistance, Portugal was freed from the enemy, all the help should be willingly paid back, and that then if the Duke of Lancaster cared to urge his claim to Castile, all Portugal would help him to do so. Richard, doubtless under the influence of John of Gaunt, gave his consent with pleasure, and numbers of his subjects came forward as volunteers from all parts of the country; citizens, clerks, merchants, all enrolled themselves for the voyage to Portugal[3]. In addition, many of the London merchants advanced large sums of money to pay the wages of the volunteers (a fact which gave much trouble later on)[4], and the rest was made up by the seizure of all Portuguese ships and merchandise found in English ports[5].

Much time was lost in making arrangements for the departure of the English volunteers, and meanwhile the regent used every effort to strengthen himself. Lisbon gave him constant support, and many other Portuguese towns by degrees declared for him, while the encouraging news which arrived from England helped to cheer his adherents. But, early in 1385, they learnt that Juan was collecting ships and stores for an attack on Lisbon, and presently ten Castilian galleys took up a position

[1] Fernando Alfonso, Master of the Order of San Thiago, and Lourenço Eannes Fogaça, Chancellor of the late King Ferdinand.

[2] He seems to have been the moving spirit in all the negotiations on the English side. See Armitage Smith, *John of Gaunt*, chap. xii.

[3] Rymer (Hague Ed.), III. iii. 175-76.

[4] See chap. iv.

[5] Lopes, cap. 48. Rymer (Hague Ed.), III. iii. 177.

outside Lisbon Harbour to waylay all vessels bound thither with provisions. Things were at their worst, when on Easter Sunday, the 2nd April, the anxious citizens of Lisbon suddenly sighted two English ships, which were bringing corn and men-at-arms to their assistance. In painful excitement they watched while a sharp encounter took place with the Castilian galleys, in which the latter were fortunately driven off, the English coming safely into harbour. They had on board 200 lancers and 200 archers, also 400 measures of wheat, and flour and bacon; and they brought news of other English ships which had put in at Setubal and Oporto[1].

With the coming of the English the tide had turned, and for John of Aviz the worst was well over. Three days later he accepted the title of King John I. of Portugal, and on the 15th April he sent royal authority to his ambassadors in England to negotiate a treaty with Richard II., and to make a special arrangement with John of Gaunt, "King of Castile." The arrival of the English archers had also put fresh heart into the Portuguese, who won a decisive victory over Castile at Aljubarrota, in August 1385. As soon as the news of this reached England John of Gaunt sent word to the King of Portugal that he was now determined to go to Castile and make good his rights there, if only John of Aviz would supply him with ships for the purpose. Meanwhile negotiations for the proposed alliance between England and Portugal went actively forward, and on the 9th May 1386 the Treaty of Windsor was signed by the emissaries of the two kings. By this treaty the two countries entered into a perpetual league and alliance against all powers except the Pope, the Emperor, and John, "King of Castile[2]." Neither king was on any account to give counsel,

[1] Lopes, *João I.*, Part II. cap. 2.

[2] The name under which John of Gaunt appeared. See the text of the treaty in Rymer, III. iii. 200.

aid, or assistance to the enemies of the other, nor to enter into any alliance without the knowledge of his new confederate. These and most of the other articles are political in their bearing, but there are two clauses which, though also partly political in character, had an important effect on the commercial relations between the two countries.

One of these is Article 2, by which it was agreed that all the subjects of one king, prelates, dukes etc. . . and merchants were to be secure in the dominions of the other king, there to stay, reside and trade with his subjects, and that they should be treated in these dominions as though they were natives, according to their rank, so long as they paid the right duties and customs, and observed the laws of the country. The other is Article 9, whereby "if in the future it happens that anything is done contrary to the stipulations of the present treaty by the subjects of one of the said kings against those of the other, whether incarcerations . . . depredations, or robbery of persons or things, the king whose subjects committed these injuries shall be responsible, and obliged to repair them, and replace them as they were before, and punish the delinquents as quickly as possible, within six months at most."

These two clauses formed a kind of charter for the merchants of either country when visiting the other. The treaty contained a stipulation that it should be confirmed[1] by all future Kings of England and Portugal, and as this provision was faithfully carried out during the whole of the fifteenth century each king made himself personally responsible for the damage done by his subjects, and undertook in the most solemn terms to see that all such damage

[1] Within a year from their coronation. A convention was signed on the same day, by which King John of Portugal promised to lend Richard ten galleys for six months, or longer if necessary, as part of the promised help to John of Gaunt. Rymer, III. iii. 203.

was quickly made good to the injured party. Whether the kings always took up this responsibility is another matter, and it can hardly have been expected that they would be able entirely to prevent injustice, but the frequent references to the treaty of 1386 in the petitions of English and Portuguese merchants show that its terms were borne in mind, and acted upon wherever possible. The bearings of this alliance on the commercial relations between England and Portugal have been dealt with as far as possible in another chapter[1], but though it is idle to attempt in any way to measure the immediate effects of the Treaty of Windsor it is worth while in passing to notice some curious figures given in the Customs Accounts of Bristol at this period[2].

During the four years from Michaelmas 1378 to Michaelmas 1382 the average number of pieces of cloth shipped every year in Bristol for Portugal was about 750, but the numbers decrease progressively, beginning with 1,067 in 1379, and ending with 533, the number of cloths sent to Portugal in 1382. This was four years before the Treaty of Windsor; four years after it, Michaelmas 1390 to Michaelmas 1391, the number of cloths sent to Portugal from Bristol was 2,158, almost one-third of the entire number shipped in Bristol during that year, and nearly three times the average number for the years 1379-82. Assuming the year 1391-92 to have been in every way exceptionally favourable it is still clear that the cloth trade between Bristol and Portugal received a powerful impulse about this time. The figures are unfortunately not forthcoming for the succeeding years, nor for the other English ports, the accounts in most cases giving few or no particulars as to the ships mentioned; but there is a great deal of indirect evidence for the years following the Treaty of Windsor which bears witness to the growing

[1] See chap. iii.

[2] *K.R. Customs.* Bdle. 16, Nos. 4, 5, 9, 11, 13, 19.

importance and regularity of the trade between England and Portugal at this time[1].

The events that followed the signature of the treaty may be briefly told. In due time John of Gaunt arrived in Portugal with an army, and had his first interview with the new king, with whom he made a formal compact, offering him as wife his daughter Catherine, who would inherit the claim to Castile. King John I., however, put aside this claim, choosing as his wife instead, Philippa, daughter of John of Gaunt by his first wife, Blanche of Lancaster, and the marriage was celebrated with all ceremony in February 1387. But, after all, the joint invasion of Castile by the Duke of Lancaster and the King of Portugal failed hopelessly. The Castilians rose indignantly against the ruler whom the Portuguese wished to thrust upon them, and after a short struggle the invaders returned to Portugal. Shortly afterwards the duke made terms with Castile and went back to England, while a momentary truce was concluded between Castile and Portugal. Yet, in spite of the poor result of the joint undertaking, the events of the last few years had drawn England and Portugal together as nothing else could have done. The King of England had recognised John I.'s position in Portugal when his fortunes were almost at their lowest; English support had helped him to secure his kingdom; and in the eyes of the world as well as in those of the two countries concerned, the alliance between the English and Portuguese nations was henceforth an established thing. During the fifteenth century, England and Portugal were included as allies in many important treaties[2], and on several occasions the two countries were able to be of great assistance to each other[3].

[1] See chap. iii.

[2] Many are mentioned in Santarem, *Quadro Elementar*, etc., Vol. XIV.

[3] In 1397, when John I.'s crown was endangered by an insurrection,

Moreover, with the accession in England of Henry IV., son of John of Gaunt, and therefore brother-in-law to the King of Portugal, there was a great increase in the cordiality already existing between the two courts. In 1400, John I. was received into the Order of the Garter; he was the first foreign sovereign upon whom this honour was conferred[1], but three of his sons and all succeeding Kings of Portugal became Knights of the Order. Ambassadors came and went frequently between the two courts, and letters on personal and commercial matters were constantly exchanged. As soon as possible Henry confirmed the treaty of 1386[2], and shortly afterwards the bond between the two houses was strengthened by the marriage[3] of John's natural daughter, Beatrice, to Thomas, Earl of Arundel, one of the foremost English nobles at this time.

This marriage seems to have led several Portuguese subjects to settle in England, for petitions from some of them still exist[4]. In the same way, Philippa's

he sent to England for archers and men-at-arms to increase his strength, and exported at the same time 500 lances. An English squadron also assisted at the Portuguese capture of Ceuta in 1415, and Portuguese cross-bowmen fought for England in the war with France, renewed by Henry V. (See Rymer, III. iv. 141, 145. Mathew de Pisano, *Guerra da Ceuta*, 35. Waurin, *Chronicles*, III. 371, 385, etc.)

[1] Beltz, *Memorials of the Garter*, liv.

[2] Rymer, IV. i. 64.

[3] Wylie, *Henry IV.*, II. 330 *et seq.* An account of the wedding is given in *Trans. For. Records*, Series II. No. 153. Sect. xiii.

[4] *Anc. Petitions*, 4227, 11175. See Appendix I. No. 11. There are isolated notices of Portuguese subjects living in England before this time, and there were Portuguese scholars at Oxford and Cambridge. Later Patent Rolls also contain entries of Portuguese merchants receiving letters of denization in England, but in most cases, owing to lack of sufficient details, it is exceedingly difficult to discover traces of the foreigners of any particular nationality living in England during the Middle Ages. Enquiries with regard to the Portuguese Archives and the Corporation Records of London have hitherto revealed only the absence of definite information as to Portuguese subjects living for commercial or other purposes in England at this time. It is most probable that in official English documents the Portuguese were included among "Spaniards."

marriage brought over English subjects to settle in Portugal. Her own household was largely English, an English parson was her chancellor, and her suite contained a number of English ladies who afterwards married into Portuguese houses. Many English customs were borrowed by the Portuguese, and among other things, French, the language spoken at the English court, was adopted at the court of John I.[1] It was part of John's policy to favour English merchants, many of whom began to live or keep their agents permanently in Lisbon[2]. In 1389, he extended to them all the privileges and liberties hitherto enjoyed by the merchants of Genoa and Pisa, and from this time on the English began to rise into the position of the "most favoured nation" in Portugal[3]. Several Kings of England and Portugal since Diniz and Edward I. had looked with satisfaction on the growing friendship between the two countries, but it had been reserved for John I. to conclude a lasting alliance, which, as set forth in the Treaty of Windsor, and ratified by his marriage with Philippa of Lancaster, became the keynote of Portuguese foreign policy, both for himself and his successors.

The descendants of John I. and Henry IV. played an active part in maintaining the alliance. The treaty of 1386 was renewed and confirmed both by Henry V. and Henry VI.[4], and during the minority of the latter, two of John and Philippa's children visited their English cousins. Pedro, Duke of Coimbra, their second surviving son, came in 1424[5] and spent some time in England, where he was well received. In his later years this prince

[1] Wylie, *Henry IV.*, II. 330. Fonseca Benevides, *Rainhas de Portugal*, 247.

[2] See chap. iii.

[3] *Trans. For. Records*, Series II. No. 154.

[4] Palgrave, *Kalendars and Inventories of the Exchequer*, II. 88.

[5] *Mon Francisc.*, II. 168. See also Devon, *Issues of the Exchequer*, 394-95.

was regent for his infant nephew, Alfonso V., in whose name he renewed and maintained the alliance with England[1]. In 1429, Isabella, daughter of John and Philippa, came to England on her way to Flanders to marry Philip, Duke of Burgundy[2].

This marriage is worth attention as a confirmation of the three-cornered friendship between England, Portugal, and Flanders, which had been growing up since the days of the crusades. The alliance between England and Flanders, or rather Burgundy, broke down in 1434, but the Portuguese duchess did not forget her connection with England, and through her mediation many truces were concluded between the two countries, while, at her request, negotiations were on several occasions entered into for the continuation of friendly commercial intercourse between England and Flanders[3].

Another member of John's family, with whom the English House of Lancaster had friendly dealings, was the famous Prince Henry the Navigator, third son of Philippa, and therefore grandson to John of Gaunt. This prince, after assisting at the capture of Ceuta in 1415, gave himself up entirely to the direction of voyages of exploration, and the work he did in this way was of the utmost value for his own country, and eventually for the whole commercial world. During his lifetime many important discoveries were made on the West Coast of Africa, and before he died Portuguese mariners were bringing back gold and other precious African products from the land of Guinea[4]. As the result of his lifework, Portugal began to grow wealthy and important, and to lay the foundations of a commercial empire. But more than this, by breaking down the veil of terror and superstition through which mediæval

[1] Rymer, V. i. 65. [2] Ibid. IV. iv. 151.

[3] Rymer, V. i. 56, 85, 119, 158, 161, 175; ii. 149.

[4] Azurara, *Discovery and Conquest of Guinea*. Ed. Beazley and Prestage, II. 236.

civilisation regarded the unknown parts of the world, Prince Henry prepared the way for the great discoveries of the end of the century[1]. It is therefore important for English people to remember that by birth this prince was half English, and that his connection with England was kept up during a great part of his life. Henry V. allowed him to receive custom free supplies of lances, staves, horses, and other goods, to be used from time to time in his enterprises[2], and when informed of his great virtues he even begged him to be captain of his armies[3]; but fortunately for Portugal the invitation was declined. According to a contemporary chronicler the valour of the English acclaimed the Prince's work[4], and in 1443 he was installed as a Knight of the Garter[5]. He himself kept an agent in Galway, to whom on one occasion he sent an African lion, knowing that "never before had such a beast been seen in that part[6]."

The outbreak of the Wars of the Roses and the downfall of the House of Lancaster in England destroyed somewhat of this intimate relationship between the English and Portuguese courts, but the alliance had by this time lasted too long to be lightly thrown aside. Alfonso V., the king then reigning in Portugal, made no difficulty about recognising Edward IV. as King of England, and even proposed for him a marriage with his own sister Catherine[7]. At one point, however, the disturbed condition of England very nearly led to a breach of the long peace between the two countries. The Earl of Warwick, acting in the interests of Henry IV., had authorised his captain, Fauconberg,

[1] See C.R. Beazley, *Prince Henry the Navigator*.
[2] Rymer, IV. iii. 5.
[3] Azurara, *Guinea*, II. 24.
[4] Ibid. 8.
[5] Beltz, *Memorials of the Garter*, 161.
[6] Azurara, II. 278.
[7] Morse Stephens, *Portugal*, 164.

to plunder any vessels he could seize near the coast of England, especially those from Flanders, because of the help given to Edward by the Duke of Burgundy. Fauconberg happened to capture twelve magnificent Portuguese vessels, returning with rich cargoes from Flanders, which so enraged the King of Portugal that he meditated the instant despatch against England of an Armada which he had prepared for Africa. Just when all was ready, however, he received the news of the deaths of the Earl of Warwick and Henry VI., and was fortunately persuaded to send the Armada to Africa as originally intended, contenting himself with an embassy to Edward to obtain compensation for his injured merchants[1]. When this had with difficulty been obtained, peace was re-established between the two countries, and in 1475 Portugal appeared once more as an ally of England in a treaty between Louis XI. and the Duke of Burgundy[2].

When Alfonso V. was succeeded by his son John II., Edward IV. received the ambassadors of the new king with all possible honour. The treaty of 1386 was confirmed once more, and Edward won John's heart by recognising his claim to the sole lordship of Guinea, and forbidding for the future all private trading expeditions thither on the part of English merchants[3]. Some years later it happened that Edward's brother-in-law, Lord Scales, came to Portugal with a large retinue, on his way to fight the infidels in Spain; when John, glad of the opportunity to show his friendship for England, loaded him with honours and kept him at his side for a month, quartering his English followers in the houses of the highest Portuguese families, and fitting out for his homeward journey a ship richly laden

[1] Ruy de Pina, *Chron. Alfonso V.*, cap. clxii. See also chap. iv. below.

[2] Santarem, *Quadro Elementar*, III. 125.

[3] Garcia de Resende, *João II.*, cap. 33.

with everything he could possibly require[1]. On the death of Edward IV., John confirmed the Treaty of Windsor with Richard III., and it was suggested that the English king should marry Joanna, daughter of Alfonso V.[2] The Portuguese princess could not agree to this proposal, however, and in a short time afterwards Richard was deposed from the English throne.

Henry VII., himself descended from John of Gaunt through his mother, made haste to claim his relationship with the King of Portugal, who sent an ambassador to congratulate him on his accession[3]. Shortly afterwards, in 1489, an important embassy was despatched from England to treat of the renewal of the ancient alliance. By this time, through her discoveries and trading enterprises, Portugal had become famous in the world of commerce, and in giving power to his ambassadors for the confirmation of the Treaty of Windsor, Henry expressly mentioned the importance of this treaty for commercial purposes[4].

During the remaining years of the fifteenth century nothing happened to disturb the peaceful relations of the two countries. In 1492 Margaret, Duchess of Burgundy, probably relying upon John II.'s professions of friendship for Edward IV. and Richard III., sent Perkin Warbeck to Portugal[5] before he made his attempt in Ireland, possibly in the hope that the Portuguese king might take up his cause. But though he received him, John gave him no support, and remained true to his word with the Tudor sovereign in England[6]. Three years later John died, and was succeeded by Manuel, "The Fortunate," during whose

[1] Ruy de Pina, *João II.*, cap. 21.
[2] Morse Stephens, *Portugal*, 165.
[3] Bern. Andreas, *Henry VII.* (Gairdner), 11, 12, 47.
[4] Rymer, V. iii. 194. An account of the embassy is given in Machado's Journal, printed in Bern. Andreas, *Henry VII.* (Gairdner).
[5] Bacon, *Henry VII.*, 108.
[6] Santarem, *Quadro Elementar*, Vol. XV. 2.

reign the Portuguese at last completed the discovery of the sea-route to India and the East. The new king was at first much occupied with the discoveries and the glowing prospect which they were opening out for his kingdom, but he did not forget the policy of his ancestors, and in 1499, on the eve of the sixteenth century, the ancient alliance with England was renewed once more[1].

Having thus briefly traced the beginnings of the Anglo-Portuguese alliance, and noted the chief points in the history of the diplomatic relations between England and Portugal in the Middle Ages, it is time to turn to the purely commercial relations of these countries during the same period. In the following chapters it will be seen that while the trade between England and Portugal was from the first equally advantageous for both countries, yet the firm alliance so early established between them and so long maintained, had important results in furthering the growth and development of this trade.

[1] *Santarem*, XV. 2.

CHAPTER II

EARLY COMMERCIAL RELATIONS BETWEEN ENGLAND AND PORTUGAL

First traces of Portuguese merchants in England — Their treatment in England — Episode of *La Cardinale* — Dealings of Henry III. with Portuguese merchants in Bordeaux — Nature of Portugal's trade with England— Commercial policy of King Diniz of Portugal—Disputes between the Portuguese merchants and Edward I.'s French subjects—Settlement by arbitration—Recognised position in England of the Portuguese merchants—Carta Mercatoria —Favourable policy of Edward III. towards Portuguese merchants—The English king's treaty with the merchants of Lisbon and Oporto—Decision of an English admiral with regard to captured Portuguese merchandise.

THE Patent Roll of the fourth year of King John contains the following entry: "To all the merchants of the land of the King of Portugal, etc. Know that we have granted you that you may come safely and securely into our land, and return with your goods and merchandise, paying the lawful customs which others pay who come into our land with their merchandise. And when you come here we have taken you, your goods and your merchandise, into our protection and safe-keeping[1]". Two years later similar Letters Patent were issued, for the merchants of Portugal "and other merchants of Spain[2]", granting them full permission to trade in the dominions of the English king, with a special clause to protect

[1] *Rot. litt. pat.*, 1201-16, ed. Hardy, 20.
[2] Ibid. 44.

them from being arrested for debt in cases where they were not the chief debtors nor sureties for them. Thus, at the very beginning of the thirteenth century, Portuguese merchants had already found their way to England, and had judged it worth while, for the sake of their trade with that country, to secure from the English king his formal acknowledgment and sanction of their position as traders in his domains.

The English were not at this time a highly commercial people, and though English products, such as wool, tin, and lead, already found a large market in the commercial world, England's trade with foreign countries was as yet almost entirely carried on by foreign merchants. Many dangers, from piracy, shipwreck, or arrest, had to be braved by the foreign merchants who brought their goods to English markets, and, until the English would face these dangers themselves, the supply of foreign products in England depended on the visits of the foreign traders who brought them. Yet though matters stood thus, no great effort was made to encourage foreign merchants to continue their visits. The control of commerce in England was entirely in the king's hands, and foreign merchants were dependent on royal favour for permission to carry on their trade. "No alien merchant could enter England or leave it, nor take up his abode in any town, nor move from place to place, nor buy and sell, without paying heavy tolls to the king[1]". Before Magna Carta, at any rate, foreign merchants had no defined status in England; they simply had to buy the king's protection, and even this might be granted conditionally, under terms which left plenty of room for unjust extortions.

In spite of such obstacles, however, foreign merchants found it well worth their while to carry on trade with England, and among the foremost of

[1] M'Kechnie, *Magna Carta*, 464-73.

those who, for this purpose obtained Royal Letters Patent in the early years of John's reign were, as has already been mentioned, the merchants of Portugal. Besides the two grants of freedom to trade noticed above, there is other evidence to show that Portuguese merchants were also beginning to settle in the dominions of the King of England. In a list of the inhabitants of Dublin, supposed to belong to the end of the twelfth century, occurs the name of a native of Portugal, already established in that important centre of trade[1], while in a royal order belonging to the year 1220, a certain Bartholomew of Portugal is mentioned as one of four citizens of London trading together, and his rights in a matter of arrested goods are recognised by royal authority equally with those of the three Englishmen[2]. As early as 1208 another Portuguese merchant obtained from King John a special safe-conduct, giving him the right to trade securely throughout the king's domains, with entire freedom in coming and going, so long as he paid the right and lawful customs[3]. These were the rights nominally secured by the barons seven years later for all merchants trading in England, but the much-discussed forty-first article of Magna Carta did not remain in force, and the necessity of securing royal safe-conducts was by no means obviated. Under Henry III., it is true, merchants belonging to certain nationalities, such as the Lombards and the Provençals, found great favour at court, but other foreign traders had still no guarantee of security in England, except the Letters Patent of protection which they could purchase from the king. The Portuguese merchants were well aware of this, and in one year, 1226, over a hundred special safe-conducts[4] were secured

[1] *Calendar of Hist. Doc. of Ireland*, 3.
[2] *Rot. litt. claus.*, ed. Hardy, I. 419.
[3] *Rot. litt. pat.*, 1201-16, 87.
[4] *Cal. Pat. Rolls*, 1225-32, 42, 52.

from Henry III. by merchants of Portugal, for themselves, and their goods and merchandise.

Considering the hard struggle for independence from which the Portuguese kingdom had but recently emerged[1], this early activity of the Portuguese merchants is the more remarkable. It is possible, however, that the exceptional anxiety which they showed on this occasion for letters of protection from the English king was due to the seizure at sea, by his orders, of a large Portuguese ship, *La Cardinale.* The fate of this ship and its cargo, as it appears in the Close Rolls for the years 1225-26[2], is a good illustration of Henry's arbitrary methods in dealing with foreign merchants, and at the same time it gives some idea of the uncertain conditions under which the Portuguese merchants had to carry on their trade with England. In September 1225, certain of Henry's knights and servitors, on their way home from Gascony in a large vessel, fell in with the *Cardinale,* manned as it was by thirty Portuguese mariners and merchants, and finding that there was on board a valuable cargo of tallow and oil, without more ado captured ship, men, and goods. The prize was taken to Porchester, whither three royal officials were despatched to watch the unloading of the cargo. An inventory was made of the merchandise found on board, and part of it was delivered to the royal officials, to be handed over to the Mayor of London for the king's use. The oil and tallow were stored in Porchester Castle till they should be needed for one of the king's ships, but the *Cardinale* itself was repaired and apparently incorporated with the English fleet. The luckless Portuguese crew, who stayed in Porchester to learn the fate of their ship, received a dole of half a mark each from the Treasury,

[1] For the early struggle of the Portuguese with the Moors, see Schäfer, *Geschichte von Portugal.*

[2] *Rot. litt. claus.* II., 63, 66, 69, 84, 89, 92, 116, 119.

but the owners of the *Cardinale* soon showed that they were not prepared to submit quietly to the loss of their goods. In December 1225 Henry was induced by an urgent petition to order the release of 40 marks' worth of the merchandise on behalf of six Portuguese scholars at Paris; their parents, it appeared, had been sending the necessary funds for their support in this way, and they were left in great distress by the non-arrival of the goods. Some months later the Portuguese owners themselves entered into negotiations with the king, the result of which was that in May 1226 a royal order was issued for the delivery of the greater part of the captured merchandise, though the ship seems to have remained in the king's hands.

There is, however, sufficient evidence to show that in spite of such accidents as the above Portuguese merchants were in the habit of visiting England for trading purposes, and that the safe-conducts which they secured from English kings at this time were intended for use in this country as well as in the continental possessions of these kings. This is the more interesting, as the flourishing trade carried on in early times between Portugal and Gascony, and the natural opportunities thus afforded for the purchase of Portuguese commodities by English subjects in Bayonne and Bordeaux have tended rather to disguise the fact that at the beginning of the thirteenth century direct commercial relations already existed between Portugal and England. Nevertheless it was sometimes more convenient for the English to trade with the Portuguese through their fellow-subjects in Bordeaux or Bayonne, and Henry III. was glad to deal with them himself when business took him to Gascony. Thus in January 1243 he bought from nine Portuguese merchants in Bordeaux a quantity of wax and rabbit skins to the value of over £400, and about the same time he borrowed £300 in Bordeaux money from one John Johannis, a merchant of Portugal, who with his fellows received from the king a special safe-conduct[1] in Bordeaux for the ensuing six months. In Gascony, however, the Portuguese merchants had to encounter the rivalry of the active and enterprising Gascons, as keen after their own interests and as hardy in facing the perils of the sea as the Portuguese were themselves. Towards the end of the thirteenth century this rivalry deepened into open jealousy and mutual distrust, to such a degree that the Kings of England and Portugal then reigning found it almost beyond their powers to keep the peace; but in the middle of the century the subjects of both kings were seemingly on friendly terms.

Some idea of the nature of the trade carried on between England and Portugal at this time can be obtained from scattered references to Portuguese merchants in the English records, and from the mention of certain English products in a commercial edict issued in 1252 by Alfonso III. of Portugal[2]. It would seem that at first the most valuable commodity imported into England by the Portuguese was wax, which was largely used for sealing important documents, and of which great quantities came to England from Portugal during the whole mediæval period. In 1258, for instance, two Portuguese merchants are mentioned as receiving part of a sum of 67 marks, 3s. 10d., owing to them for 3,535 lb. of wax bought by Henry III. for his own use[3]. Among the other articles brought by the Portuguese to England at this time were skins and leather, several kinds of which are mentioned in the Corporation Records of London

[1] *Cal. Pat. Rolls*, 1232-47, 360, 368, 369.

[2] Ribeiro, *Dissert. Chronol.*, III. 59-72. It is an exceedingly interesting edict, issued with the object of keeping down prices in Portugal. It contains an apparently exhaustive list of the commodities known to Portuguese trade at this time, with a price assigned to each.

[3] *Pat. Roll* (42 Hen. III.), m. 3. See Appendix I. No. 1.

as coming from Spain and Portugal[1]. The early poverty of their country prevented the Portuguese at first from bringing to England any large quantity of the special products such as wine, dried fruits, olive oil, and the like, with which the ships of later Portuguese merchants coming to England were almost entirely laden. During the long quiet reigns of Alfonso III. and Diniz, however, Portuguese commerce grew apace, and at the beginning of the fourteenth century the merchants of Lisbon were already able to export wines, figs, grapes, spices, and other wares, though it is not till rather later that there is any definite mention of these commodities as being brought from Portugal to England. In exchange for these goods the Portuguese merchants brought home various English products. Those mentioned in Alfonso's edict include several articles of London make, and a certain kind of English cloth—"cobitus de Ingres tinto in grano"—which is valued at 45 solidos as against 3 livros, the price of "cobitus de melior escarlata framenga." The other articles mentioned are "melior alfres de auro de Londres," which is worth 6 livros, "meliores cordæ de dona cum auro et argento de Londres," 6 livros, and "aliæ cordæ quæ veniunt de Londres," 25 solidos. There is evidence, however, that in many cases the Portuguese merchants who came to England went on from thence to Flanders, and it is probable that they frequently made a round, exchanging their own wares in England for wool, which they then carried to Flanders for an exchange in cloth, which would be of far greater use in Portugal.

In 1279 Alfonso III. of Portugal was succeeded by his son Diniz, whose accession seemed to mark a general awakening of the national faculties of the Portuguese. The independence of their nation was

[1] *Calendar of Letter-Books of the City of London*: Letter-Book A, 206-7.

no longer threatened either by the Moors or by their Spanish neighbours, who had at length accepted Portugal as a new and separate kingdom. Diniz could therefore turn his attention to the internal development of the country. He recognised the importance of seafaring for Portugal, and its favourable position for trade with foreign countries; he sought to attract a larger population to the coast, and with this end improved several of the seaports, and took steps to preserve their harbours. The fleet also received his special attention, and in 1317 he placed at its head as admiral, Emanuel Pessanha, a Genoese of tried capacity in all that related to seamanship[1]. He had full jurisdiction over the Portuguese fleet, and this arrangement caused great satisfaction, especially in England, where many of the new admiral's relations were highly esteemed denizens, which gave a certain sense of security to English subjects dealing with Portuguese mariners.

Diniz was fully aware of the importance for his merchants of keeping on good terms with the King of England, who was also lord over the rich province of Gascony. An ordinance issued in 1293 shows that England and Flanders, with the north and west coast of France, supplied by far the most important foreign market for Portuguese goods at this time[2], and the friendly letters which Diniz from time to time addressed to Edward I. and Edward II. indicate that it was part of his policy for commercial reasons to increase as far as possible the cordiality already existing between the English and Portuguese crowns. Nevertheless, it became clear towards the close of the thirteenth century that between the merchants of Portugal and the French subjects of Edward I. a serious breach of the peace was impending. The

[1] Schäfer, *Geschichte von Portugal*, I. 316.

[2] Ribeiro, *Dissert. Chronol.*, III. 170. It is an agreement as to dues to be paid by Portuguese ships laden for foreign parts.

ports of Portugal at this time harboured numbers of pirates, and foreign ships carrying valuable cargoes were frequently liable to attack in Portuguese waters, while foreign merchants in Lisbon sometimes had to take sanctuary in a church to save their lives[1]. Though this did not greatly concern the English merchants, who were hardly yet embarking in foreign commerce, the natives of Bayonne and Bordeaux suffered great annoyance from these depredations. According to the custom of the times, they retaliated upon the merchants of Portugal wherever they were to be found, and after much damage had been done matters came to a crisis about 1293. The danger of an outbreak of hostilities seemed to Diniz so great that he wrote a pacificatory letter to Edward I., in which he skilfully tried to throw the blame of recent misdeeds on to the Castilians, who were already in more or less open hostility against Bayonne, but Edward in reply expressed himself unable to acquit the Portuguese of all blame[2]. The English king knew, however, that a serious disturbance of the peace with Portugal was likely to prove disastrous. The merchants of Bayonne, Portugal, and Castile were constantly coming into contact with each other; goods, for instance, belonging to merchants of Portugal were frequently carried in ships of Bayonne[3], while the Portuguese would carry goods for the Castilians, and so on; thus under the strained relations already existing between Bayonne and Castile an open breach with Portugal would be most harmful to the trade of Gascony. Edward therefore wrote commissioning two officials in Gascony to investigate, together with emissaries from Portugal, the complaints of the men of Bayonne with a view to their peaceable settlement[4].

[1] Rymer, *Fœdera* (Record Edition), I. 789.
[2] Rymer, I. 789.
[3] *Cal. Pat. Rolls*, 1292-1301, 34.
[4] Ibid.

The disputes dragged on notwithstanding, till February 1294, when an attempt was made to smooth matters over through the mediation of the Count of Flanders[1]. It was agreed that royal letters should be issued in Gascony, Portugal, and Castile, guaranteeing the freedom and safety in those parts of all merchants belonging to one or another of them, notwithstanding any recent outrages. But such safe-conducts could not be effectual while all parties were conscious only of their own injuries, and much as they both desired peace Edward and Diniz could not continue to neglect the complaints of their subjects. Accordingly the whole matter was at last referred to arbitration, and in April 1294 Edward announced that the method of settlement had been agreed upon. Two commissioners on each side were to receive full powers to enquire into the alleged acts of violence, and to award compensation wherever it might seem to them just. If the four could not agree, a fifth arbitrator of known impartiality was to be chosen, and the decision of the majority was to be binding. As the discussion was expected to prove a long one, the Kings of England and Portugal issued new safe-conducts for each other's subjects, and to avoid all possible danger of further hostilities the Portuguese were specially enjoined not to have their goods carried in Castilian ships for the present, nor to carry Castilian goods in their own ships till the breach between Castile and Bayonne had been healed[2]. Diniz sent to England John Suger and Peter Martin as the two Portuguese commissioners, and in the course of the year 1295 the affair was settled. Edward wrote to Diniz at once announcing the result, and at the same time he sent a letter to Bayonne acquainting his subjects there with the new form of peace and concord with Portugal, and begging them to observe it strictly. He also issued orders to his officials in London, to deliver without delay

[1] Rymer, I. 797. [2] Ibid. 799.

certain merchandise which had lately been arrested at the suit of some merchants of Portugal, in the ships of one Thomas Sely and other London merchants; and to see to it that the Portuguese merchants received their money for the same. Similarly Edward ordered the officials of Portsmouth to release merchandise and a ship belonging to Portuguese merchants, which had been arrested in that port by royal command[1].

Beyond the occasional arrest of their merchandise in English ports, as in this case, the disputes of the Portuguese with the French subjects of the English king had no ill effects on the commercial relations of Portugal with England. From about the middle of the thirteenth century there are many signs of the growing importance of these relations, and of the gradual recognition of the Portuguese in England as traders who belonged to a friendly nation, and whose presence at English markets was on the whole very welcome. As early as 1258 Henry III. had issued Letters Patent in their favour, not only for the small number mentioned by name in the grant, but for all other merchants belonging to the King of Portugal and coming to England with their goods, the letters to remain in force as long as peace should be maintained between the King of England and the said King of Portugal[2]. Edward I. made it part of his policy to encourage all foreign merchants, but the Portuguese he regarded with special favour through the friendly attitude maintained towards himself and his subjects by King Diniz. After the peaceful termination of the dispute of 1294 Edward on several occasions issued special safe-conducts for the merchants of Portugal in his domains[3], to which Diniz responded with similar letters in favour of Edward's subjects; and it was not many years later

[1] *Miscellaneous Rolls* (Chancery), Bdle. 14, No. 8.
[2] *Pat. Roll* (42 Henry III.) m. 13. See Appendix I. No. 2.
[3] Rymer, I. 860; *Cal. Pat. Rolls*, 1292-1301, 482.

before Diniz and Edward II. were congratulating each other on the friendship and concord which had already existed so long between the merchants of Portugal and the subjects of the English king[1].

An interesting indication of the recognised position of the Portuguese merchants in England at the end of the thirteenth century is afforded by a record of the appointment by the Corporation of London in 1283 of brokers[2] of the merchandise coming from Portugal. There is nothing to show that this was the first time such brokers had been appointed; indeed, it seems very probable that the office was already a regular one, for about five years later the Corporation Records mention the swearing in of fresh brokers of the merchandise coming from the same parts. The Portuguese merchants were to be found in other English ports besides London; the Patent Roll of '21 Edward I., for instance, shows some of them at Sandwich buying wine and whalebone off a ship brought in by certain merchants of Bayonne[3].

But it was not long before the increasing prosperity of the Portuguese attracted the jealous attention of English traders—and particularly of the citizens of London. Again and again the Londoners had opposed Edward I.'s policy of favouring foreign merchants, and in 1285 the king had confiscated the city's charters, but in 1298 he restored them, and the corporation then set about making new restrictions on the freedom of foreigners in London. Thus it happened that in 1300 a very tiresome restriction, though one much in favour with mediæval corporations, was laid upon the Portuguese merchants who had taken up their abode in that city. Precept

[1] Rymer, II. 58. See chap i. above.

[2] *Cal. Letter-Books, City of London*, A., 206. For the duties of the broker, and his important position in mediæval commerce, see W. Mitchell, *Law Merchant*, 90-2.

[3] *Cal. Pat. Rolls*, 1292-1301, 16: *Cal. Close Rolls*, 1288-96, 283.

was given them that in future they might no longer keep their own hostels, for eating and sleeping, but that they must lodge only in the houses of freemen of the city; a day was appointed them by which the change of residence must have been effected, and in case of failure to comply with these instructions they were threatened with the loss of all their possessions[1]. The Portuguese could now be supervised in their dealings with one another, and in their retail dealings, matters in which the London citizens were exceedingly jealous; they could thus also be forced to leave the city if their stay became undesirably long, while their hosts made profit during their visit out of the charges made for their entertainment.

Much as Edward must have resented this interference with his commercial policy, he was not just then in so favourable a position towards his London subjects as to make a protest against it. Three years later, however, the Portuguese merchants, together with those of many other important trading nations, received from the English king a grant of privileges which gave them at once complete rights of trade all over England, and a definite status in English law. Various reasons have been put forward for Edward's policy in granting the charter of 1303 to foreign merchants[2], but it is certain that he was anxious to attract more foreign traders to his kingdom, and that he was determined no longer to endure the narrow-minded attitude of the town corporations in this respect. England lay almost outside the regular commercial traffic; her ports were out of the way of the ships which carried on the coasting trade of Flanders, France, and the Spanish Peninsula, and the Portuguese merchants themselves had already shown that they preferred seeking a Flemish market for their goods to facing the perils of shipwreck on

[1] *Cal. Letter-Book*, C, 65.
[2] Schanz, *Englische Handelspolitik*, I. 383-88.

the inhospitable English coast[1]. As England could not do without the products of other countries it was important that the effects of her geographical isolation should not be enhanced by the unreasonable treatment of those foreigners who did visit the country. Moreover, in the present case another consideration probably carried much weight with the hard-pressed monarch, namely, the possibility of securing a substantial pecuniary advantage for himself as well as more attractive conditions of trade for foreign merchants. Hitherto the chief profit to the Crown had probably been derived from the fees paid in the Chancery and Wardrobe for letters of protection and other royal concessions to foreign merchants, or from forced purchases of wines or wax, and other goods, at the king's price or for his use. But now a new source of revenue might be devised to supplement the existing ancient custom on staple commodities exported by native merchants. In 1303, therefore, Edward entered into negotiations with the foreigners trading to England, Germans, French, Spanish, Portuguese, and all others, with the result that certain privileges which had been secured to the merchants of Gascony in August 1302, in return for the payment of an extra fee of two shillings per ton of wine imported, were in the following year extended by an agreement known as Carta Mercatoria to all foreign merchants, in consideration of a new scale of charges on merchandise exported and imported by them.

Henceforth, then, the merchants of Portugal among others could hope to trade in England under more favourable conditions. Full security in England was now guaranteed to them, and they were exempted from all special restrictions and extra payments such as murage, pontage, or pavage. Henceforth they might reside in any town or borough in the kingdom, subject only to the civil and municipal laws of the

[1] *Anc. Corr.*, XX. 18.

country, and the Crown promised not to seize their goods without giving compensation in full. Other stipulations contained in Carta Mercatoria provided for fair dealing between foreign and native traders; and it was also enacted that half of the jury in all cases where a foreigner was concerned should themselves be foreigners. In return for all these benefits each foreign merchant was henceforth to pay the New or Petty Custom, as it was termed, consisting of an increase of 50 per cent. in the amount already paid on wool and leather, a butlerage of 2s. a ton on wine, and a poundage of 3d. on other exports and imports[1]. It must be pointed out, however, that the value of the concessions made in 1303 varied considerably with the character and policy of successive rulers of England, and that, though foreign merchants could no longer be legally oppressed by the king or government, they still suffered frequently from the jealous hostility of native traders and the citizens of the big towns, combined with a great lack of interest in their welfare on the part of the authorities.

As far as the merchants of Portugal are concerned, there are indications that, though the personal relations of their King Diniz were as friendly with Edward II. as with Edward I., their trade with England was not so securely carried on during the reign of Edward II. as during that of Edward I.[2] The new king was on two occasions persuaded to order his officials to cease collecting the Petty Custom, with the intent, as the citizens of London hoped, that the privileges and securities of which it was the price should thereby fall into neglect[3]; and although in return for letters of protection for

[1] Carta Mercatoria (31 Ed. I.) is printed in the Appendix to Hall's *History of the Customs Revenue*; in the *Liber Custumarum*, 205 *et seq.*; in *Rot. Parl.*, V. 422a, etc. See also Schanz, I. 391, and Lindsay, *Merchant Shipping*, I. 403.

[2] For instances of Portuguese merchants plundered in English ports during Edward II.'s reign, see chap. iv.

[3] Schanz, I. 393.

his subjects issued by Diniz, he was ready to grant special safe-conducts for the Portuguese in his kingdom[1], there is no likelihood that these safe-conducts were any more strictly observed by his officials and other subjects than those of Carta Mercatoria. As soon as Edward III. came to the throne, however, the aspect of affairs changed again, and the merchants of Lisbon and Oporto began to receive such consistent favour and protection in England, that before the first half of his reign was well over, they were able on their own authority to conclude an advantageous commercial treaty with the English king.

One reason for Edward III.'s policy in this respect is doubtless to be found in the exigencies of the French war[2], but he also clearly recognised the importance to England of the Portuguese commerce, which was by this time in a flourishing condition. The visits of the Portuguese merchants now not only supplied England with a large number of valuable commodities, such as wax, fruit, leather, salt, and cork, but in addition they helped considerably to swell the royal revenue by the customs paid at the English ports. An interesting indication of the progress of the commercial relations between the two countries is seen in the hire, by four Portuguese merchants in 1338, of a ship of Southampton, with which to go to Spain and Portugal for wines, olive oil, and other goods—a fact which shows a certain amount of confidence on both sides. Edward III. approved of the transaction, granting the four merchants his special protection, from January to Whitsuntide[3]. In this same year a grant was made by Alfonso IV. of Portugal to a certain Gascon merchant, which affords evidence that the subjects

[1] Rymer, II. 58. *Cal. Pat. Rolls*, 1307-13, 106. See also 1321-24, 235.

[2] See p. 7 above.

[3] *Cal. Pat. Rolls*, 1338-40, 1.

of the English king had already begun to take up their abode in Lisbon for trade purposes. The merchant, an native of Old Bayonne, had, according to his own account, lived in Lisbon for five years, but was now afraid that he might be made to suffer because the English had stolen goods off Portuguese ships trading to Flanders and Normandy. Alfonso granted him full security to carry on his trade unmolested, and sent notice to his officials to this effect[1]. It was with one of the daughters of this king that Edward, a few years later, proposed a marriage alliance for one of his own sons, but though this marriage, after it had been agreed upon, was broken off by Alfonso[2] in the most unexpected and inexplicable way, Edward did not allow the favourable attitude which he had hitherto maintained towards the merchants of Portugal to be affected by the strange behaviour of their king. Very soon after the failure of the marriage negotiations, a Lisbon merchant received from him a new and special favour, which affords a good example of the advantages to be obtained at this time in England by foreign merchants whom the king happened to regard with a friendly interest. The Portuguese merchant in this case received royal permission to ship eighteen and a half pieces of English cloth, which he had bought in Southampton with the proceeds of the sale of nine tuns of oil, direct to Portugal, instead of taking it first to the staple at Calais[3].

About this time the Black Death reached Portugal, and under its dread influence enterprise was at a standstill. Lisbon with its large population suffered especially, and its foreign commerce was much disorganised. But, as soon as the terrible shadow had passed away, a fresh vigour began to show itself

[1] *Trans. For. Records*, Series II. No. 153, Sect. ix.
[2] See chap. i.
[3] *Cal. Close Rolls*, 1346-49, 476.

in Portugal, and now Edward III.'s consistent protection of Portuguese merchants and their trade bore fruit in a curious way. It would seem as though the merchants of Lisbon and Oporto, disappointed that the expected matrimonial alliance between England and Portugal should have come to nothing, determined to take the matter into their own hands, and to secure for themselves, at any rate, a satisfactory arrangement with the English king. If once a formal treaty were signed between England and Portugal, Edward's subjects, when they met Portuguese merchants on the sea, could no longer pretend that they were acting in the interests of their king in arresting the ships with the goods they contained, as belonging to enemies of England. Moreover, Flanders was already allied with England, and a treaty with Edward III. would thus afford an additional means of securing Portuguese ships on their way to the Flemish cloth markets.

In 1352 two Portuguese merchants came to Edward with letters from Alfonso IV., stating that he had taken under his protection all the subjects of the English king coming to his realm by land or sea. Edward in reply, as he was expected to do, issued similar letters of protection[1] to Portuguese merchants in his domains, with a number of special safe-conducts to individual merchants of Lisbon and Oporto. But, more than this, the two merchants informed Edward that certain envoys of the King of Portugal were coming to England about Christmas time, with full powers for carrying through a treaty of closer mutual friendship between the two royal houses. Edward willingly issued special letters of protection for these envoys, but when they eventually came it was found that the King of Portugal had no hand in the matter; the envoys, in fact, had their powers not from him, but from the merchants, mariners, and commonalties of the Portuguese sea

[1] Rymer, III. 247.

coast, and the cities of Lisbon and Oporto. Edward III. would doubtless have preferred a political alliance with Alfonso himself, but, failing this, he was very willing to treat on commercial matters alone with these enterprising merchants.

Thus came about the interesting commercial treaty of 1353, signed by the King of England on behalf of his people, and Alfonso Martin Alho on behalf of the merchants of Lisbon and Oporto. The position is fully explained in the preamble, which begins as follows: "Sachent touz que, comes les bones gentz, marchauntz, mariners, et les comunaltes de la marisme, des citees et villes, de Ulixbon et de port du Portugal du roialme et de seignurie de Roi de Portugale eient envoye Alfonso Martyn dit Alho, lour message et procuratour devers le tres excellent prince, monseur Edward par le grace de Dieu Roi d'Engleterre et de Fraunce: de treter des amistes et fermes alliances entre le dit Roi . . . , pur lui et pur sez subgitz, et les gentz, marchauntz . . . et comunaltes . . . avantdites pur eux et chescun de eux."[1] A certain amount of deference was paid to Edward III. as the King of England, in that he was asked to decide whether the treaty should last indefinitely, or for a certain period, and accordingly he fixed fifty years as the limit; otherwise the two parties secured terms practically equal, to their mutual advantage, the preamble goes on to state.

The first few articles of the treaty are concerned with securing the merchants belonging to either party from any kind of injury at the hands of the other party; it was enacted that the merchants and mariners of either side might go securely and freely by land and by sea between all the ports and cities belonging to either party, and henceforth all relations whatsoever between the two parties were to be peacefully conducted. All discussions, dissensions, and discords raised, or damage done

[1] See the text of the treaty in Rymer, *Fœdera*, III. 264.

in time past on either side were to cease, and remain annulled without any action or recovery for all time, and if any harm were done henceforth by one party, to the other, it was to be suitably redressed by the lords or great men of both sides.

Then follow several articles of great importance at this period in a treaty of this kind, dealing as they do with disputed ownership in the case of goods captured in sieges or other hostile encounters. In case the King of England or his people should take from the enemy any town, castle, or port, in which should be found goods belonging to the merchants of Lisbon and Oporto, or ships containing merchandise belonging to the same merchants, it was agreed that the King of England or his captain should cause these goods to be produced, in whose-soever hands they might be, and should loyally do his utmost to restore the said ships or merchandise to their owners, so long as the latter were not armed nor giving aid of any kind to the enemies of the English king. If, however, any Portuguese merchant should be found in arms, or giving aid to the enemies of England, he was to lose not only his goods, but also his life. If English subjects should capture ships belonging to the enemy, in which should be found goods that belonged to the merchants of Lisbon and Oporto, these goods were to be taken to England, and there safeguarded until the owners should make good their claim to them. And, in similar circumstances, "the men of the aforesaid seaboard and cities" were to do the same by the subjects of the King of England. The treaty concludes with a provision that the fishers of Lisbon and Oporto might come freely to fish in the ports of England and Brittany, and wherever else they pleased, paying only the customary dues to the lord of the country.

Though Alfonso had held aloof from the negotiation of the treaty, he evidently accepted the settlement with a very good grace, for shortly afterwards he wrote to Edward III. asking for the restoration of some Portuguese merchandise which had come into English hands, and quoting as his authority this same treaty of 1353, to which Edward alluded in his reply[1] as "the compact so amicably entered into between us." The decision of the case in question shows that both parties were bent on keeping strictly to the letter of its terms. The merchandise had been taken from Portuguese merchants by the French, from whom some English sailors in their turn had recaptured it. The latter brought the goods before the English admiral[2], and having explained the circumstances under which they had captured them, they were allowed to keep them as lawful prize of war. The King of Portugal, however, wrote and expostulated, saying that the admiral had judged without reference to the treaty of 1353, and that the goods belonged by right to his own subjects[3].

Edward III., anxious to please Alfonso, brought the matter before his own council, and had it fully discussed. The result was that the admiral's decision was approved, and a royal letter was therefore sent to Alfonso, explaining that, though the goods in question originally belonged to Portuguese merchants, they had passed entirely out of their possession before ever the English laid hands on them. Edward declared that he was always ready to observe the terms of the agreement of 1353, but that unfortunately these goods did not come under those terms. He therefore advised the Portuguese merchants to proceed against the French, who had committed the original

[1] Rymer, III. i. 138.

[2] This case is noteworthy as one of the earliest occasions on which the decision of an English admiral is mentioned. See Marsden, *Select Pleas in the Admiralty Courts*, Intro. XIV, XLI, etc.

[3] The title of belligerents to such "recaptures," though admittedly just, was destined to be the cause of constant international friction down to the beginning of the last century.

act of violence, rather than against the English, who were in no way guilty. In conclusion, Edward promised that while it would be neither just nor reasonable for him to deprive his subjects of their lawful gains, yet if it should happen that at any time goods actually belonging to the Portuguese should be seized in the ships of his enemies, they should be restored at once, and in every other way he would endeavour to obey the wishes of the King of Portugal.

The commercial treaty of 1353 would have held good till the beginning of the fifteenth century, but before that time, as has already been shown, circumstances had arisen which brought England and Portugal far more closely together.

CHAPTER III

GROWTH AND DEVELOPMENT OF THE TRADE BETWEEN ENGLAND AND PORTUGAL

Entry of English merchants into trade with Portugal—Prosperity of Lisbon—The wine trade—Position of English merchants in Portugal—Portuguese merchants in England under Edward III. and Richard II.—The Treaty of Windsor, and the flourishing state of the trade during the years following it—Portugal's trade with England, as seen in the "*Libelle of English Polycye*"—English merchants acquire new privileges in Portugal—Irish merchants in Portugal—Petitions of English merchants to Alfonso V., 1454 and 1458—Commercial effects of the alliance of 1386—Embassy of John II. to Edward IV.—Embassy of Henry VII. to John II.—End of the mediæval period.

IN the last chapter it was shown that the earliest trade between England and Portugal was carried on almost entirely by the Portuguese, and that English merchants could at first only obtain Portuguese goods when they were brought to England. From the middle of the fourteenth century, however, the commercial relations of England and Portugal became more important, and at the same time more interesting from the English point of view, because now at length Englishmen began to take an active part in the trade. It was quite in keeping with the general development of English wealth and enterprise at this time[1] that native merchants should begin to secure some of the large profits of foreign commerce

[1] Cunningham, *Growth of English Industry and Commerce*, I. 293-94.

by making trading expeditions of their own to foreign countries, and of such countries Portugal was by no means the least attractive to English merchants. In the flourishing commerce of Lisbon there was to be found a reward for many hardships endured on the way. Practically the chief city of a country with a good climate and a fertile soil, Lisbon had, ever since the expulsion of the Moors, thriven under the special care of successive Kings of Portugal, and, long before the discoveries of the fifteenth century, it was famous for the large number of foreign merchants who lived and traded there. According to the chronicler Lopes, there were often as many as 450 foreign and native merchant ships anchored in the mouth of the Tagus, giving every facility for profitable exchanges of goods[1], and more important still, the wine, for which Portugal was beginning to be famous, could be obtained in large quantities in Lisbon, whence, according to Lopes, many thousand tuns of it were exported every year[2]. It was this which formed the chief attraction for English merchants.

As the war between England and France dragged on, and the English hold upon the vineyards of Gascony grew ever less secure, the value of the Portuguese wine trade for England gradually increased. There is evidence that, by the middle of the fourteenth century, Portuguese wine had been coming into England fairly regularly for some years, though it had not yet taken the prominent position among Portuguese exports to England which it was to hold at a later period. As early as 1304 certain merchants of Bayonne are mentioned as lading a ship at Lisbon with "wines, spices, and other wares to the value of 312 marks" for a trading voyage to England[3], and six years later the cargo of a Lisbon merchant who

[1] F. Lopes, *Chron. Fernando*, Intro.
[2] Ibid.
[3] *Cal. Pat. Rolls*, 1301-7, 210.

was wrecked at Hove was shown to have consisted largely of grapes[1], proving that the products of the Portuguese vines were known in England at the beginning of the fourteenth century. As the population of Portugal began to increase, and as the merchants found the wine trade more profitable than any other, the cultivation of vineyards took the place of corn-growing in Portugal. In 1338 four Portuguese merchants had hired an English ship for the express purpose of trading to Spain and Portugal for wines and olive oil[2], and some years later the importation of wine from the Spanish Peninsula had become so important as to call for special mention in a royal ordinance of 1366[3]. For Portuguese wines especially, the market in England was already so good, towards the end of Edward III.'s reign, as to attract foreign merchants to take part in the trade, for a charter of 1372 mentions the lading of 109 tuns of wine in Lisbon by a Genoese merchant, almost certainly bound for England[4], and a few years later a certain merchant of Bruges, whose ship was wrecked off the English coast, turned out to have had on board a large cargo of Portuguese wines, which he was bringing to Bristol for sale in England[5]. Moreover, the fact that, during the latter half of the fourteenth century, special privileges were on several occasions conferred upon English merchants in Portugal makes it probable that they themselves were proving good customers for the Portuguese wine-sellers.

To add to these inducements, of a good opportunity for all kinds of trade, and a plentiful supply of a valuable commodity for which there was a constant demand, English merchants visiting Portugal had the knowledge of the long-established friendship between the Kings of England and Portugal, and of the treaty

[1] *Cal. Pat. Rolls*, 1307-13, 252.
[2] Ibid. 1338-40, 1.
[3] Rymer, III. 781.
[4] F. Michel, *Commerce à Bordeaux*, I. 335.
[5] *Rot. Parl.*, III. 546.

of 1353, whereby the Portuguese people had undertaken to do no harm to any English merchants who might visit their country. Though there is no mention of this treaty after 1357, it cannot have been wholly without effect in encouraging the English to set foot in Portugal, and this effect was increased by the Portuguese kings, who granted special privileges to English merchants in their kingdom. The royal edict, usually taken as the first grant of privileges to the English in Portugal, is one which belongs to the reign of Pedro I. (1357-67), and in which, curiously enough, the English are apparently not mentioned by name, though Scotch merchants appear among the foreign traders to whom the grant was made[1]. The edict was issued in 1363, and its purpose was to confirm to all foreign merchants in Portugal their right to lade their ships as they chose, instead of employing the carrier whom Pedro had attempted to appoint. It was not long, however, before the increasing number of English merchants coming to his kingdom induced Ferdinand, who succeeded Pedro in 1367, to grant them particular facilities of their own for the more convenient conduct of their trade. The great difficulty of ensuring a just administration of the law in cases where native and foreign merchants stood opposed to each other, had led to Edward I.'s enactment that half of the jury in all such cases should be composed of fellow-countrymen of the foreigners concerned. In Portugal this difficulty was now surmounted rather differently, and apparently as a special favour for English merchants alone. According to Ferdinand's grant of 1367[2], the judge of the custom-house at Lisbon was appointed sole judge in all lawsuits between English and Portuguese merchants, and all other judges were forbidden henceforth to take cognizance of such

[1] Brit. Mus. MS., *Lansdowne*, 190, f. 4.

[2] *Trans. For. Records*, Series II. No. 153. Printed in Postlethwayt, *Dictionary of Trade and Commerce*, art. "Treaties."

cases. In this way a fair hearing was secured to the English, for a judge appointed, because it was Ferdinand's "desire to favour the English merchants," was likely if anything to favour them himself rather than the Portuguese. To the English traders, bewildered by new customs and a strange language, the possession of a judge whom they could trust, must indeed have been a boon[1].

The alliance formed by Edward III. and Ferdinand in 1373, and its renewal in 1380 with Richard II.[2] may have helped in some measure to strengthen the bond between the subjects of these kings, and the expedition of the Earl of Cambridge in 1381 gave excellent facilities for trade, which were probably not neglected[3]. In Portugal, of course, as elsewhere, foreign merchants had to submit to a number of restrictions on their freedom of trade, imposed for the sake of protecting and furthering native enterprise. In 1375, for instance, Ferdinand issued a charter to the effect that foreigners might only buy goods "of averdupois" in Lisbon itself[4]; and during his reign he made various other provisions for the good of the navigation and commerce of his kingdom, especially with a view to increasing the number of native ships and shipbuilders[5]. Nevertheless, his anxiety for the welfare of his fleet did not prevent Ferdinand from occasionally setting aside his own enactments, for fear of discouraging foreign traders from coming to Portugal, and thus in 1383, on petition of two Englishmen, he ordered that in spite of his previous command that all merchandise should be carried in Portuguese ships only, all English merchants should be allowed to embark

[1] A hundred years later the English merchants in Lisbon quoted it as one of their most valuable privileges.

[2] See p. 9.

[3] See F. Lopes, *Chron. Delrey Don Fernando*, cap. cxxxi.

[4] Santarem, *Quadro Elementar*, I. 21.

[5] *Monarchia Lusitania*, VIII. Book xxii. cap. xxx.; Schäfer, II., 103, 104.

and transport to their own country such goods as they desired, in their own ships, and without any fear of molestation on the part of the royal officials[1].

Whether as the result of Ferdinand's encouraging attitude or not, the voyages of English merchants to Portugal certainly increased in number during the latter part of Edward III.'s reign, for, by the year 1375, when an inquisition was taken at Queensboro' as to the rates of hire for sailors going to different parts of Europe, the port of Lisbon had come to be regarded as one of the usual places to which English ships now sailed, and there was already a customary rate of transport thither[2].

The Portuguese merchants who came to England during this same period seemed to have enjoyed the utmost amount of protection and security compatible with the troublous times in which Edward III. reigned. Not only had he formed an important treaty with them, but he evidently did all that lay in his power to secure the observance of its terms by his officials and other subjects. Edward III.'s attitude in commercial matters was strongly on the side of law and order in the interests of foreign merchants[3], and any particularly grievous tale of wrong done to Portuguese merchants was sure to elicit from him an indignant command for restitution or redress. Thus in December 1371 the mayor and bailiffs of Bristol, and many other ports, received peremptory orders to see to it that the Portuguese merchants coming to these ports should on no account be molested, and to have it publicly proclaimed throughout the towns and their suburbs that these merchants should be treated in every way as

[1] *Trans. For. Records*, Series II. No. 153.

[2] *Black Book of the Admiralty*, I. 139: "The jurymen doe say that by auncient custome a marriner is to take for hire from the Poole of London to Lisbone 20 shillings (and) the portage of a tun."

[3] See a paper by Dr Cunningham on the *Commercial Policy of Edward III.*, in *Trans. Roy. Hist. Soc.*, N.S., IV. 197.

friends and well-wishers. If through enmity any Portuguese goods happened to have been arrested already, they were to be released immediately and restored to their owners[1]. Three days later a similar letter was sent[2] to the seneschal of the Prince of Wales in the county of Cornwall, stating that the king had heard that he had arrested, without cause, certain merchants of Portugal in Dartmouth and Falmouth, and ordering him on pain of forfeiture instantly to set free all such merchants, and allow them to go whither they pleased without injury. On the same day special safe-conducts were issued to the masters of several Portuguese ships, with licence to trade between England and Portugal for the space of a year[3], free from all interference on the part of English officials. Three years later the Portuguese merchants again began to complain, and in September 1374 another proclamation was issued, almost identical in words with the former ones, and most strictly forbidding the molestation of Portuguese subjects coming to England for the sake of trade, or for any other honest cause whatever[4].

The nature of the complaints of the Portuguese merchants during the early years of Richard II.'s reign is sufficient to show the alteration caused by the death of Edward III. in the conditions of their trade. Their stories now show insubordination on the part of inferior servants of the king, the interfer-

[1] Rymer, III. 929. The other ports were Barnstaple, Exeter, Dartmouth, Fowey, Plymouth, Melcombe, Weymouth, Southampton, Chichester, Lynn, etc.

In *Letter-Book G of the City of London* (see p. 290 of the Calendar), there is a notice of a similar proclamation received by the Corporation on the same day, 3rd December.

[2] Rymer, III. 929.

[3] Ibid.

[4] Rymer, III. 1013. Sent to London, Southampton, Exeter, Plymouth, Dartmouth, Bristol, the Cinque Ports, and Falmouth. Notice of the receipt of these letters by the Corporation of London is contained in *Letter-Book G*. (Calendar, p. 327.)

ence of interested persons in the settlement of disputes as to arrested goods, delay in the administration of justice, and the fruitless appeal of suits from one court to another[1]. In short, the consistent policy of Edward III. was abandoned, and in its stead was a kind of disorder, in which foreign merchants must shift for themselves. It is, indeed, doubtful whether Richard II.'s ministers had either the power or the inclination to deal consistently with the foreign merchants coming to England at this time, for a strong reaction was just setting in among the English influential classes against the prominent position which foreigners had so long held in England as compared with themselves[2]. The result of this movement is to be seen in a new tendency in English legislation at this time towards the advancement of native interests at the expense of those of foreign nations, while the complaints and petitions of foreign merchants in England afford ample evidence that the authorities took small care of their feelings or convenience.

Moreover, besides the reaction against all foreign merchants in England, and the consequent indifference of English officials to the welfare of the Portuguese, the commercial relations between England and Portugal during the early years of Richard II.'s reign illustrate the further progress of the movement with which this reaction was connected, and the beginnings of which were already noticed during the reign of Edward III., namely, the entry of English merchants into competition with foreigners abroad[3]. As far as Portugal is concerned, for instance, the last twenty-five years of the fourteenth century form a period of transition, during which the character of the trade relations altered

[1] See chap. iv.

[2] Cunningham, *Growth of English Industry and Commerce*, I. 377, 394.

[3] Ibid. 373.

imperceptibly, the English merchants gradually overtaking the Portuguese, and finally almost passing them in the race for the profits arising from the commerce they carried on together. One reason for this is to be found in the rapid growth of the English cloth industry, by means of which England was now able to produce woollen goods which found a ready and profitable sale in almost all foreign markets. It seems to have been partly in taking these goods across the sea that English merchants learnt the advantages of taking an active part in foreign commerce; in Portugal, at any rate, the merchants who began during these years to come over from England seem at first to have dealt almost entirely in cloth, for it was as cloth merchants that they became known, and as cloth merchants that they received trading privileges from successive Portuguese kings[1]. Hence, not only was there no longer the same necessity[2] as there had been in the time of Edward I. to encourage foreign merchants to visit England's shores, but also the influence of her own merchants was all against any favour being shown to aliens. For practical purposes, the only drawback to the positive maltreatment of foreign merchants in

[1] In this connection, the *Particular Accounts* of the customers at Bristol, which still exist for the years 1378-82, and 1390-91, give some interesting details. By 1378 the cloth trade between that port and Lisbon was already in a flourishing condition, and about two-thirds of the cloths shipped for Portugal are entered as belonging to English merchants, who either went over with them or sent them to their factors already established in Lisbon. The proportion of English to Portuguese ships engaged in the trade was roughly 2 : 5. Ten years later, from September 1390 to December 1391, the accounts record the departure of twenty ships laden with cloth for Portugal; all the ships without exception were English, and out of a total of over 2,000 cloths only three apparently belonged to Portuguese merchants (*K. R. Customs Accounts*, Bdle. 16, Nos. 4, 5, 9, 11, 13, 19, 23). In one of the earlier accounts twenty cloths are entered as belonging to King Ferdinand himself. (Bdle. 16, No. 11.)

[2] It would seem, on the other hand, that the trade with Portugal was so profitable in Richard II.'s reign that steps had to be taken to check the smuggling of English goods into that country. See Appendix I. No. 7.

England now lay in the certainty of reprisals when the English merchants went abroad.

At this point, however, the commercial relations between England and Portugal assumed a new aspect owing to the circumstances attending the death of Ferdinand and the accession of John I., which have already been described[1]. By the terms of the Treaty of Windsor, as has been seen, the Kings of England and Portugal made themselves each responsible for the protection in their own domains of the subjects of the other king, and as soon as Portugal settled down again after the events of the years 1383-87 John showed that his part of the promise at least had been no empty word. The new king owed his position greatly to the prompt action of the citizens and merchants of Lisbon and Oporto, and commercial matters from the beginning received his earnest attention[2]. Ordinances of 1394 and 1395 relieved all foreign merchants in Lisbon from a number of tiresome regulations, and at the same time John's subjects were strictly forbidden, on pain of instant and severe punishment, in any way to insult or molest foreigners living in, or coming to, Portugal for the sake of trade[3]. The English merchants in particular, as has been seen, received in 1389 privileges hitherto enjoyed only by the Genoese and Pisans, and in 1400 John I. issued a new charter, conferring fresh favours on English merchants, and confirming them in the enjoyment of the privileges of the Genoese[4].

Probably, however, the royal grants by which the English merchants in Portugal benefited most were the regulations framed during John's reign for the better ordering of their cloth trade in Lisbon.

[1] Chap. i.

[2] Several merchants were members of John's council during his regency, and a merchant called Lopo Martins afterwards became chief magistrate in Lisbon.

[3] Santarem, *Quadro Elementar*, I. 21. The ordinances are transcribed in *Trans. For. Records*, Series II. No. 155.

[4] Postlethwayt, art. on "Treaties."

Several of these regulations are mentioned with gratitude in a petition presented in 1454[1] to Alfonso V., John's grandson, which shows that they were highly valued by those for whom they were framed. According to them, for instance, John, seeing that on account of the frequent long disputes as to the quality of their cloths the English merchants could not reload their ships and return within a month as they used to do, which was causing many complaints on the part of the ship-owners, ordered that henceforth the cloths should all be examined on the day of purchase, and that a broker should be present in every case to seal the goods. If any dispute arose it must be brought forward at once, and decided upon there and then by the judge of the custom-house and two merchants sworn on the Gospels, after which no further complaints were to be made[2]. It was also arranged, to make it easier for the English merchants to get their money from the purchasers of their cloths, that as soon as any goods had been delivered the vendors should give a list of them, with the sum owing in each case, to a certain Alfonso Bernaldez, who was appointed as proctor for the English merchants, and who, with the porter of the custom-house, was to see that they received their money at once. If the Portuguese merchants delayed payment, their goods were to be distrained; and if after nine days they still had not paid their debts their goods were instantly to be sold, according to instructions given to Nuno Vaz, the comptroller, that the English might be sure of having their money without delay[3]. As another special favour to the English cloth merchants, John remitted one-fourth of the "sisa" or import duty on the cloths which they brought into his kingdom[4].

[1] *Trans. For. Records*, Series II. No 154. Printed in Schanz, *Englische Handelspolitik*, II. 498-522.

[2] *Petition of* 1454, cap. 11.

[3] Ibid. cap. 12.

[4] Ibid. cap. 23.

But while Portugal was thus amply fulfilling its share of the engagements entered into in 1386, it can hardly be said that during Richard II.'s lifetime much regard was paid to the Treaty of Windsor in England. There are, indeed, many indications that during the last few years of the fourteenth century the Portuguese merchants received but scant courtesy at the hands of their new allies. This was partly due to the unfortunate fact that John was obliged to raise considerable loans in England at the time of his accession, which loans he afterwards found much difficulty in repaying. Many of the English merchants, therefore, who had advanced large sums of money to the King of Portugal, felt themselves justified in recouping themselves by arresting the goods of his subjects wherever they could lay their hands on them. In spite of urgent remonstrances on the part of the Portuguese, this state of things lasted through the remainder of Richard's reign, and it was not till the accession of Henry IV. that any adequate attempt was made to deal with the matter[1]. Nor was this all that the Portuguese had to suffer. A new import duty was suddenly imposed on wine, and Portuguese shipmasters who protested against it were detained until they saw fit to pay the sum required. This threw the "council and good men" of Oporto into consternation, and obliged them to revive an old custom of mutual insurance against embargoes in foreign lands[2]. Also, according to the petition of one Diego Alfonse[3], a citizen of Oporto, Portuguese merchants were frequently detained in English ports against their will, even when they were driven in simply by stress of weather, for the sake, as it would appear, of forcing them to sell their goods at a sacrifice rather than let them spoil.

[1] This episode is described more fully in chap. iv. below.
[2] Ribeiro, *Dissert. Chron.*, I. 317.
[3] *Patent Roll* (20 Richard II.), m. 38.

With the accession of Henry IV., however, the aspect of affairs grew brighter. For the first time the Portuguese merchants began to benefit from the Treaty of Windsor. The English creditors of the King of Portugal were no longer allowed to act on their own authority in arresting Portuguese merchandise, and several proclamations were issued, forbidding, under heavy penalties, all attempts to molest Portuguese subjects for this or any other reason[1]. In May 1404, Henry Pay, "the Rover of Poole," was specially warned not to attack vessels belonging to Spain or Portugal[2]. Petitions of this period show that Henry IV. had a great deal of trouble in restoring order after the deposition of Richard II.; the Patent Rolls for the early years of his reign contain many entries relating to ships seized at sea contrary to existing alliances, and among these several are entered as belonging to Portuguese merchants. Even when order was restored, there is no reason for supposing that the position of the Portuguese merchants in England was in any way a specially favoured one; privileges such as those granted to the English by John and his successors were never enjoyed by the Portuguese in the land of their allies. Under most of the English kings of the fifteenth century, an attempt was made to secure justice and fair treatment for them in carrying on their trade, but this was the most they might expect.

Nevertheless, their unprivileged position does not seem to have troubled the Portuguese merchants very much, for during the early part of the fifteenth century their trade with England seems to have been particularly brisk. It has been shown that some hundreds of pieces of cloth were by this time shipped every year to Portugal from Bristol alone, and besides cloth the Portuguese were busily engaged

[1] See chap. iv. below.
[2] Wylie, *Henry IV.*, I. 444.

in exporting English wheat and barley, tin and lead, arms and armour. The quantity of wheat produced in Portugal had diminished by degrees as the male population betook themselves to sea, or turned to the more profitable business of vine-cultivation, till at length this country was obliged to seek elsewhere for the means to supply the needs of its own people. England, on the other hand, was still able to produce quantities of cereals over and above the amount required for home consumption. During part of Richard II.'s reign the export of English corn was forbidden[1], but this injunction must have been disregarded, for in the Patent Roll of 1387 there is mention of a licence to ship corn to Bordeaux, Bayonne, or Portugal[2], and by the time of the Treaty of Windsor the Portuguese had evidently begun to reckon on a supply of wheat or barley from English markets. It was of great importance for Portugal that the supply of foreign corn should not fail, and in 1399 John I. issued an ordinance for the special protection and safe-conduct, even in case the war between England and France should be renewed, of all merchants of Flanders, Brittany, and other countries, bringing bread to sell in Lisbon[3]. Even so the supply was not always sufficient, for John had sometimes to press merchants into the wheat trade[4], and about 1413 he was obliged to send a special ambassador to the King of England on account of the urgent need of bread for the citizens of Lisbon, to arrange for a large quantity to be sent as soon as possible[5]. The French Rolls

[1] Hall, *Customs Revenue*, Appendix I. 233, 238. *Rot. Parl.*, III. 141, 154. (6 Ric. II.)

[2] *Cal. Pat. Rolls*, 1385-89, 281.

[3] *Trans. For. Records*, Series II. No. 155, fol. 55. These merchants petitioned for equal security in Portugal with the English merchants. The document is printed in Schanz, II. 497.

[4] See *Anc. Petition*, 10838.

[5] Brit. Mus. MS. *Vespasian* C. XII. fol. 156. See Appendix I. No. 10.

of 1413 and 1414 contain several entries of licences to export corn to Portugal—in one case as much as 100,000 qrs. being sent[1].

Though not so necessary as corn, English armour, tin, and lead also found a good market in Portugal at this time. The first of these was, of course, chiefly imported for royal use. In 1397 John exported 500 spears, and in 1414-15, during the preparations for the expedition to Ceuta, he exported altogether 750 lances, and 6 harnesses for men-at-arms[2]. Three years later 300 lance staves were exported for the use of the Infant Dom Henry, and in 1421 two Portuguese ambassadors left England with 600 more lances[3]. In 1405 a large supply of lead was bought in England for the use of the King of Portugal, and on another occasion Alfonso V. exported 3,000 lb. of tin and 2,000 lb. of lead[4]. The custom accounts for Bristol, also, contain entries of several shipments of tin, lead, or pewter to Lisbon or Oporto[5].

The Patent Rolls of the earlier years of Henry IV.'s reign give some interesting details with regard to the merchants engaged in the trade between England and Portugal. In some cases English and Portuguese merchants are seen trading together, as for instance a certain John Lucas of Plymouth, and Fonsus Martyn, and Rigo Gonsalvez of Portugal, who freighted their ship *La Trinite* at Lisbon for a mutual trading voyage[6]; or the merchants who laded *La Katerine* with wine and olive oil for England, Andrew Dymanges, John English, and Peter Marchaunt, who are all described as subjects of the King of Portugal[7], but one at least of whom must have

[1] *French Roll* (1 Henry V.), m. 14. For other references see *Deputy Keeper's Report*, 44, Appendix, 543, etc.

[2] Rymer, III. iv. 141; IV. ii. 88, 101.

[3] Ibid. IV. iii. 5; iv. 34.

[4] Ibid. IV. i. 80; V. ii. 71.

[5] See chap. v. below.

[6] *Cal. Pat. Rolls*, 1401-5, 277.

[7] Ibid. See also 276, 281.

been of English origin. Another point of interest that appears from the petitions, is the fact that foreign merchants were also engaged in carrying on this trade. Several petitions are presented in the name of one Michael de Mane, who is described as a merchant of Piedmont living in Portugal, whence he carried on business with his partner Richard Garner, also from Piedmont, who lived in London. They apparently traded chiefly in fruit, but also in wine, hides, and wax, which Michael bought in Portugal and despatched to Richard in London. On one occasion the King of Portugal, finding one of their ships on the point of departure with 900 couples of fruit, valued at £315; 16 tuns of wine, at £147, 10s.; 201 ox hides, at £40, 4s.; and 4 bales of wax, at £29, 8s., forced the master, in spite of the valuable cargo, to sail first to Harfleur for wheat, which was badly needed in Portugal, but in getting which the Portuguese ship fell into the hands of certain English sailors. Michael de Mane therefore petitioned the King of England, and a commission was issued to the royal serjeant-at-arms, to cause restitution to be made, or compel the malefactors to appear before the king and council within fifteen days[1].

The remaining years of Henry IV.'s reign passed without bringing much change in the commercial relations of England and Portugal. Both countries enjoyed a short period of peace and quiet, during which commerce throve and prosperity increased. John and Henry were both careful not to disturb the alliance existing between their kingdoms, and, except for occasional complaints of theft, their subjects seem to have acquiesced very willingly in a friendship which was advantageous to both parties. In 1412 a royal letter was despatched to Portugal on behalf of a London citizen named Thomas Fauconer, whose ship had been seized in the most

[1] *Anc. Pet.*, 10838, 10852; *Cal. Pat. Rolls*, 1401-5, 507, 508.

audacious way by one of John's own officials[1]; but the matter was evidently settled at once, for no further trouble was caused. In the same year there is an interesting entry of 96 pipes of wine of Algarve bought from a Portuguese merchant named Oliveiro Martin, for the use of the King of England, at the rate of £4 per pipe; the usual rate at which Portuguese wine seems to have been sold at this time[2].

As the century advanced, however, the relations between the merchants of the two countries became less peaceful. The revival of the French war had a disastrous effect in emboldening English pirates or privateers to prey upon all sea-going commerce, regardless of the alliances of their sovereign; and, among others, Portuguese merchant ships suffered severely. The Portuguese were not slow to retaliate, and by degrees there ensued a terrible state of confusion, in which reprisals and counter-reprisals formed the order of the day[3]. In October 1436 a royal proclamation was issued in England[4], followed in February 1437 by special letters to the customers at Bristol and other ports[5], insisting on the better observance of the existing alliance with Portugal, and prohibiting, under severe penalties, any infringement of its terms. Some months later, in August 1437, the King of Portugal issued similar orders to his officials, forbidding any of his subjects to molest English merchant vessels[6]; but there is nothing to show that these steps had the desired effect. On the contrary, there is evidence that during the middle of the fifteenth century the plunder of English and Portuguese ships was at its height.

No serious diminution of the trade between the two countries seems to have followed as a consequence

[1] Rymer, IV. ii. 8.
[2] Devon, *Issues of the Exchequer*, 328.
[3] See chap. iv.
[4] Rymer, V. i. 35.
[5] Ibid. 37.
[6] Ibid.

of this, though the merchants who carried it on took more special precautions to secure themselves against violence. Letters of special protection against reprisals were obtained by many English merchants from the King of Portugal[1], and the Portuguese merchants in their turn applied to the English government. The French Rolls of Henry VI.'s reign contain numerous entries of royal licences or safe-conducts for Portuguese ships or shipmasters trading to England[2], and on two occasions a general safe-conduct was issued for all Portuguese ships coming to English ports. The merchants of Portugal brought goods which were always welcome in England, and so long as they reached harbour safely, they were sure of a good market. The writer of the *Libelle of English Polycye*, a poem supposed by internal evidence to belong to the year 1436, has given a good description of the trade of Portuguese merchants with England at this time. Though he has many sharp words for the merchants of other countries, he regards the Portuguese with favour, partly as the ancient allies of England, and partly because they brought goods worth having, so different from the

> "Trifles, trifles that litelle have availede
> And things wyth whiche they fetely blere our eye[3],"

too often exchanged by foreigners for good English cloth. Of Portugal the writer says:

> "The marchaundy also of Portyngale
> To diverse londes torne into sale
> Portyngalers wyth us have trought one hande
> Whose marchaundy cometh moche into Englande
> They bene our ffrendes wyth there commoditez
> And wee English passen into these countrees.

[1] Some details as to these safe-conducts are given in chap. iv.

[2] For references see *Deputy Keeper's Report*, 48, Appendix, 217, etc.

[3] *Libelle of English Polycye*, in Wright, *Political Songs*, II. 173.

Here londe hathe oyle, wine, osey, wax and grayne
Fygues, reysyns, honey, and cordewayne;
Dates and salt, hydes and such marchaundy[1]."

No change seems to have taken place in the status or condition of Portuguese merchants in England, for many years after this description was written, and during the remainder of the mediæval period interest centres rather on the English merchants in Portugal, where they were acquiring a privileged position[2] which became even more valuable as the great Portuguese navigators of the fifteenth century raised their country above all other commercial nations[3]. The favours bestowed by John I. on English residents in Lisbon were continued by Edward[4], his son, and Alfonso V., his grandson, with additions in some cases which greatly increased their utility. It has already been mentioned that during John's reign a certain Alfonso Bernaldez was appointed proctor or consul for the English merchants in Lisbon[5], an appointment rendered necessary, as the English explained, by the constant annoyances which arose from their having to carry on business in a language which they understood very imperfectly. The English residents seem to have

[1] *Libelle of English Polycye*, in Wright, *Political Songs*, II. 162. The author of the poem complains, however, of the preference for Flemish markets so often shown by the Portuguese:

"And if they would to Flanders passe forth bye
They schulde not be suffred ones nor twyes
For supportynge of our cruel enemyes."

[2] Apart from the fact already mentioned (fn. p. 17) that it is difficult to find evidence of Portuguese merchants living in England during the Middle Ages, whereas the English "factory" in Lisbon was well established by the beginning of the fifteenth century, there was far more reason for special privileges in the case of the English cloth merchants, whose trade was of high value to Portugal, than in that of the Portuguese, who only brought to England goods which, though valuable, could be equally well supplied by many other nations.

[3] See Beazley, chap. xx., and Morse Stephens, chaps vii. and ix.

[4] Portuguese "Duarte," after his great grandfather, Edward III.

[5] See p. 56.

elected him themselves, and his election was confirmed on John's death by Edward, and later in the name of his infant successor Alfonso V.[1]. Again, for the convenience of merchants who wished to take wine back to England in exchange for their cloths, Edward took steps to prevent unfair charges being made by the collectors of the export duties. The rate of payment was an "almude"[2] and a half of wine from every tun exported, but, as the English preferred to pay the duty in money, the head of the custom-house and the receivers of the customs contrived to cheat them systematically, charging them on all wines, cheap and dear alike, the price of an "almude" and a half of the most costly. To remedy this Duarte issued a charter[3] to the effect that henceforth the English merchants should pay in every case according to the price at which they bought each wine, and in no other way[4].

In most cases, the English who took up residence in Lisbon were factors or agents for merchants in England, and King Edward himself had his English factor, a certain John Chirche, who made trading voyages to England and elsewhere at the king's bidding. On one occasion, for instance, he came to England for sixty sacks of Cotswold wool, which he was allowed by a special favour to export custom free, and which he then took to Florence "for the provision of cloths of gold brocade and silk for the king's own use"[5]. So many of the English had, indeed, begun to live in Lisbon that, in Alfonso V.'s reign, at any rate, they already had their own chapel of San Domingos in that city, where notices referring to their trade were sometimes posted, so that none

[1] *Trans. For. Records*, Series II. No. 153, 30th May 1439.

[2] An almude is $\frac{1}{26}$th of a tun.

[3] Cited in the English petition of 1458, cap. 37. Schanz, II. 520.

[4] The Portuguese vintages mentioned in this connection are "Ribatejo, D'Almadaa, D'Azoya de Villa Longa, Pedra da Estrema, Ribas d'Alemquer."

[5] *French Roll* (15 Henry VI.), m. 5.

might be able afterwards to allege ignorance of the Portuguese king's decrees[1].

Some of the most interesting of the grants to English subjects made by Alfonso V., who came to the throne in 1438, are those to .Irish merchants, of whom a large number were evidently engaged in trade with Portugal. The geographical position of Ireland lends itself to this trade, and as early as 1353 the Irish were mentioned among the subjects of Edward III., who received by his treaty with the Portuguese merchants full permission and security to go and trade in Portugal. Whether as the result of this or not, an extensive trade had sprung up between Ireland and Portugal before the end of the fourteenth century, and in 1379 the Irish petitioned in Parliament that "pur profit le Roi et grant relevation de sa Terre d'Irlande," the merchants of Portugal might come safely into Ireland with their wines and other merchandise, and that their own merchants might be allowed to go freely to Portugal and Lisbon[2]. During the fifteenth century this trade increased; Portuguese ships visiting Bristol would cross to Ireland and back again before returning home[3], while Irish ports like Waterford carried on a large share of their commerce directly with Portugal[4]. Among the municipal archives of Waterford, for instance, there is recorded a complaint against absenteeism on the part of the mayor and members of the corporation during their year of office, in which Portugal and Flanders are mentioned as the foreign lands which chiefly tempted these functionaries to forsake their charge[5]. It has already been noticed that Prince Henry the Navigator had his own agent in Galway, and it seems probable

[1] Mentioned in an ordinance of 1471, *Trans. For. Records*, II. 154. See also Appendix I. No. 15.

[2] *Rot. Parl.*, III. 86a.

[3] See *K. R. Customs Account* $\frac{19}{4}$ 1466, 15th and 28th February.

[4] *Hist. MSS. Com.*, X. v. 267.

[5] Ibid., 313.

that many Irish merchants had their factors in Lisbon. Piracy near the Irish coasts, however, seems to have been nearly as prevalent as in the English Channel, and in any case the Irish merchants were held responsible in Portugal for the misdeeds of their fellow-subjects the English. Consequently, it was equally necessary that they should secure themselves against reprisals, and during Alfonso V.'s reign several special safe-conducts in Portugal were obtained by Irish merchants. Merchants from Limerick and Galway are mentioned in this connection, and the language of one grant seems to show that the four persons in whose favour it was issued were already resident in Lisbon[1].

Among other royal grants issued for English subjects in Lisbon during Alfonso's reign two of special interest may be mentioned. In 1448 there was confirmed for a certain Nicholas Brown, an English merchant living in Lisbon, a long list of privileges which he had received from Alfonso's father, King Edward, exempting him from the payment of any special taxes, excises, imposts, services, or any other charge which might be imposed by the king or council in Portugal. No one of any condition whatsoever was to be lodged in his house, nor take his bread, wine, cloths, straw, nor any other thing belonging to him, under a penalty of 6 milreis[2]. Some years later, Alfonso granted a very special favour to one John Redy, another English merchant, who received a licence to carry arms at his pleasure on any occasion, night or day, throughout the whole of Portugal, notwithstanding the royal ordinance to the contrary[3]. Also,

[1] *Trans. For. Records*, Series II. No. 153. Grant dated 12th July 1465.

[2] *Trans. For. Records*, Series II. No. 153. Grant dated 10th December 1448. See Appendix I. No. 13.

[3] Ibid. Grant dated 22nd October 1462. The carrying of arms in Portugal had been forbidden to foreigners in 1442, and refused to the English in 1454.

in 1452, all the English, Flemish, German, and French merchants resident in Lisbon received a grant of privileges very similar to those given to Nicholas Brown, with the addition of an important assurance that their houses henceforth should on no account be taken for the king's use by the royal harbinger. All breaches of the royal commands to the harm of the foreign merchants were also henceforth made punishable by a fine of 6 milreis[1].

In 1454, however, the English cloth merchants then living in Lisbon, finding that general grants of this nature still left room for a great deal of annoyance and incivility on the part of the customs' officials, and others of Alfonso's subjects with whom their trade brought them into contact, presented the Portuguese king with a list of twenty-eight of their grievances, with petitions for redress[2]. Alfonso realised as John I. had done the importance for Portugal of foreign trade, and always sought to encourage foreign merchants to remain in Lisbon; therefore, on this occasion the English received a satisfactory answer to almost all their petitions. They complained of dishonesty and favouritism on the part of the customs' officials, of delayed payments and similar irregular proceedings in other quarters, and of frequent unjust arrests of their own persons. Alfonso accordingly ordered the prompt despatch of all business, at times convenient to the merchants as well as to his officials, who were to proceed in all respects fairly and honestly on pain of fine or dismissal. As to cloths lost or stolen after they had been placed in the custom-house, the doorkeeper was to be held responsible for them; disputes as to the value of the cloths were to be brought forward at the time of purchase, and settled at once; and English merchants, if arrested on suspicion of wrongdoing, were to be instantly released on satisfying

[1] Postlethwayt, *Dictionary*, art. "Treaties," 28th March 1452.
[2] Printed in Schanz, II. 498-516.

the magistrates as to their peaceful intentions. Four years later the English appealed to Alfonso again for the confirmation of his replies to the petitions of 1454, and for further ordinances with regard to the working of some of the regulations issued in that year[1]. Again they received a favourable reply to their requests; and the two sets of petitions and answers formed together a most important charter for the English merchants in Lisbon[2].

Thus by about the middle of the fifteenth century the English had received privileges in Portugul which, as the Portuguese complained, placed them in a more advantageous position for trade than Alfonso's own subjects, while a number of the ordinary taxes and burdens of government borne by the Portuguese themselves were lightened or removed in their case. The answers of 1454 and 1458 were confirmed by Alfonso V. in 1461, by John II. in 1491, and by Manuel in 1497[3]; and therefore at the time when Portugal was beginning to rise into first-rate commercial importance the position of the English in that country was such that they could take full advantages of its new prosperity.

It is difficult to form any estimate as to how far this privileged position of the merchants of England in Portugal was due to the old alliance between the two countries, or whether it was not rather the result of the valuable nature of their trade. In this connection, it is interesting to notice that the author of the *Libelle of English Polycye*, who seems to have had a keen judgment in commercial affairs, attributes the flourishing condition of Portugal's trade with England to the firm alliance existing between the two countries, and this opinion was also held by the famous traveller known as

[1] Printed in Schanz, II. 516-22.
[2] A fuller account of these petitions is given in chap. v.
[3] Schanz, II. 522-23.

Giles de Bouvier. In his description of Portugal, written about the middle of the fifteenth century, occurs the following passage:—"En cedit royaulme croist de bons vins et grant foison figues et raisins, qu'ils meinent vendre en Angleterre pour ce qu'ils sont aliez avec eux"[1]. The alliance was certainly very much in the minds of the Portuguese merchants who came to England, for it is mentioned in almost every petition presented by them to the English king, and there can be little doubt that the Treaty of Windsor acted during the fifteenth century as an inducement for the Portuguese to come to England. It is probable, therefore, that the English were similarly encouraged to send their cloths to Portugal, by the knowledge of the promises made on their behalf by John I., and confirmed by his successors. It seems certain, also, that John himself was influenced by his alliance with the King of England in granting the earlier privileges to English subjects in his country, and in seeing to the welfare of those who took up their abode there. As soon as the English had established their "factory" in Lisbon, however, the Portuguese people seem to have observed the convenience of having the indispensable woollen goods brought to their door, and to have welcomed the cloth merchants of their own accord. In 1454 and 1458 the English residents in Lisbon complained of many things, but in none of their complaints is there any evidence of jealousy or hostility on the part of the Portuguese people, while some years later, in 1482, the latter actually petitioned that the wearing of all garments, save those of English cloth, should be forbidden[2].

It would seem, therefore, that it was the great popularity of the English merchants and their cloth in Portugal which led to their very favourable reception there, and that important as the com-

[1] Cited in Fr. Michel, *Commerce et Navigation à Bordeaux*, I. 334.
[2] Santarem, *Quadro Elementar*, XIV. 226.

mercial clauses of the Treaty of Windsor may have been at first in directing English trade to Portugal, their effect was afterwards greatly enhanced by the character of this trade. While the Portuguese could supply wines and fruits which were not produced in England, the English brought woollen goods, for which the demand in Portugal at this time must always have been greater than the supply, and thus the trade of each country was supplementary to that of the other, in such a way that neither need fear encroachment in its own particular province. Nor could English and Portuguese merchants easily come into collision in foreign lands, for, with the exception of salt, perhaps, their respective countries produced no two commodities alike. During the latter part of the fifteenth century, indeed, the only possibility of a disturbance between them lay in the newly-discovered Portuguese lands on the West Coast of Africa, where the King of Portugal, naturally enough, claimed the monopoly of trade for his own subjects, but where, also naturally enough, English and other foreign merchants tried hard to force their way in. In 1481, for instance, several Englishmen were in treaty with a Spanish nobleman[1], for whom they had undertaken to fit out a strong fleet for Guinea, when John II. sent a special embassy to Edward IV., begging him to observe that he was sole lord of that territory, and to forbid the present and all future attempts on the part of his subjects to infringe the rights of the King of Portugal. Edward IV. did as he was requested, and no further complaints seem to have been made. In all other ways the commercial relations between the two countries during the closing years of the fifteenth century seem to have been of the friendliest, England's cloth trade to Portugal maintaining its high standard, while

[1] The Duke of Medina Sidonia. Garcia de Rescende, *João II.*, cap. 33.

the Portuguese wine trade with England steadily increased[1].

In conclusion, the account given by Roger Machado of his visit to Portugal as an ambassador, in 1489, may be noticed as an interesting piece of contemporary evidence as to the popularity in Portugal at this time of the English and the English alliance[2]. After a short visit to Spain, Machado and two other envoys, Thomas Savage and Richard Nanfan, arrived at Elvas on the 9th April. Immediately on their arrival a prominent citizen sent them a present of wine, barley, preserved fruits, and other delicacies. This example was presently followed by the whole town; and four days later they proceeded to Villa Viciosa, where they were equally well treated. The Chancellor of Portugal met them here, with many other important personages, and delivered a speech to the effect that the king was overjoyed at their visit, and that they were welcome to Portugal, "not as strangers, but as though they belonged to his own kingdom, because he held his cousin the King of England as his own brother, true friend, and old ally; wherefore his ambassadors were the most welcome in his kingdom of those of all nations whatsoever." After Easter the envoys were accompanied to Beja, where they were to have their audience with the king. The whole city was decorated with banners in their honour, and, as they approached, cannon shots were fired. After the royal interview they were *fêted* by different persons in every possible way, and when their stay of three weeks was over, during which all expenses were defrayed, they left for Lisbon each the richer by a very valuable present from the king. In

[1] The Bristol accounts mention the arrival of many ships laden entirely with wine from Portugal during these years. See chap. v.

[2] See *Life of Henry VII.*, by Bern. Andreas (ed. Gairdner), 157, etc. The object of the embassy was to treat of the confirmation of the Treaty of Windsor, and for the continuation of commercial intercourse between the two countries.

Lisbon they were lodged in the royal hostel, and again treated with all respect and honour. A certain Edward Brandon, originally a Portuguese subject, but afterwards a naturalised Englishman, took charge of them, and entertained them on several occasions. In this city the English envoys also met a number of the English merchants then living in Portugal, Thomas Smith, Thomas Tirry, William Cabol, Thomas Baker, and others of London and Bristol, who helped to show them about the city. The ambassadors took the opportunity to lade two ships for themselves with salt and sugar for England, and in July they at last returned to their own country. The result of the embassy was that the Treaty of Windsor was confirmed by Henry VII. in August 1489, and by John II. of Portugal in the following December[1].

But the mediæval period of commercial history was now almost at an end, for, with the discoveries of Columbus and Vasco da Gama, the world of trade began to assume the wider dimensions and the new aspect under which modern conditions gradually became necessary. At the opening of the sixteenth century everything began to undergo a change; a new commercial policy was abroad, and trade was beginning to be organised on a different footing. Among many changes one of the greatest was that in the relative positions of the great commercial nations of Europe. Through their discovery of the sea route to India, the Portuguese became for a short time the chief trading nation in Europe, while the prosperity of the Italian merchants, who had hitherto carried on the trade with the East, gradually fell away. For England, the effects of the discovery of the New World, if less immediately obvious, were scarcely less important, because she acquired thereby for the first

[1] Rymer, V. iv. 4, 5.

time a central position in the commercial world[1]. At this point, therefore, the mediæval history of the commercial relations between England and Portugal ends, and a new story must begin of the English and Portuguese merchants in later times, and under more modern conditions. But, in order to complete the sketch already given, it remains to examine briefly certain questions connected with international trade in the Middle Ages, and the conditions under which it was carried on, according as the merchants of England and Portugal were affected by them in their dealings with each other.

[1] Cunningham, *English Industry and Commerce*, I. 474.

CHAPTER IV

RISKS AND VICISSITUDES OF THE TRADE

Danger of shipwreck — Cases of shipwrecked Portuguese merchants robbed by English subjects—Their petitions for compensation or restitution—Procedure in such cases —Other dangers, piracy, unlawful arrest, detention in English ports—Some periods worse than others—The war between England and France in Edward III.'s reign —Violent treatment of Portuguese merchants in England during Richard II.'s reign, chiefly on account of the debts of the King of Portugal—Gascon and English merchants robbed by the Portuguese—The French war renewed by Henry V., and the increase in the number of Portuguese merchants plundered by the English during the middle of the fifteenth century—Reprisals of the Portuguese on English merchants in Portugal — Special letters of exemption granted by the King of Portugal.

IN the two previous chapters it has been shown that the commercial relations of England and Portugal during the Middle Ages were, from the beginning, of a friendly nature, and that during the fifteenth century in particular the strong alliance between the two countries combined with the profitable character of their mutual trade to produce conditions very satisfactory for the development of that trade. While the more enterprising of the Portuguese merchants and mariners were engaging in the new and profitable trade with the African Coast, the English found their opportunity to secure their position in their own country's trade with

Portugal, where, as has been seen, they soon acquired very valuable privileges. Similarly, though the Portuguese merchants who came to England during this period obtained no special privileges from the king, yet they were known to the English authorities as friends and allies, and all attempts to molest them were forbidden. Almost throughout the mediæval period the utmost peace and concord existed between the rulers of the two countries, and even before their formal alliance royal safe-conducts and other special grants for the merchants of each kingdom were frequently exchanged.

Yet such were the conditions under which mediæval commerce was carried on that in spite of these favourable circumstances a great deal of uncertainty still attached to the trade between England and Portugal, and, though the majority of English and Portuguese merchants must have gone backwards and forwards securely, no account of the commercial relations of these countries would be complete without some notice of the misadventures of those who did not do so. Of the many risks which in early times all Portuguese merchants had to run in bringing their ships to England, one of the most serious was shipwreck, to which they were, of course, always liable, but the terrors of which were at this time more than doubled by the prevailing custom of treating wrecked cargoes as salvage. According to merchant law in England, if a ship were wrecked or driven ashore by a tempest, so long as any living creature survived the catastrophe, whether man, woman, horse, dog, or cat, no part of the cargo was to count as wreck of sea, but all was to be kept safely under the charge of the sheriff and coroner, or the bailiff of the place where the wreck occurred, from whom it might be claimed at any time within a year and a day[1]. No great inducement was thus offered to

[1] *Little Red Book of Bristol* (ed. Bickley), I. 67.

English coast dwellers to lend their help in rescuing distressed mariners; but even when such mariners came safely to land the people on the shore frequently took advantage of their comfortless plight to lay violent hands on the whole or part of the cargo. In such cases all that foreign merchants could do was to petition the English king or his council for relief, and to await such steps as they chose to take on their behalf. Numbers of such petitions from Portuguese merchants still exist[1], and many are recorded in the *Patent and Close Rolls* of the period with a notice as to the steps taken in each case. The usual method adopted was that of royal commissions to investigate and to decide upon the complaints of the shipwrecked merchants. These commissions were generally issued to justices belonging to the county in which the wreck occurred, who conducted their enquiry by the examination of witnesses from the neighbourhood.

For instance, a petition presented by two Lisbon merchants during Edward II.'s reign sets forth that as they were returning from Flanders their ship grounded on a sandbank by the port of Romney, whereupon seeing danger they "took to their boats and landed at the town of Romneye, where they made an agreement, as they assert, with the men of that town, and with others of Lede and Winchelsea, to deliver their ship and goods, for which the men were to receive the value of one-fourth of the goods as soon as they should come ashore with the ship and cargo." Subsequently the salvors sought to obtain one-third of the goods, and, because the merchants would not agree, they carried off half of the cargo, and of the remainder they still insisted on taking one-third as their fee, whereby the two merchants lost £1,000 or more, according to their

[1] See *Index of Ancient Petitions*, in *Lists and Indexes*, No. 1 (Rolls Series).

own account. In reply to their petition for a remedy, a commission was issued to the constable of Dover Castle[1], to enquire into the whole matter, and to see whether the evidence obtainable supported the statements of the Portuguese merchants. This was in November 1313, and, in March of the following year, the enquiry into the case having been made, a royal commission of *oyer* and *terminer*[2] was issued to certain justices, by virtue of which they were to decide the case, and make due restitution to the injured merchants.

In 1318, again, two merchants of Portugal complained on behalf of themselves and their fellows, that whereas on a voyage to Flanders with a ship laden with wine and other goods they, on account of contrary winds, anchored in Padstow, where the ship was cast ashore, "but the mariners escaped to land, and afterwards carried all the goods and wares which were in the ship, whereby the said goods ought not to be wreck of sea"; yet a number of the inhabitants of these parts, many of whom are mentioned by name, had carried away the goods so salved as though they were. A commission of *oyer* and *terminer* was issued to three justices to decide on the case[3], but apparently their proceedings were too slow for the impatient merchants, for, nearly three months later, the King of Portugal wrote to Edward II.[4], setting forth once more the particulars of the case, and begging for the prompt satisfaction of the claims of his merchants. This letter must have had some effect, for, in the course of the next few years, some of the malefactors concerned were outlawed for non-appearance to answer the charges laid against them, and pardoned only on condition of surrendering at the king's prison in the county

[1] *Cal. Pat. Rolls*, 1313-17, 67.
[2] Ibid. 142.
[3] Ibid. 1317-21, 169.
[4] *Anc. Corr.*, XXXIV. 159.

of Cornwall[1]. Procedure by means of these commissions seems often to have been lengthy and unsatisfactory, and one case in particular, that of a merchant called Martin de Beck, of Oporto, will show how the issue of a commission of *oyer* and *terminer* by no means implied that a case would then be heard and determined at once. In 1318 the ship of this merchant was cast ashore at Brighteston[2], in the Isle of Wight, where the inhabitants instantly seized the cargo and refused to give it up. In November a commission of *oyer* and *terminer* was issued[3], and Martin petitioned[4] that the justices might choose their jury among the men of Southampton rather than among those of the Isle of Wight, who had themselves been guilty of the trespass. Some investigations must have been made, and in 1320, during which year two fresh commissions were issued, twenty-six persons were mentioned as suspected of complicity in the matter[5]. In 1322 two further commissions of *oyer* and *terminer* were issued[6], and the list of suspected persons rose to fifty-six; but still Martin received no compensation. At last, in 1336, he appealed to Edward III., mentioning forty-six of the offenders by name, and begging for justice. A commission to hear and determine the case was again issued[7], and it is possible that after this the outraged merchant and his companions received compensation, for their petition does not occur again.

It was not always quite by accident, moreover, that the ships of foreign merchants were wrecked off the English coast; and the petitions of Portuguese subjects in England show cases in which a wreck

[1] *Cal. Pat. Rolls*, 1317-21, 403.
[2] Now Brixton.
[3] *Cal. Pat. Rolls*, 1317-21, 296.
[4] *Anc. Petition*, 1595.
[5] *Cal. Pat. Rolls*, 1317-21, 538.
[6] Ibid. 1321-24, 315.
[7] Ibid. 1334-38, 298.

was caused under circumstances giving rise to grave suspicion. Such was the case of two Portuguese merchants called Piers Garcie and Martin Domynges, who hired an English shipmaster to take their valuable cargo to Flanders. The Englishman steered straight for Yarmouth instead, where he left the ship and cargo in the hands of two men and a boy; the ship was cast ashore in his absence and wrecked, whereupon the honest shipmaster claimed and secured the greater part of the cargo as compensation[1]. A similar case was that of the *Saint Marie of Portugal.* In December 1382 this ship, laden with 3,000 couples of fruit, 40 tuns of bastard wine and wine of Algarves, a pipe of grain, two quintals of wax, and other merchandise, was brought to Southampton by her owners for purposes of trade. There she was boarded by certain Englishmen who, in the absence of the master, took her outside the port, whereby through incautious navigation she was wrecked. Thereupon the English intruders, according to the account of the Portuguese merchants, seized the merchandise which had been on board, to the value of 2,000 marks, and imprisoned certain of the crew of the late ship. The damaged owners instantly appealed to the English king, and after some delay a commission was issued to three justices to enquire into the case[2]. But the affair dragged on for two years before any further steps were taken, and it was not till 1385 that the chief offender was at last summoned to the King's Bench, where a verdict was, however, given in favour of the defendant[3].

Besides the danger of shipwreck, whether caused by accident or by design, the Portuguese merchants who visited England in the Middle Ages had to face many other dangers, of which the chief were,

[1] See Appendix I. No. 4.
[2] *Cal. Pat. Rolls*, 1381-85, 256, 357.
[3] Marsden, *Select Pleas in the Admiralty Courts*, Introd. xlviii.

perhaps, attacks from pirates or privateers at sea, and unlawful arrest or undue detention in English ports. In the first case, the offenders were not, of course, by any means always English, but the complaints of Portuguese merchants, against English subjects who seized their goods and ships by force, are sufficiently numerous to give a clear idea of the hardships thus inflicted, while for the present purpose the steps taken in such cases alone are immediately interesting. There seems always to have been a certain amount of piracy round the English coast in the Middle Ages; but some periods were worse than others in this respect. The Portuguese seem to have suffered most from English pirates after the outbreak of Edward III.'s war with France, and during the continuation of this war under Henry V. and Henry VI. When the Hundred Years' War broke out in 1338 Portugal was not yet formally allied with England, and though the king did his utmost to prevent his subjects from molesting any merchants, save those of France and her allies, it was by no means easy to secure the ships, even of nations known to be friendly to England, from the attacks of English privateers. At the beginning of the war Edward issued a series of proclamations[1] in favour of the merchants of Portugal, Spain, and other friendly lands, but, as the years went on, the complaints of these merchants became more and more bitter. Between Edward III. and Alfonso IV. of Portugal a vigorous correspondence was carried on; the King of Portugal brought forward complaint after complaint from his merchants, and the King of England sought to pacify him and them by describing all the remedies and precautions that were being taken. Thus, for instance, Alfonso wrote[2]

[1] 1338, 5th, 15th, and 20th January; 8th and 15th February, etc., *Cal. Close Rolls*, 1337-39, 229, 236, 288, 303, and Brit. Mus. MS., *Bibl. Harl.*, 6072, fol. 162.

[2] *Anc. Corr.*, XXXVIII. 126.

informing Edward that a ship laden with cloths to the value of 36,000 gross turnois of silver, belonging to Portuguese merchants, had been seized off Winchelsea and taken to Dartmouth, where the merchants were robbed of their goods on the pretext that they came from a hostile country. He also stated that others of his subjects had been similarly ill-treated by the men of Bayonne, and begged Edward to provide a remedy. In June 1343 Edward replied that the sheriff of the county had been ordered to make enquiries, and to cause justice to be done to the Portuguese merchants, and that, with regard to the injuries said to have been inflicted on Alfonso's subjects by the men of Bayonne, royal orders had been sent to the officials there to "cause the things attempted by them unduly in this matter to be reformed"[1].

Almost immediately after this, Edward received another letter from Alfonso, describing further seizures by English subjects of cloth and other goods from Portuguese ships in the port of Brest. The English king's reply to this letter must again have been conciliatory, for, in answer to it, Alfonso issued a proclamation to the effect that none of his subjects, on pain of death, should injure the subjects of the King of England, and at the same time he requested that Edward would issue a similar order in return. In January 1344 Edward replied to this request, stating that he had once more ordered speedy justice to be done to all Alfonso's injured subjects, and that wherever it seemed expedient proclamation was to be made against any further molestation of Portuguese merchants[2]. Special letters to this effect were sent on the same day to Bordeaux, Bayonne, London, Sandwich, Winchelsea, Southampton, Bristol, and Dartmouth, as the ports

[1] *Cal. Close Rolls*, 1343-46, 218.
[2] Ibid. 257.

most frequented by these merchants[1]. The disorder caused by the war was, however, beyond the reach of letters and proclamations. A very short time had passed before Edward III., who was now negotiating for an alliance with the Portuguese king, received from him an account of an unusually serious trespass committed by his subjects of Bayonne. In spite of the special letters of protection for Portuguese merchants so lately issued, the admiral of the fleet, belonging to the city of Bayonne, had seized and plundered four large Portuguese ships laden with cloth, fish, and other goods, while three other ships, laden with goods of avoirdupois, had similarly been plundered near Guernsey by the masters of two vessels also belonging to Bayonne. With Edward's sanction the Portuguese king sent two of his own subjects to act as procurators on behalf of his injured merchants, and to see after the restitution of the stolen goods[2].

The story of a Portuguese merchant, known as John Alfons, of Tavile or Tavira, may serve to illustrate the rough and ready methods of some of the English privateers. This man had laden a ship with 300 couples of figs and grapes worth £90, and was on his way to Flanders, when he was overtaken by certain English mariners, who forced him to bring his ship into Sandwich. There they seized the whole cargo, and obliged the luckless Portuguese merchant, in addition, to seal letters of acquittance to them of all actions real or personal, laying stress on the fact that this was all done in honest warfare, "because the King of Portugal was hostile to the King of England." As soon as he was released, John appealed to the English authorities, and the case was finally brought before the king at

[1] Rymer, II. ii. 1243 (Record Ed.) The letters sent to Bordeaux, slightly different from the others, are in *Gascon Roll* (17 Edward III.), m. 3.

[2] *Gascon Roll* (20 Edward III.), m. 2.

Westminster. But when the pirate chief, who appeared for himself and his companions, saw his accuser within reach, he seized the terrified merchant by the beard, and threatened him with a knife, hoping thus to awe him into silence; fortunately for John Alfons, however, the contempt thus shown to the royal presence so incensed the king that he ordered the pirate to be imprisoned without delay, with instructions that he was not to be released before he found security to make good all the losses caused to the Portuguese merchant and others by his misdeeds[1].

In this case the injured party was fortunate in securing a hearing before the king, but all foreign merchants cannot have been equally lucky. Some years later, in 1353, Edward III. concluded his treaty with the merchants of Lisbon and Oporto, and in all probability the formal recognition of these merchants as friends and allies of the English king had some effect in removing the doubts as to their good faith which were so often felt by English privateers. Nevertheless, so long as the war lasted, there was always the danger that the Portuguese, like all other friendly nations trading to England, might be wilfully mistaken for enemies, and treated accordingly. Evidence that Portuguese merchants were still complaining of this towards the end of Edwards III.'s reign is afforded by the proclamations of 1371 and 1374, already mentioned[2], which were intended to prevent any futher maltreatment of these merchants, and by an order sent in 1374 to Philip de Courtenay, admiral of the fleet in the West of England, to release twelve Portuguese ships, at present unlawfully detained in English ports[3]. In 1381, four years after the death of

[1] *Anc. Corr.*, XXXVII. 64, 165. *Cal. Pat. Rolls*, 1334-38, 443. *Cal. Close Rolls*, 1337-39, 130.
[2] See chap. iii.
[3] *French Roll* (48 Edward III.), m. 19. See Appendix I. No. 5.

Edward III., a somewhat similar commission was issued[1], to Edmund, Earl of Cambridge, William Beauchamp, and others, to enquire into and make a report to Chancery concerning the capture by the king's subjects in the ports of Plymouth, Dartmouth, Fowey, etc., of ships belonging to Portuguese merchants, and laden with wines, cloths, armour, leather, and other merchandise, which were presumably to be released as soon as the result of the commission should be made known.

The issue of this commission was probably due to the instigation of the Portuguese ambassadors, who were at that time in England treating for the renewal with Richard II. of the alliance of 1373 between Edward III. and Ferdinand[2], for during the remainder of Richard's reign very little regard seems to have been paid to the welfare or security of Portuguese merchants coming to England.[3] The indifference of the English authorities at this time must indeed have caused great annoyance to all foreign merchants visiting England, but to the Portuguese it was specially disastrous, because a number of Richard's subjects regarded them as their lawful prey, owing to circumstances which arose in the years 1383-86, while John I. of Portugal was struggling for his crown. The story of their troubles on this account is a long one. For the hire and equipment of all the Englishmen who volunteered to fight for Portugal in 1384 and 1385 a far larger sum of money was required than could possibly be furnished immediately by John himself. Such enthusiasm was felt in England for his cause, that at first numbers of London merchants and other wealthy persons advanced large sums as

[1] *Cal. Pat. Rolls*, 1377-81, 631.

[2] Rymer, IV. 94 (Record Ed.)

[3] For cases of Portuguese ships plundered during the early part of Richard II.'s reign, see *Cal. Pat. Rolls*, 1381-85, 142, 260, 286, etc.

loans, and by means of this, with the appropriation of all Portuguese ships and merchandise found in English ports, the difficulty was tided over for the moment. But in a few months John's need became more pressing than ever, and when he sent powers to his ambassadors to negotiate a treaty with Richard II., he commissioned them also to raise loans in England[1] for his immediate necessities, upon security of his person, goods, and kingdom. They accordingly did so fairly extensively, and, as before, found their creditors among the rich merchants of London and other English towns.

There is still preserved a notarial instrument dated 16th April 1386[2], containing the bond of the two ambassadors, Fernando, Master of San Thiago, and Laurence John Fogata, to repay to Sir Thomas Moreaux, Sir Henry Grene, and other merchants of London, the sum of £1,000 in Lisbon, or elsewhere in Portugal, within two months after demand, or at Michaelmas next at latest. Richard Scrope, Dean of Chichester, and others were appointed attorneys of the Portuguese envoys, who undertook, if they failed to pay on the day named, neither to bear arms nor be armed till full payment had been made. In case of failing to pay at all they were to be accounted false knights. This was probably the form under which all these loans were made, and when, as might have been expected, the short term specified expired without bringing John much relief from his financial difficulties, the question of the "debts of the Master of San Thiago" became one of painful interest to numbers of English merchants.

But so long as the Portuguese merchants brought their ships to English ports with rich cargoes of commodities, for which there was always a high demand, the keen creditors had no fear of ultimate

[1] Rymer (Hague Ed.), III. iii. 202.

[2] *Diplomatic Document*, 1279, at the Public Record Office. An abstract is given in *D. K. Report* 48, Appendix, 592.

loss. Already, in July 1385, three persons, including the Mayor of Southampton and a certain John Gonsales, evidently a Portuguese subject, had been appointed on petition of the Master of San Thiago himself, "who is bound in divers sums of money to the merchants of London, for payment whereof three ships of Portugal are at his suit arrested in the port of Southampton, to sell the same at the best price, and pay the moneys arising therefrom to the said merchants, until fully satisfied the said sums[1]"; and, from the subsequent action of the English merchants, it is easy to realise that in their eyes the true security for their loans had lain, not in the prospect according to the bond of exposing the arms of the Portuguese envoys reversed and accounting them false knights, but in the regular visits of the Portuguese merchants with their valuable shiploads of fruit, wine, wax, and oil.

The Portuguese merchants evidently represented this view of the matter to John their king, for, in due course, he wrote to Richard II., saying that it would be a scandalous thing if the merchants who had lent money to his envoys should make reprisals on the goods of Portuguese merchants when they came to English shores. In order to avoid anything so disastrous, he asked the King of England to order all his English creditors to appoint a proctor, who could set forth their claims to him, as he wished to pay them immediately[2]. Richard expressed himself equally desirous of avoiding the scandal of reprisals, and promised that the creditors should present their claims before the envoys of Portugal, all except those unavoidably absent, who were to send proctors to John himself[3]. This occupied some time; the proctors went to Portugal, but the claims

[1] *Cal. Pat. Rolls*, 1385-89, 9.
[2] Santarem, *Quadro Elementar*, XIV. 120.
[3] Ibid. 124.

had to be examined, and the most careful enquiries made, till at length the English merchants took the matter into their own hands, and began to procure the arrest of Portuguese ships and their cargoes wherever they possibly could.

The arrestors were acting entirely on their own authority, for, under the special terms of the Treaty of Windsor, the Portuguese were guaranteed royal protection in England; and the first course the sufferers pursued was to appeal for redress to the king and his council. These and similar petitions are framed in a notably despondent vein, and show the terrible disadvantage at which the merchants of Portugal were placed when their ships were arrested, owing to the perishable nature of their goods[1]. Not satisfied with seizing the goods of the Portuguese, the English creditors sometimes even put the owners themselves into prison as a precaution[2]. This state of things lasted during the remainder of Richard II.'s reign, much to the vexation of all persons concerned. In 1390 John wrote to the English king stating that so many of the citizens of Oporto had been plundered and imprisoned in Flanders and England that the authorities of that city had asked for permission to seize any Flemish or English merchants whom they could find in Portugal, to sue them for the damages done by their fellow-countrymen. John explained that for this time he had given orders that the real offenders only should suffer for their misdeeds, but he implied that, unless steps were soon taken, he might not be able to restrain the wrath of his officials[3]; and when at length Henry IV. ascended the English throne he received from the merchants of Portugal a long series of complaints against their unfair treatment by the English, with a

[1] See Appendix I. No. 7, *Petition of Julian Piers of Oporto.*
[2] Appendix I. No. 8, *Petition of John de Lere.*
[3] Santarem, *Quadro Elementar*, XIV. 122.

demand for the better observance of the Treaty of Windsor.

This document is very interesting[1], giving a good idea of the extent to which treaty obligations could be disregarded under a king like Richard II., and also of the freedom which his subjects enjoyed, to take advantage of foreign merchants in any way they pleased. Henry was entreated, in the first place, to forbid his subjects to go to sea armed for war, and to allow them only to carry arms for their own safety, because of the many injuries suffered by the ships and crews of the King of Portugal; where losses had been caused by his subjects he was requested to order their indemnification by the bailiffs and people of the port from which the armament had set forth. He was informed that though the English had robbed Portuguese merchants—even selling their goods against their will—yet, when the Portuguese had applied to the justices and authorities of the kingdom, they had only received the reply that "such persons were under the protection of the king's government, and in his service of war, and that therefore the authorities had no action over them." After fruitless appeals to the justices, and to the king's council, the Portuguese had complained to their own king, who had written about them several times to the King of England; but in spite of the stipulations of the late treaty of alliance, they had never yet obtained justice in England. The Portuguese merchants declared that the offenders were well known in England, and that, nevertheless, they were allowed to go unpunished, and publicly received everywhere.

Another sore grievance was the fact that certain ships which had been laden for Flanders had been forced to remain in English ports at the pleasure

[1] Brit. Mus. MS., *Bibl. Cott. Nero*, B. I. fol. 20. An abstract is given in Santarem, XIV. 132.

of the king, and had at last been released only after their owners had sworn not to go to Flanders, by which they lost a good and opportune occasion for selling their goods. The Portuguese also complained of a new impost, which, during the last five years, they had had to pay on the wines which they brought to England, over and above the regular custom on each tun of wine as paid to the King of England and his ancestors. They begged that, by virtue of the alliance, this impost might be removed, and that they might enjoy the same franchise in England as they used to have, just as English subjects were treated in Portugal, enjoying more liberties and greater freedom from customs duties than the Portuguese themselves, and paying no extra taxes even in time of war. Unless, indeed, Henry IV. could give some guarantee of security for them and their goods in future, the Portuguese merchants declared that they would be obliged to cease frequenting his dominions, which would cause much loss and diminution of the customs and revenues of England.

A pacificatory answer was returned to most of these complaints, but shortly afterwards Henry wrote to King John I. about the debts of the Portuguese envoys, reminding him that though his instructions with regard to the appointment of proctors had been carried out, many of the creditors had as yet received no compensation for their losses[1]. Nevertheless, steps were now taken in England to secure the better treatment of Portuguese merchants. In September 1403 a royal injunction stated that whereas the king had had intelligence that many Portuguese ships, with their goods and merchandise, had been captured on sea and brought to various English ports, where they were now detained contrary to the form of the alliance lately concluded, all ships thus detained or their equivalents in money

[1] 1403, 16th February. Santarem, XIV. 146.

were instantly to be restored to their owners, or their attorneys in those parts, and the masters and mariners were to be allowed to depart freely with their ships and goods[1]. On 16th February 1404, Henry renewed the Treaty of Windsor with John I., and at the same time forbade for the future any unauthorised action with regard to the debts of the King of Portugal[2]. Twelve days later another injunction was issued, setting forth that English subjects, who had made reprisals on Portuguese merchandise for these debts, without royal authority, must instantly make good the damage they had caused[3]. On 6th March, again, an order was sent to the sheriffs of Bristol, Southampton, Kent, and Devon, commanding them, with reference to the above order against reprisals to have it proclaimed, wherever necessary, that "no English subject, under a severe penalty, shall molest in any way any of the said Portuguese subjects or their goods, nor henceforth rob, despoil, arrest, inquiet, or in any way oppress any merchant or other subject of the King of Portugal, on sea or elsewhere, contrary to the form of the alliance signed between the two kings."

There could be no doubt of Henry's good faith, but the evil had gone unchecked so long that, in October 1405, after the marriage of his daughter Beatrice with the Earl of Arundel, the King of Portugal was obliged, before he could send over her dowry of 50,000 crowns, to write for special letters of protection on this account for the merchants who had undertaken to bring half of it[4]. Consequently, in January 1406, a last injunction was issued, to the effect that no Portuguese subject whosoever was to be molested in any way whatsoever by any private individual or royal official, whether for the debts of

[1] Rymer, IV. i. 55.
[2] Ibid. i. 62.
[3] *Trans. For. Records*, Series II. No. 153. See Appendix I. No. 9.
[4] Santarem, XIV. 161.

the King of Portugal, or under any other pretext; but that all merchants and subjects of the said king should be allowed to come and go freely, and without hindrance, in the domains of the King of England[1]. After this the matter seems to have dropped.

It is not to be supposed that the Portuguese endured so much violence on the part of the English without raising a hand in their own defence, for though all the cases examined so far have been those of Portuguese merchants spoiled by English subjects, this is due to the paucity of information as to the plunder of the English by the Portuguese, rather than to the rarity of such occurrences. From earliest times Portugal had been notorious for its pirates, and the French subjects of Edward I., at any rate, suffered much damage from them. The story of one Gascon merchant is interesting, as containing almost the first known instance of the grant of letters of "marque" or reprisal by an English king. It also gives a good illustration of the practical working of these letters. The merchant in question had laden his ship in Malaga with almonds, raisins, and figs, which he intended to sell in England, but being driven out of his course by a tempest he anchored off the coast of Portugal, where his ship was seized by an armed force and carried into Lisbon. The captors paid the King of Portugal one-tenth of the value of the prize, and divided the rest, to the value of £700. Upon this the merchant, unable to obtain restitution in Portugal, applied for letters of "marque" against the Portuguese, and especially those of Lisbon. His case was brought before John de Britannia, Edward I.'s lieutenant in Acquitaine, where he established the truth of his plea "by lawful proof of merchants," upon which the lieutenant gave him licence, "according to merchant law, to mark, retain, and appropriate" the goods of Portuguese

[1] *Trans. For. Records*, Series II. No. 153.

subjects, especially those of Lisbon, wherever he could find them within the jurisdiction of the English king. The licence was to last for five years, or until he should have repaid himself all his damage and expense, and any surplus was to be accounted for to the king. After a year or two the merchant found some Portuguese goods at Romney, in a ship from Lisbon; he accordingly arrested them, and was immediately summoned by the owners before the king and council in Parliament. Judgment was given for the Gascon merchant, however; he was allowed to keep the goods until he should receive full compensation for his own plundered property, and a mandate was issued in his favour to all mayors, bailiffs, and other officials, ordering them not to molest him for distraining the goods of Portuguese merchants[1].

This happened in the last years of the thirteenth century, and it was not till rather later that the English themselves began to come within reach of Portuguese freebooters; but there is evidence that when they did come to Portugal they were by no means immune from attack. In a grant issued to certain Portuguese subjects by Edward III. in 1374, the sum of £232, 11s. 8d. is mentioned as the value of goods belonging to two London merchants which had been unlawfully arrested in Portugal[2], while in 1412 Henry IV. called the attention of the Portuguese king to a serious trespass committed by one of his own officials against the owners of a ship called the *Thomas* of London[3]. It was about the middle of the fifteenth century, however, that the aggressions on both sides reached their highest point.

At the outbreak of the renewed war between England and France Henry V. gave special instructions to the commissioners of his fleet for the South

[1] Rymer I., 828 (Record Ed.) *Cal. Pat. Rolls*, 1292-1301, 520.
[2] *French Roll* (48 Edward III.), m. 19. See Appendix I. No. 5.
[3] Rymer, IV. ii. 8 (Hague Ed.)

of England that, in performing their duty of defending the coast, they should on no account molest any Portuguese subjects[1], but, in spite of this, as the war continued, Portuguese ships were frequently captured and detained in English ports till the owners could prove satisfactorily that they belonged to a friendly nation. Among the petitions which evidently belong to this period, there is one from a Portuguese merchant called John Pynell[2], which shows something of the trouble experienced by these merchants in proving their nationality, and consequently the fact that their country was in alliance with England. The goods of this John Pynell were seized by certain "robbers," and carried off to Shoreham, where they remained for a year in spite of the owner's strenuous efforts to obtain their delivery. He applied to the Chancellor, but his suit failed, owing to the statement made by those who had seized his goods that Pynell was a Breton, and that his goods belonged to merchants of Brittany. In order to disprove this statement he applied to the mayor and corporation of Bristol, and also of Southampton, from whom he received sealed letters, in addition to the deposition of many "respected persons," natives of England, Portugal, and Gascony, to the effect that he was known to be a Portuguese subject, and no Breton. Even this evidence seems to have been insufficient, for at last he wrote to his own king, and received from John I. a special letter[3] proving his Portuguese origin. Armed with this he then petitioned the English king, stating his lamentable case, and urging him to instruct his Chancellor to bring the case before him, with the principal offenders and those who had since bought the stolen goods.

It is impossible to mention all the similar cases

[1] Nicholas, *Privy Council*, II. 200.
[2] *Anc. Petition*, 9210.
[3] Ibid.

that appear in the records of this period, of Portuguese merchants plundered by English sailors. A certain John Preto, of Lisbon, who was in great straits through having lost his entire cargo, some 60 or 50 tuns of wine, which had been seized by English subjects from Calais, was able to induce the Portuguese ambassador, João Vasques d'Almada, to intercede for him. The latter accordingly petitioned the English king for a special safe-conduct for the ship in which his unfortunate fellow-countryman hoped to make a new venture, to compensate himself and his companions in some measure for the losses they had suffered[1]. Other Portuguese merchants, especially those whose ships were laden for Flanders, lost still more valuable cargoes. The English government dealt with such cases in several different ways; the petitions of the merchants resulted sometimes in the despatch of orders to the sheriff of the county in which the goods stolen were supposed to be, sometimes in the issue of instructions to the admiral of the fleet for that part of the kingdom, sometimes in the appointment of justices of *oyer* and *terminer*, to enquire as to the alleged misdeeds, and to administer justice to the injured merchants wherever possible[2]. Lastly, on two occasions at least during the reign of Henry VI., the complaints of the Portuguese merchants formed the subject of a royal proclamation[3].

By the first of these proclamations it was ordained that, in order to prevent the unlawful seizure of Portuguese ships under the pretext that they were carrying goods belonging to the enemy, no English subject should henceforth interfere in any way with ships carrying letters from the King of Portugal

[1] *Anc. Petition*, 9380.

[2] For an example of a commission issued during Henry VI.'s reign to enquire into a petition from Portuguese merchants, see *French Roll* (5 Henry VI.), m. 3.

[3] October 1436 and February 1437.

or the officials of a Portuguese port, containing the name of the ship and a statement to the effect that no goods belonging to the enemy were on board. If any person infringed this rule he was to be arrested and forced to make reparation, besides paying a penalty for transgressing against the royal commands[1]. On the second occasion, special letters were sent to the customers at Bristol and other ports, to the effect that, above all things, the existing alliance between England and Portugal must be kept, and that henceforth no English subject must take his ship out of any harbour armed for war, without giving security that he would in no way molest the subjects of the King of Portugal, so long as they had on board sealed letters from this king, proving that they carried no goods belonging to the enemy[2].

The merchants of Portugal had by this time grown somewhat weary of petitions to the English authorities, and were beginning to take the law into their own hands, punishing the English privateers, and recouping themselves by the indirect method of making reprisals on English merchant vessels which came to Portugal. After two such proclamations in favour of his subjects, however, the King of Portugal had to take his share in keeping the peace between the merchants of the two countries. In August 1437, accordingly, John's son and successor, Edward, issued an order to his own officials in words exactly similar to those used in the English ordinance of October 1436, forbidding any of his subjects to molest English merchant vessels carrying letters from the King of England[3]. During the years 1439 and 1440 several letters on the same subject passed between the English king and the guardians of Edward's infant successor Alfonso V., in which Henry VI. protested that he desired

[1] Rymer, V. i. 35 (Hague).
[2] Ibid. 37. [3] Ibid.

nothing more than to keep the peace between the two countries, and asked for the names of malefactors, promising to make them an example to others by the punishment they should receive. At the same time Henry wrote to Dom Pedro, regent for the young Portuguese king, restating his strong desire that the mutual alliance, contracted and confirmed in ancient days between the Portuguese and English royal houses, should be preserved inviolate by all those under his authority[1]. But, though he thus expressed himself anxious above all things to uphold the alliance between England and Portugal, Henry VI. had not the power to restrain the audacity of his subjects. In January 1445, he received two long letters from the King of Portugal, complaining of the continual misdeeds of his subjects[2]; and there is still extant another letter, dated August 1455, written in the name of Henry VI., in answer to a similar list of accusations[3].

In the latter case, the Portuguese king sent over two ambassadors to state the grievances of his subjects, and watch over their interests, while competent men were appointed in England to act in conjunction with these envoys. The letter states, in addition, that commissions and proclamations were issued, providing for the better observance in England of the Treaty of Windsor. But, in conclusion, it is pointed out that many of the English were also complaining of attacks from the Portuguese, and of much damage done to them by the subjects of Alfonso V., which disastrous state of affairs the Portuguese king was earnestly entreated to rectify, because the attempts made by the English to obtain justice from the Portuguese authorities had hitherto proved fruitless.

[1] Bekynton, *Official Correspondence of Henry VI.*, I. 190-97.
[2] *Anc. Corr.*, XLIII. 189.
[3] Brit. Mus. MS. *Cott. Nero.*, B. I. fol. 52. See also fol. 49 for another complaint about 1442.

It was certainly disastrous for English merchants, who had nothing to do with pirates or privateers, and who wished only to trade in peace with the subjects of Alfonso V., that they happened to belong to the same nation as the "robbers" of whom so many of the Portuguese were complaining. By the terms of the royal safe-conduct for these merchants, which was issued in Portugal in 1443 and successive years, the principle of reprisals upon their goods for damages suffered by the Portuguese at the hands of all English subjects was established beyond the chance of appeal[1]. The only thing left, therefore, for the English merchants to do was to obtain from the Portuguese king, by purchase or otherwise, special safe-conducts which exempted them and their companions from the action of the letters of reprisal held by Portuguese merchants. During the greater part of the reign of Alfonso V. a large number of these special safe-conducts were issued, and this made it possible for Englishmen who disliked running greater risks than were absolutely necessary, or who wished to load a specially valuable cargo, to cross to Portugal with every reasonable hope of a safe passage and a peaceful reception[2]. The period during which the exemption was to extend varied in different cases, being sometimes granted only for a year, or even a few months, and sometimes for five years or longer[3]. Occasionally a special safe-conduct was given only for one particular voyage, and sometimes it was granted merely for a single ship and cargo.

In most cases, however, some three or four merchants were included in the exemption, and

[1] Brit. Mus. MS. *Lansdowne*, 190, fol. 6. See Appendix I. No. 12.

[2] For an example of a special safe-conduct from Alfonso V., see Appendix I. No. 14.

[3] *Trans. For. Records*, Series II. No. 153. Grants dated January 1455, December 1454, July 1462, July 1465, etc.

sometimes its duration was indefinite in extent. For example, an English merchant named William Canis had already brought his ship *La Mary Redclyff* as far as Restello, a Portuguese port, when fear or prudence prompted him to seek royal protection before approaching Lisbon. As a result he fortunately obtained a grant of security to last for the remainder of his life[1]. These special grants seemed to have attained their object satisfactorily, and, as the depredations of English privateers became more disastrous to Portuguese commerce, the cloth merchants of England found it more and more advantageous to secure themselves in this way against reprisals in Portuguese waters. In January 1455, for instance, Alfonso received so many and urgent requests for protection that for once he revoked all his letters of reprisal and granted, "through his love and friendship for the English king," a special safe-conduct during the whole year to all the merchants and other subjects of the kingdom of England[2], even though some who came freely in this year of surety might have been guilty of the wrongs of which his own subjects were complaining.

Nevertheless, English merchants still suffered in other ways from the misdeeds of their fellow-countrymen. The reduction in their favour of the import duties on cloth, which had been sanctioned by John I., and confirmed by Edward, was withdrawn during Alfonso's minority, by the regent Dom Pedro, on account of the complaints of the Portuguese against the depredations of English subjects. Though the English merchants appealed most strongly to Alfonso for the old reduced rates, explaining that it was not fair that they should suffer for robberies committed by others, and that neither John I. nor Edward would have permitted

[1] *Trans. For. Records*, Series II. No. 153. Grants dated February 1442.
[2] Ibid. 28th January 1455.

such injustice, the king only answered that they must appeal to their own sovereign to punish the offenders, and so stop the offences for which they were suffering[1]. Moreover, on one occasion the English were confounded by the sudden revocation[2] of all the special safe-conducts which had been issued in their favour, while permission was given to the Portuguese for unlimited reprisals on English goods and merchandise. This unexpected action on Alfonso's part turned out to have been caused, not by any misdemeanour of the English residents in Lisbon, but by the audacity of the Bastard of Fauconberg in England, who, acting in the interests of Henry VI. against Edward IV., had seized and plundered twelve large Portuguese ships, "en rompant l'alyance qui de long temps sestoit tenue entre les roiaulmes d'Angleterre et de Portugal[3]." Alfonso is said even to have declared war on England as the result of this act of violence, but, as at this moment Henry VI. died, and Fauconberg fell into the hands of the English government, it is possible that the withdrawal of all royal protection for the time being from English merchants in Portugal was the most important step he actually took in the matter[4]. In March 1472 Edward IV. confirmed the Treaty of Windsor, and a few months later Alfonso in his turn consented to renew the alliance with England[5].

The ambassador, João D'Elvas, who took over to England Alfonso's Letters Patent of confirmation of the treaty, was, however, instructed to demand the restitution of the ships and goods which had been seized by Fauconberg. If any doubt should arise in the matter, Alfonso declared himself willing

[1] *Petition of English Merchants*, 1454, cap. 23. Schanz, II. 513.

[2] December 1471, *Trans. For. Records*, Series II. No. 154. See Appendix I. No. 15.

[3] Letter of the Mayor of London, reporting the misfortune to Edward IV., in Waurin, *Chron.*, 1447-71, 673.

[4] See account in chap. i. above.

[5] Rymer, V. iii. 15, 24.

to abide by the decision of the Duke of Burgundy, and his ambassador received full power, when restitution had been made, to give letters of quittance and safe-conducts to all Edward's subjects, to come once more in surety into the kingdom of Portugal[1]. Five commissioners were accordingly appointed in England, to enquire by the oath of upright and lawful men, or in any other way possible, concerning the manner in which the ships had been plundered, which of the accomplices of the Bastard had taken them, what their price or value was, and into whose hands they afterwards came. Such of the ships as they could find, or their money equivalent if this was impossible, the commissioners were to restore, receiving in each case the proper quittance from the Portuguese owner, to show that restitution had been made; and from time to time they were to report to the king and council on the progress they had made[2]. By 26th February 1473, the commission had succeeded so far that João d'Elvas undertook to close the matter. He promised that no English subjects should now be molested in any way on account of the misdeeds of Fauconberg, and in Alfonso's name he renounced for ever any right which the king or his subjects might have in the ships taken by the daring sea-captain[3]. Thus the incident ended peacefully enough, and the English merchants in Lisbon could once more enjoy the security granted to them by their special safe-conducts. During the remainder of the mediæval period no other serious mischance of this kind seems to have occurred.

1 Rymer, V. iii. 24. 2 Ibid. iii. 26. 3 Ibid.

CHAPTER V

GENERAL CONDITIONS OF THE ANGLO-PORTUGUESE TRADE ABOUT THE MIDDLE OF THE FIFTEENTH CENTURY

English and Portuguese ports concerned in the trade—Ships —Merchants—Cargoes—Customs duties paid at English ports—Town duties—Payments made in Portuguese ports —Petitions of the English merchants in Lisbon, 1454 and 1458—Malpractices of the Portuguese customs' officials in respect of the tithing of English cloths—The door-keeper of the custom-house—Negligence and dishonesty of the tithing officers—Disputes as to the value of the cloths—Difficulty of collecting the money due to English merchants for goods sold in Lisbon—Other conditions of the life and trade of the English in Lisbon.

TAKING the first half of the fifteenth century as the period during which the commercial relations between England and Portugal were attaining their full limits for the mediæval period, it is interesting to conclude with a brief survey of the trade as carried on by the merchants of the two countries about the middle of that century. This will take note of the ports and ships concerned in the trade, the various kinds of merchandise which made up the cargoes, and the dues paid on them, together with the regulations according to which the merchants actually bought and sold their goods. It must be pointed out, however, that an enquiry into details of this kind is limited by the amount and nature of the information to be obtained on the subject, and in the present case many interesting points must be passed over owing to an insufficiency of material rather than to their lack of importance.

To begin with, as regards ports, the English ports chiefly concerned in the trade were naturally those on the south and west coasts, of which Bristol was by far the most important. One of Alfonso V.'s decrees contains the names of nine ports of England and Wales, from which he had received petitions of merchants anxious to continue their trade with Portugal if they could obtain a special safe-conduct from him; these ports are London, Bristol, "Antona, Bastona, Certamua, Precamua[1]," Tenby, Milford, and "Chabristol[2]," some of which names are almost unrecognisable in their Portuguese version. Besides these, Bridgewater and Sandwich are mentioned in connection with the export of corn to Portugal, and there is no reason to suppose that other important ports, such as Fowey and Portsmouth, were not still taking their share in the trade. Southampton, Plymouth, and Dartmouth were the ports most frequently used by ambassadors and others who travelled to and from Portugal; the voyage took about sixteen days, and the route was a straight one from Falmouth, across the Bay of Biscay to Finisterre, and thence down the Portuguese coast.

Lisbon and Oporto were the two great centres of Portuguese commerce; almost all the Portuguese ships that came to Bristol for cloth sailed from one or other of these ports, and of the two Lisbon was considerably the more important. It had been John I.'s policy to favour Lisbon at the expense of all other cities and towns[3], and now under his grandson the remarkable results of that policy were

[1] (?) Southampton, Barnstaple, Dartmouth, Plymouth.

[2] (?) Chichester.

[3] In 1423 foreigners were forbidden to buy merchandise except in Lisbon; and in 1429 they were forbidden to buy goods of avoirdupois or provisions outside the city.

seen. A contemporary writer[1] states that at this time Lisbon was as large as London, and to the King of Portugal, certainly, the capital with its flourishing commerce and ever-increasing wealth was a source of immense profit, as well as of pride and pleasure. In the Middle Ages many advantages attached to the concentration of commerce in a few great cities, for the government was thus able to control the course of foreign trade, the levy of dues and customs, and the dealings of foreign residents with native merchants, to an extent altogether impossible in a country like England, where the ports, though small in size, were large in number[2]. Other Portuguese ports are occasionally mentioned, such as Viana in the north, and Setubal, south of Lisbon; but the little kingdom of Algarve, which forms the south coast of Portugal, was the only part outside Lisbon and Oporto whence cargoes of any great importance were at this time shipped to England. By a special favour foreign merchants were allowed to buy fruits and wine there for exportation[3], but if in order to do so they wished to take money out of Lisbon, they were obliged first to buy a licence to export coin from the customs' officials.

The ships engaged in the trade were small, and in most cases seem to have carried less than 150 tons. The vessels of the Portuguese merchants were known as carvels or caravels, and are described as light ships, or from 150 to 180 tons freightage[4]. The prow was more or less round in shape, becoming more pointed towards the stern, and there were, as

[1] Nicolas von Popplau. Quoted by Villa Franca, *João I. e a Allianca Ingleza*, 203.

[2] Some such reasons must have led to the institution of staple towns in England.

[3] Santarem, I. 24. By a royal ordinance of 1451.

[4] *Historia da Academia Real das Sciencias de Lisboa*, N.S., IV. Pt. 2, Memoir on Portuguese ships in the fifteenth and sixteenth centuries. See also Azurara, *Conquest of Guinea* (Ed. Beazley and Prestage), II. Introd. cxi.

a rule, four masts, all carrying triangular or lateen sails, with the exception of the foremast—the sails of which were round. These carvels were very small, for the largest of them in the time of Prince Henry the Navigator carried at most thirty-six men, but it was in vessels similar to those which visited English shores that the Portuguese mariners made their early discoveries on the West African Coast. The number of English ships plying between Bristol and Portugal about 1465 was rather less than the number of Portuguese ships engaged in the trade.

As regards the merchants themselves, however, there can be no question that by this time the English had considerably the larger share of the trade in their hands. In the Bristol Customs Accounts, during eight months from Michaelmas 1465 to May 1466[1], the entire cargoes of all the English ships employed in the Portuguese trade, together with the greater part of the cargoes of the Portuguese ships mentioned, are entered as belonging to English merchants. Of the Portuguese ships two only, the *Katerine*, of Lisbon, of which one Bartholomew Diaz was master, and the *St Michael* of Viana, brought cargoes belonging to Portuguese merchants. The total value of Portuguese merchandise, wine, fruit, oil, wax, and other goods, brought to Bristol during six months from November 1465, was roughly £4,800; of this sum over £4,700 was the value of the goods imported by English merchants, the remainder only, some £52, representing the value of goods imported by the Portuguese. Of 1,062 pieces of ungrained cloth, which left Bristol for Lisbon during the same period, 1,042½ belonged to English, and only 19½ to Portuguese, merchants.

The cloths belonged in most cases to companies of Bristol merchants, who sent them over to Portugal in charge of an attorney. The company of the merchant prince, William Cannynges, is frequently

[1] *K. R. Customs Accounts*, Bdle. 19, Nos. 3, 4.

mentioned, as also those of John Shipward, John Gaywood, and many others. Each company had several attorneys, who on some occasions traded also in their own names[1]. According to the Customs Accounts the value of each piece of ungrained cloth was on an average nearly £3, and English merchants paid a custom duty of 1s. 2d. per piece exported. The Portuguese and other foreign merchants paid more than this; on each piece they were charged 2s. 9d. custom duty, in addition to a subsidy of 1s. in the £ on the value of the cloth.

The kind of cloth described as "sine grano" was that usually exported from Bristol to Portugal at this time, though other varieties were also very popular with the Portuguese, such as Welsh cloths, and kersies, while there is an occasional mention of pieces of "scarlett" or "Kendall" being shipped for Lisbon. Of other commodities, two pieces of silk, worth 10s. each, were exported on one occasion, and on another 12½ tanned hides, worth 30s. At other times quantities of lead, tin, pewter, and alabaster are mentioned, while, in later years, during the reign of Henry VII., it is not unusual to find a consignment of corn[2]. As a rule, however, the bulk of the cargo of a ship sailing for Portugal from Bristol would be composed of cloth. It is interesting to compare these results with a list of English manufactures and merchandise exported by a Portuguese ambassador in 1428 for the use of the King of Portugal and his son[3]; as the articles were intended for royal use the list contains the names of many specially

[1] Among forty English merchants who owned the cargo of the *Mary Grace*, brought into Bristol from Lisbon, 16th December 1465, it is interesting to notice the name of Richard May, an English merchant, whose safe-conduct from Alfonso V., obtained in August 1452, is still extant.

[2] *K. R. Customs Accounts*, Bdle. 19, Nos. 6, 7, 10, 10a, 11, 14, 15.

[3] Rymer (Hague), IV. iv. 134. Translated in Anderson, *Historical Deduction*, I. 255. The ambassador received licence to export all the goods custom free.

fine kinds of cloth, which do not appear in the Bristol Customs Accounts, together with certain other goods made by skilled English workmen. In Anderson's translation the list reads as follows:—

1. Six silver cups gilt.
2. Woollen goods—
   Two pieces of scarlet.
   One piece of sanguine dyed in grain.
   Two pieces deblodio[1].
   Two pieces of Mustrevilliers.
   Two pieces of marble colour.
   Two pieces of russet of Mustrevilliers.
   Two pieces of black cloth of Lyre.
   One piece of white cloth.
   Three hundred pieces of Essex streits.
3. Two thousand pewter vessels, dishes, plates, saucers, etc.
4. Two beds with curtains of largest size.
   Four beds with curtains of a middling size, red and green.
   Four red and green pallet beds.
   Two green beds with curtains.
   Eight pieces of red cloth.
   Four pieces of green.
   Sixty rolls or balls of worsted, red, white, green.
5. Twelve dozen of lances.
   Twenty-six saddle horses.

The list of commodities mentioned in the Customs Accounts of Bristol, as coming from Portugal about the middle of the fifteenth century, is a long one, and shows how far the Portuguese nation had progressed since the early years of its history. First of all, there is wine, of which some tuns came to England in almost every ship from Lisbon or Algarve; between November 1465 and May 1466, for instance, six ships brought over altogether 498 tuns, and of this amount one ship alone brought nearly 150[2]. The value of this wine is not entered in the Customs Accounts, because a fixed duty was paid on each tun, regardless of value, but from other

[1] ? of blue.
[2] *K. R. Customs*, Bdle. 19, No. 4.

sources it seems to have been about £4 a pipe, or £8 a tun. The names of several different kinds of Portuguese wine are mentioned in one of Alfonso V.'s decrees[1], but none of these names occur in English records, where the only special kinds of wine mentioned as coming from Portugal are bastard wine[2], wine of Algarve[3], and osey[4]. Besides these, a kind of sour wine (vinum acre) appears in the Customs Accounts as coming in considerable quantities from Portugal. This is generally called "viniacre" or "vinaigre," and was probably the home-made vinegar still used in the south of Europe, for its value is always entered as £2 a tun, whereas a tun of ordinary wine would have fetched four times this price.

Of other Portuguese commodities, wax (valued at £2 the cwt.), oil (at £4 the tun), honey (£2, 10s. the tun), and dried fruit (£2 the tun), came in large quantities, together with cork at 26s. 8d. the cwt., and salt at 8s. 4d. the tun. But besides these, which had formed the cargoes of Portuguese merchant ships for many years, a number of new commodities were beginning to appear. Sugar[5], which is not mentioned in the *Libelle of English Polycye*, is entered in the Bristol Customs Accounts for 1466, and from this time an increasing quantity of it was brought every year into England; this was one of the chief products of the Island of Madeira, and its entry into England at this time among the more purely Portuguese products is one of the first indications of the results of Prince Henry the Navigator's work. About the same time the Portuguese began to import alum, soap[6], and woad, commodities which they had not yet brought, but which they could now obtain

[1] See fn. p. 65.
[2] *Cal. Pat. Rolls*, 1401-5, 507.
[3] *Rot. Parl.*, IV. 89a.
[4] *Libelle of English Polycye*; in Wright, *Political Songs*, II. 162.
[5] Valued at £2 the cwt.
[6] Valued at 24s. and 10s. the tun respectively.

from abroad; of grain, resin, and dates, also, though they had formerly imported a certain amount of these into England, the Portuguese could henceforth obtain larger supplies from their new African possessions[1].

The duties levied in English ports on these commodities were not at this time excessive; on wine, English and Portuguese merchants alike paid the subsidy of 3s. per tun, while on all other kinds of merchandise, exported or imported, including all varieties of cloth except the ordinary undyed pieces mentioned above, they paid a subsidy of 1s. in the £ value. The Portuguese in addition paid petty custom at 3d. in the £ value, according to Edward I.'s original agreement with the foreign merchants; and this small impost, with the additional duties paid on cloths, formed the only extra fiscal burden imposed on the Portuguese in England as compared with native merchants. But the customs and subsidies levied for the royal revenue were not the only payments that had to be made on merchandise coming to English ports. There were, besides, certain town dues, which varied in different ports, but which, though smaller in amount than the royal customs, yet helped to diminish the profits of merchants trading between England and Portugal.

It is impossible here to make any general statement as to these town dues, but, with regard to Bristol, it is interesting to notice some information contained in a grant made to that city by Henry VI. in 1439[2]. After granting the town of Bristol in farm to the mayor and commonalty for twenty years, with Court of View of Frankpledge, Hundred Court, wreck of the sea, wrecks royal, waifs and strays, etc. for a sum of £102, 15s. 6d., together with other charges, making up the amount to £160, the

[1] See Azurara, *Conquest of Guinea*, II. 236. Grain was worth £20 a tun.

[2] Bush, *Town Duties of Bristol*, 31.

charter continues as follows :—" Moreover, in aid of repairing and amending as well the walls of the key of the town as of the other walls and pavement of the said town, we have granted to the mayor etc., . . . that during this time they may take of things for sale, coming to the town aforesaid, as well by land as by water . . ." ; then follow the rates. A few examples, of those chiefly concerning the trade with Portugal, will give some idea of the scale of charges[1] :—

From every merchant vessel, arriving with merchandise, every time	6d.
Every two quarters of salt for sale . . .	$\frac{1}{4}$d.
Every cask of wine	2d.
Every cwt. of wax	1d.
Every frael of figs and raisins . . .	$\frac{1}{2}$d.

(Almost every other kind of merchandise, 1d. per £ value).

It is more difficult to discover what payments had to be made in Portuguese ports, but some light on the nature of the most important charges is thrown by the petitions of the English merchants in 1454 and 1458, mentioned in a previous chapter. As regards the wines exported by English merchants, it has been shown that the ordinary export duty levied was an "almude" and a half per tun, and that King Edward, to prevent unfairness, ordered that the charge made in each case should be in proportion to the value of the wine. In 1454, however, the English complained that the receivers of the customs used to wait till they saw the ships laden and ready to start, when, knowing that the merchants would pay anything rather than be delayed, they would demand as large a sum on

[1] Bush, *Town Duties*, 35. In addition to town dues other small charges were made in English ports, such as weighers', porters', and brokers' fees, but, though the last was often an expensive item, such charges formed part of the necessary outlay of merchants of all countries in the Middle Ages. The brokerage charged in London on wax from Lisbon in the fourteenth century was 4d. per bale. See *Calendar of Letter-Books G.*, 209.

wines costing 1,500 reis as on those costing 2,500 or even 3,000 reis. Alfonso V. gave instructions that the merchants were to pay only according to Edward's book of rates, and that if the officials did not observe these instructions they were to appeal to the royal overseer[1], but, in 1458, the same grievance was brought forward again, showing that the royal commands did not always restrain the greed of the customs' officials. As a matter of fact, the custom-house in Lisbon seems at this time to have been corrupt in all its proceedings; the customs were farmed out to a number of unscrupulous individuals, of whom many were Jews, and though the king might remonstrate with these "rendeiros," or receivers, as they were called, he was in no position to prevent them from making the most of the many opportunities they had, to swindle foreign merchants and extort money from them under false pretences.

Other export duties mentioned by the English are the "portagem" and "tavolla" on goods of avoirdupois, and the "tavolla da impossicam" on salt, but the only other charge on exportation to which they objected was that made for licences to export coin from Lisbon when they wished to buy fruit or wine in Algarve[2]. The price of this licence varied from 100 to 300 reis, in proportion to the value of the money to be exported. The English, however, considered this unfair, because no more trouble was involved in making out a licence for a large sum than for a smaller one, and, on their complaining of it in 1458, the price was fixed at a uniform rate of 200 reaes brancos[3].

When their ships were laden, and all the export duties had been paid, the English merchants had

[1] Veedor da nossa fazenda. See *Petition of* 1458, cap. 37. Schanz, II. 520.

[2] Ibid. cap. 36. Schanz, II. 519.

[3] It is probable that at this time "reis" were worth about ½d., and "reaes brancos" just under 1d., of our money.

still to obtain a bill of discharge[1] from the clerks of the custom-house and harbour before they were allowed to sail. The clerks received a salary from the king for this purpose, and had therefore no warrant for making any extra charge, but the merchants were in the habit of giving them 50 or 100 reis, according to the size of the ship. This custom was often abused, for the clerks practically had the merchants in their power, and in 1454 the English complained bitterly that their ships were often detained four or five days, until they consented to pay for the discharge such sums as the clerks were pleased to demand. The king therefore ordered his clerks to discharge each ship at once, or at latest on the day following that on which the shipmaster applied. Payment was in future not to exceed 100 reis for a ship with a forecastle, or 50 for other vessels; and if the clerks made any further charge they were to be fined, while the penalty for the third offence was dismissal from office[2]. Unhappily the position of the English merchants was not much mended, for having by diligent watching procured the conviction and punishment according to this decree of certain of the clerks, who had exacted too much for discharging some German ships laden with salt, they found that the post held by these clerks in the custom-house gave them every opportunity of avenging themselves on their accusers. Moreover, as the English pointed out in 1458, the fact that a ship was built with a forecastle, generally present only for purposes of defence, was no index to the amount of cargo which she was carrying. They suggested that they should pay for their bills of discharge as they paid the custom duties, according to the weight of their merchandise; 50 reis, they

[1] This apparently corresponded with the famous "cocket" issued at the English out-ports, *i.e.*, Letters Patent of discharge under the seal of the cocket.

[2] *Petition of* 1454, cap. 18.

proposed, for anything from 100 to 50 tons, and 30 or 20 reis for smaller cargoes. Alfonso V., however, declined to make any further alteration in the charges[1].

As regards import duties in Portugal, those mentioned by the English are the "sisa" or excise, and the "dizima" or tithe. John I. had made a reduction of a quarter of the sisa in favour of English merchants, but Dom Pedro, while regent, had withdrawn this favour, and the English in 1454 petitioned in vain for the old reduction. Though they set forth that the extra charge was causing them much loss in their trade, while it was most unjust that they should suffer for the misdeeds of disreputable persons who fled at the approach of honest men, many of which misdeeds, also, had been done before Alfonso came to the throne, and had been settled long ago, yet they found the king obdurate in his refusal to reduce the duty paid by the English[2].

But far more than of the sisa the English merchants complained of the dizima or tithe on their cloths, or rather of the manner in which it was levied. The fact that it was taken in kind, one piece in ten, or one-tenth of each piece, being measured off in the custom-house and set apart for the receivers of the customs, gave rise to a terrible amount of annoyance. Immediately the ships of the English merchants arrived in Lisbon they had to expect a visit from the custom-house officers and clerks, who came to take account of all the merchandise and cloth on board; and, when this was done, the English complained, they went on to ransack the private chests of the merchants, even in the absence of the owners, seizing anything that took their fancy, or carrying it off under

[1] *Petition of* 1454, cap. 35. Schanz, II. 519.
[2] Ibid. caps. 23, 24. Schanz, II. 513.

pretence of taking it to the custom-house, on the way to which it would mysteriously disappear[1]. Their cloths, as soon as they were inventoried, had to be disembarked and taken to the custom-house, there to remain till the tithing officers[2] had finished with them; and the English complained that, not content with this, the officials insisted on carrying off their bedding, and even the chests containing their own clothes, keeping them in the custom-house for a fortnight or three weeks in case any pieces of cloth should be concealed within them, during which time the English merchants had to go about in the soiled clothes and linen which they had been wearing on board ship, much to their shame and disgust[3]. In 1454, therefore, the English appealed to the King of Portugal against these malpractices, with the result that a decree was issued ordering that the cargoes of their ships should only be examined in the presence of the owners, and that all their private chests should be removed and put on one side before the officials turned their attention to the merchandise. Nevertheless, when once their precious cloths were in the hands of the Portuguese customs' officers the English merchants had still many trials to endure before they saw the purchase money for these cloths safely in their own pockets.

The first enemy whom they had to encounter was the door-keeper or porter of the custom-house, whose duty it was to arrange the cloths on the shelves of the custom-house, and to look after them as long as they remained there. For the more delicate materials most careful handling was necessary, and the merchants' chances of an advantageous exchange depended greatly on the cloths being released to them before they had time to become creased, or grow dusty and faded with exposure. Thus it is easy to understand the painful anxiety of the

[1] *Petition of* 1454, cap. 1.

[2] Dizimeiros.

[3] *Petition of* 1454, cap. 2.

merchants when they saw the indifferent attitude of the door-keeper, through whose negligence and bad management the cloths would sometimes actually be trodden under foot, the owners having to wait while merchants who had arrived a week or a fortnight later than they received attention first[1]. Moreover, when they tried to enter the custom-house themselves, to see how their cloths were being treated, or even to show them to a possible purchaser, the English merchants received scant courtesy from the door-keeper, who sometimes shut the door in their faces, and sometimes went so far as to strike them, giving them "many blows about the sides[2]." Such treatment injured the pride of the English very grievously, because, as they said, though they were but strangers in Portugal, yet in their own country they were esteemed honourable and well-to-do, and every man had a clear right to look after his own goods.

But the worst accusation brought against the unscrupulous door-keeper was that of dishonesty in appropriating or conniving at the appropriation of cloths left at the custom-house under his safe keeping. The English complained that they frequently found on their return fewer cloths than they had left in the custom-house; as many as ten or twelve rolls of cloth would sometimes be missing, while, if the packs happened to have been opened, one or more of the smaller pieces would invariably disappear. The door-keeper always disclaimed all knowledge of the matter, saying that he could not tell whether such cloths had ever been there or not. The English therefore suggested that he should either be forced to make good all such losses from his own private property, or else that a clerk should be appointed to keep a list of all the cloths coming into the custom-house. Both these suggestions were adopted.

[1] *Petition of* 1454, cap. 3.
[2] Ibid. cap. 4. Schanz, II. 500.

King Alfonso sent for the door-keeper and ordered him to amend his ways; he was to arrange the cloths as the merchants wished, and in such a way that they should not suffer; he was to do no violence to the merchants, and the door of the custom-house was to be kept open the whole afternoon; the cloths were to be tithed in proper order, and a ledger was immediately to be made in which a list could be kept of all the merchandise which came to the custom-house. This ledger was to be placed in a chest with a lock, to which each of five clerks, who were to keep the list, was to possess a key, and if anything was ever again found to be missing, the door-keeper was instantly to make good the losses of the owners[1].

When the business of tithing was taken in hand, more troubles awaited the English merchants. All the cloths were then laid open and arranged where they could easily be seen, when, to the disgust of the merchants, the hall of the custom-house would gradually fill with gentlemen, knights, squires, and other citizens, who had no business there, but who came out of idle curiosity, and were admitted through the servility of the tithing officers. These intruders not only occupied the time of the officials by talking to them when they ought to have been at work, but also they even interfered in any sales that might take place after the tithing, ordering the measurers to give extra measure to certain influential persons, or capturing for a mere song some specially valuable piece of cloth as it came under their notice, thus often spoiling the contents of a whole pack[2]. To add to this, the tithing officers themselves were very irregular in their attendance, coming sometimes very late, and going away again almost within an hour. Some days they would not even come at

[1] *Petition of* 1454, cap. 5, and replies to caps. 3, 4, 5. Schanz, II. 499-501.

[2] Cap. 6.

all, and, out of consideration for the large number of Jews who were receivers of the customs, they refused altogether to tithe cloths on Saturdays, though, just because no Jews did business on this day, it was the freest of all at the custom-house[1]. The result was that the cloths were often detained for a whole month, or even two, though the English declared that the tithing could easily be finished within a week. To reform these abuses, Alfonso V., in 1454, ordered that none but those having business at the custom-house were to be allowed admission at the time of tithing, and that at this time no other business whatever was to be transacted. He also ordered that the tithing officers should come at 6 A.M. every week-day, Saturdays included, from 15th March to 15th September, staying at least three hours; and during the six remaining months of the year they were to come at 8 A.M. In 1458 the English pointed out that nothing had been said as to how long the tithing officers were to stay during the six winter months, an omission which was the more important for them, because this part of the year was even busier than the other half, so that haste and despatch during these months were absolutely necessary. At their suggestion, therefore, it was arranged that during the winter the tithing officers should come at 8 A.M., and stay till midday, and then again after dinner at 2 P.M., remaining till 4, by which arrangement business could be got through regularly and quickly[2].

But another delinquency of the tithing officers tried the patience of the English even more than their irregular attendance. By means of a royal decree to the effect that not more than four vendors and four purchasers should enter the custom-house at one time, these officers used to keep out any particular merchants as long as they pleased,

[1] Cap. 28.
[2] *Petition of* 1458, cap. 39.

till those who had cloths and goods to be tithed, were obliged to pay heavy bribes for permission to enter the hall where the tithing was carried on. In 1454 the English begged Alfonso V. to suspend this decree, and to allow them to enter the custom-house freely as before[1]. The king, however, ordered, that while their ships were being unloaded, the merchants should agree among themselves as to the order in which they would enter the custom-house, and that they should give a list of their names in this order to the judge of the custom-house[2], keeping another copy themselves, by which they could see to it that they went in four by four in order without favouritism or bribery. They tried this for a while, but, in 1458, they complained that the tithing officers did not allow the man with the list to enter, and so continued to tithe according to favour; whereupon Alfonso commanded the judge of the custom-house to be more diligent in seeing that his orders were obeyed, and imposed a penalty of 2,000 reaes brancos, half of which sum was to go to the accuser, upon any tithing officer who should be convicted of tithing otherwise than according to the list of the merchants[3].

In all the transactions of the custom-house at Lisbon the rendeiros or receivers of the customs seem to have exercised an undue influence. The English stated in 1454 that ever since the customs had been farmed out, though at first the judge of the custom-house might tithe fairly, he would soon be surrounded by ten or a dozen rendeiros, whose outcries were so loud that the miserable merchant, who was being tithed, would be intimidated and his voice drowned[4]. Then the judge would take to tithing according to the pleasure of the rendeiros, who would seize as their tithes the best pieces they could find, and leave the worst to the merchants. Another cause of exasperation to the English was

[1] *Petition of* 1458, cap. 9.
[2] Juiz d'alfandega.
[3] *Petition of* 1458, cap. 40.
[4] Ibid. cap. 27.

the secret understanding that existed between the judge of the custom-house, the rendeiros, and the persons whose business it was to measure the cloths in the custom-house, whether for tithing or other purposes. They declared that the measurers[1] often measured off 15, 18, or even 20 ells[2], instead of 10, for ordinary purchasers, and that at tithing time they were persuaded, by some of the other officials who said they wished to take their salary in cloth, to make an extra allowance of from 6 to 8 ells on every 10 measured off for the tithe. The owners of the cloths complained bitterly against thus having to pay not only the necessary customs' duties, but also the fees of the clerks who levied them, and begged Alfonso to order that if these officials wished to take their payment in cloth they should take it from among the tithes already cut off, and not from the packs still belonging to the merchants[3]. This would hardly have suited the rendeiros, however, for they would thus have lost a portion of their profits, and the king's reply was diplomatically framed so as to appease the English, without making any great concession. With regard to the shouting and hustling while tithing was going on, he decreed that his former charters were to be kept, and that sufficient provision against such behaviour had already been made in answers to other complaints. As to the misdemeanours of the measurers, if any merchant should complain of a mistake in measurement, all parties concerned were to return at once and have the cloth remeasured by some official of the custom-house who was known to be above suspicion, when, if any mistake were found, it should instantly be corrected, the measurer paying a fine for the first two offences, and receiving his dismissal for the third. Nothing was said as to the payment of the fees of the officials, but Alfonso ordered that all payments on the cloths of the English merchants

[1] Medidores. [2] Varas. [3] *Petition of* 1454, caps. 13, 14.

should be made according to his own instructions, and as in the case of other persons.

When at last the tithing was over, the merchants were free to dispose of their cloths. Many sales took place in the custom-house, immediately after the tithing, and here again the English had to contend with difficulties, caused by the unequal lengths and textures of their goods, together with the possible existence of small blemishes in the interior of some of the packs. The suspicions of the Portuguese traders were easily aroused, and the cloth merchants were often drawn into long disputes, and even lawsuits, on account of some alleged defect in goods recently sold by them. The purchasers refused to pay for the cloths until the dispute had been settled, and as the case could be carried from one court to another, the cloth merchants frequently had to waste precious months in Lisbon, when, for the sake of their business, they ought to have been on the way home. In 1454 the English protested[1] against these protracted lawsuits, and suggested a revival of John I.'s legislation on the subject[2]. The matter was settled rather differently by Alfonso. He ordered that in the case of cloths sold in the custom-house the purchasers should be instructed to examine them at once, to see if they contained any flaw for which they could claim a rebate. If such were discovered, they were to call the judge's attention to the fact, and the latter was to settle the point in the presence of both parties concerned. There was to be no appeal from his judgment up to the value of 600 reaes brancos; but, if the dispute concerned a higher sum of money than this, he was to call in the chief and clerks of the custom-house, together with the chief royal accountant[3], upon whose advice he was to deliver a final judgment against

[1] *Petition of* 1454, cap. 11.
[2] See p. 56.
[3] Almoxarife e escrivæs d'alfandega e contador mor del rey.

which there should be no appeal. If, however, the purchasers took the cloths away without raising any discussion about them at the time, no cognisance was to be taken of any complaints which might be brought forward afterwards. In the case of cloths sold in the warehouses of the English merchants, the purchasers were ordered as before to examine them at once, and if they found any fault in them they were to take them, either the same day or the next morning, to the judge of the custom-house, who, when he had seen them, was to proceed as in the former case.

Two things in this arrangement greatly displeased the English merchants. In the first place, they objected to the calling in of the clerks of the custom-house to decide in disputes as to the value of their cloths, because, as they explained, these clerks bore a grudge against them, and therefore did them all the harm they could contrive to do while performing this office[1]. Secondly, when disputes arose as to cloths sold in their own warehouses, they very much disliked taking them to the judge of the custom-house. They complained, in 1458, that even in rainy weather the judge forced them to bring the cloths to his own house, where he would keep them two or three days, to the detriment of the goods, making the owners go backwards and forwards continually. The cloth merchants begged once more for a revival of the methods of John I. and Edward, under whom the cloths were either taken to the custom-house, or left in the shop for the judge to come and see them. It was ordered, therefore, that in future all such cloths should be taken to the custom-house, and on no account to the private house of the judge, who was on the contrary to come at once and examine them in the custom-house. The much-condemned clerks of the custom-house were at the same time excluded from taking part in the

[1] *Petition of* 1458, cap. 31.

disputes, and at the request of the English they were also deprived of another office which they had apparently used vindictively. Until the year 1458 the clerks had been allowed to undertake the tithing of cloths in case the officers, whose duty it was, were otherwise engaged, but they were now forbidden to do so in future, and the "contador mor" or chief accountant was ordered, if necessary, to appoint one of his own subordinates to do the work[1].

The English merchants seem to have suffered much inconvenience in collecting the money owed to them for goods sold in Lisbon. John I. had ordered that payment should be made within nine days at most; but in 1454 the English complained that the Portuguese officials were allowing as much as two months to elapse before they would proceed against their fellow-countrymen; that sometimes two or three years would pass before they could get their money; and that many of the "rendeiros" would buy cloths and then use their official influence to prevent the judge of the custom-house, who by an ancient grant judged all matters relating to the trade of the English, from taking cognisance of the case, or hearing the appeals of the creditors. The English explained[2] that in this way harm was done not only to themselves, but to the Portuguese traders, from whom they bought fruit and wine for the return journey, because through not being able to obtain their money from the purchasers of their goods the English could not afford to pay their own debts. The king therefore ordered that whenever a sale took place the broker, through whom the negotiations were conducted, should seal the merchandise and should make a note in his ledger of the day, month, and year in which the purchase was made, whether in the custom-house or in the warehouse of an English merchant. Any day within a week from

[1] *Petition*, cap. 34.
[2] Ibid. caps. 10, 12, 26.

the time the merchandise was sealed the purchaser might come to take it away, and within another week from the day he received it he was to pay the price for it. If he failed to do so, the parties concerned were to appeal to the judge, who, if he still refused to pay, was to send the purchaser to gaol, whence he was not to be released until he paid his debts in full, though he might even be a royal official or the holder of special privileges. For the English merchants this was an exceedingly important decision, and in 1458 they appealed for its better observance, saying that the judge was not sufficiently prompt in hearing their appeals, and that though of their own accord they sometimes allowed the debtors two or three months' grace, yet even then they could not always get their money. They therefore begged that the judge should hear any suit as soon as the term of payment had expired, and that if he proved negligent the governor of the civil courts should be charged with seeing that the royal ordinances were kept[1].

According to their own account many other conditions of their life and trade were very trying to the English merchants in Lisbon. They complained, for instance, that the brokers, through whom they effected their sales and purchases, took advantage of their ignorance of Portuguese regulations to omit the formalities necessary for the conclusion of a valid contract[2]; also, they declared, the Portuguese merchants who bought their goods, paid for them in coins so small that even the royal officials refused to pass them, and detained the English ships till the dues had been paid in larger money, such as "reaes brancos"[3]. Moreover, as strangers living in a foreign city they from time to time experienced much unpleasantness from the strict watch kept over them, and the restrictions imposed upon them

[1] *Petition*, cap. 42. [2] Ibid. cap. 16.
[3] Ibid. cap. 19.

as precautions for the safety of the city. In 1454 they described how, in the time of the vintage, they were always very busy over their merchandise, and how because the days were short they were obliged to go to supper very late in the evening, with the result that when they left the eating-house, to return to their warehouses, they would suddenly be arrested by the city magistrate[1] and his men, with great violence and discourtesy, for being out of doors after the evening bell. They pointed out in their petition that it was quite easy to distinguish foreign merchants and mariners from the loose characters who neither lived with a citizen nor had any means of livelihood—an utterly different type from the well-to-do English merchants—and they therefore appealed to the king, begging that such arrests might be discontinued in future; more especially because it had already happened that when they were thus arrested thieves had gone to their shops and stolen their cloths, pretending them to be their own. If the magistrate should doubt their word as to their peaceable intentions at such an hour, the merchants suggested that he might send back to the eating-house, or to another merchant, or to the lodgings where they passed the night, to ask if they were known there; for this small amount of respect was customary with regard to all foreign merchants in other countries[2].

In reply to this request a decree was passed, ordering that if under such circumstances the English merchants should be found without arms, and should explain their position to the magistrate when he met them, they were to be taken to the house where they said they supped; and, if they were found to be speaking the truth, they should be allowed to go safely to their lodgings or warehouses even though the evening bell were past. But when they went on to beg for permission to carry arms in Lisbon, the English

[1] Alcaide. [2] *Petition*, cap. 20.

merchants found the Portuguese king quite obdurate. Though they explained in graphic terms how at vintage time they were obliged to keep much of their wine, oil, and honey on the wharf, how when they went to look to their safety by night, after supper, and after the evening bell, they would often be attacked by men disguised and armed, who wounded them and robbed them of their mantles and cloaks, jewellery, and money, and how all these misfortunes befell them because they were not allowed to carry arms for their own defence, though in England all Portuguese subjects were freely allowed to do so; in spite of all these arguments the king declared himself unable to make any change in the existing ordinances which forbade to all foreigners the carrying of arms in Portugal[1]. He consented, however, on the further representations of the English, that for want of an armed watch they were sometimes robbed of all their goods, even as they lay on the wharf, to order the city magistrate with his men to keep special watch all night against robbery or assault on the river bank[2].

This long list of complaints and grievances, of which an abstract has now been given, throws incidentally so much light on the conditions of life and trade for the English merchants in Lisbon, that the absence of any similar information with regard to the Portuguese in England is to be regretted. Much can be learnt from the English records of the fourteenth and fifteenth centuries about the "foreign merchants" then living in England[3], among whom the Portuguese are in all probability to be included; but up to the present very little detailed information is available with regard to merchants belonging to particular nationalities. In the absence of such

[1] *Petition*, cap. 21. [2] Ibid. cap. 22.

[3] See in particular a paper by M. S. Giuseppi, in *Trans. Roy. Hist. Soc.*, N.S., IX., on "Alien Merchants in England in the Fifteenth Century."

information, however, it may be hoped that the practices of the English officials, particularly those of the custom-house, did not show the same intolerable corruption which called forth the bitter complaints of the English merchants in Lisbon. The farming out of the customs almost unavoidably leads to the use of questionable methods in levying and collecting them, and, popular as was this system abroad, it was happily not adopted in England. It is true that a great deal of English commercial legislation in the fifteenth century was aimed directly against foreign merchants, and it can hardly be supposed that the English officials always acted with courtesy, or even absolute justice, towards the aliens with whom they had to deal, but it is probable that in England the merchants of Portugal were spared a great many of the annoyances connected with the custom-house, which figure so largely in the two petitions of the English merchants in Lisbon.

PART II.: MODERN

By A. B. Wallis Chapman

CHAPTER I

COLONIAL RIVALRY

(1487-1580)

Relative position of the English and Portuguese nations in the beginning of the sixteenth century—Growing estrangement—Influence of Spain—Effect of the English Reformation — Commercial relations — Trade through the Low Countries—The spice trade—Direct trade—English export of cloth — Barbary trade — Sugar — English attempts at trade with the Indies and with Africa—Portuguese jealousy —Action of Philip II.—Attitude of Elizabeth—English piracies and Portuguese retaliation—Protest of English merchants against piracy — Proposed cloth staple in England—English trade with Portugal and with Barbary compared — Negotiations with Portugal concerning the African trade—Treaty of 1576.

THE three hundred years, from 1500 to 1800, witnessed a complete change in the positions occupied by England and Portugal in the rank of European nations, and, consequently, a profound modification of their relations to each other.

In the beginning of the sixteenth century the Portuguese were distinctly in advance of the English as the colonising, exploring, trading nation. English manufactures, and, consequently, English trade, were but little developed. According to the "Venetian Relation" (1500), England imported "nothing for her own subsistence."[1] In other words, her imports, with

[1] *Venetian Relation*, p. 228.

the doubtful exception of wine, consisted wholly of luxuries. Portugal, on the other hand, producing but little beyond wine and oil, fruit and salt, was yet, relatively to its area, one of the wealthiest nations of Europe. The School of Explorers, founded by Diniz and Henry the Navigator, had not only given to the Portuguese the supremacy of Africa: their possession of the Cape route to the East had unlocked the door of the Indies, and they were bent on retaining sole possession of the key.

The list of Portuguese exports to Antwerp, given by Guicciardini, shows from what varied sources the nation drew its wealth. It includes jewels, pearls, gold (in bulk and wrought), spices, drugs, "excellent amber," musk, civet, ivory in great quantities, rhubarb, incense, aloes, "the Indian colour called by the Portuguese anil," cotton, sugar (from St Thomé, Guinea, and Barbary), wine "of Madeira, so excellent, it is like Malvoisie"; from Portugal itself—salt, wine, oil, sumach, and dried fruits; and from Barbary—leather, gums, skins, and feathers. The value of all these products was enormous. The spices alone amounted annually to 1,000,000 crowns; and the sugar was worth 100,000.

The contrast is curious with the English list, consisting chiefly of woollen manufactures, of which about 250,000 crowns' worth were sent annually to Antwerp; besides these, the English exported tin, lead, skins, saffron, leather, dairy produce, and, curiously enough, Malvoisie, which they brought from the Levant[1].

In other words, England was at this time a poor country, directly dependent on its own products for subsistence; and Portugal a rich one, dependent on its trade for its wealth.

Superiority in trade involved naval efficiency, and this, too, Portugal possessed. Portuguese vessels were freighted by the English for the Levant

[1] L. Guicciardini, *Descrittione di lutti in Paesi Bassi.*

trade[1]; Portuguese pilots aided English captains in their early attempts at exploration; a charter, granted in 1501 to the Bristol adventurers by Henry VII. was granted to certain English and Portuguese.[2] Portuguese shipbuilders were employed by that fosterer of the English navy—Henry VIII.[3]. Neither as sailors, merchants, nor explorers, could the English in the sixteenth century vie with the Portuguese, and consequently the ancient amity between the two nations seemed in no danger of disturbance.

The political revolutions in England had not hitherto affected English relations with Portugal. Two years after the accession of Henry VII. the great treaty of 1386,—the treaty of mutual peace and freedom of trade,—was renewed and confirmed[4], and during the next thirty years the political relations of the two countries were in the main uneventful. By 1524-25, however, there were signs that the interests of these old allies might draw them in opposite directions.

The first disturbing element was the rising power of Spain. Hitherto, dread of Spain had driven Portugal nearer to England. Now, Charles V. courted the Portuguese alliance. The first step was the marriage in 1518 of his sister Eleanora to the King of Portugal; then, in 1524, the Emperor himself annulled his engagement with the English Princess Mary to marry the Portuguese Infanta, prompted in part by the huge dowry of the latter. The marriage opened the way for the subsequent union of Spain and Portugal; and from this time onward, the rulers of the two countries acted in great measure as allies. The Portuguese and the Emperor acted together against the Turks (1535); arrests of ships were made at Lisbon in the Imperial interest

[1] Anderson, *Historical and Chronological Deductions of the Origin of Commerce*" (Combe's Edition), II. 60.

[2] W. Busch, *England under the Tudors*," I. 162.

[3] M. A. S. Hume, *Life of Sir Walter Raleigh*, 4.

[4] Rymer, O., XII. 378.

(1538); and Charles V. and his successor remonstrated against damage done to Portugal[1].

This coalescence was intensified by the overshadowing question of the Reformation. One of the strongest characteristics of the House of Avis was religious enthusiasm: moreover, the pretext which Henry VIII. put forward for his divorce touched the honour of the Portuguese king; the latter's father, Emanuel, had successively married two sisters, and the Pope did not fail to point out the analogy between this case and that of Katherine of Aragon, who had married two brothers; thus should the dispensation be declared invalid in the second case, its force in the first would certainly be affected[2]. The Emperor emphasised the point by declaring that the Portuguese honour was involved as well as his own[3]; and Portugal was reported to be among the nations with whose armed intervention England was threatened[4]. The definitely religious side of the quarrel appeared in the wrath excited by the appearance of some heretical placards at Lisbon, attributed to the English[5]; and in the flight of the "Novos Christos" to England where their reception, after all, was not particularly hospitable[6]. There was no direct result of these differences which, of course, disappeared on the accession of Mary, but they deepened the hostility which was springing up from other causes.

Neither religious discord nor European strife produced the depth of antagonism which was excited by colonial rivalry. In fact, during the first eighty years of the sixteenth century, the old tie between England and Portugal, the bond of a

[1] See *Hen. VIII. St. P. Cal.*, for date 1538, Nos. 1213, 1070; and for 1535, Nos. 744 and 1022.

[2] Ibid. 1535, No. 569.

[3] Ibid. 1531, Nos. 265, 468.

[4] Ibid. 1535, No. 901.

[5] Ibid. 1539, No. 340.

[6] Ibid. 1537, Appendix No. 38.

common commercial interest, was fretted almost to breaking point by the competition of the two nations for the wealth of Africa and the Indies.

But the old tie was strong; a steady trade existed between England and Portugal, chiefly through the Low Countries. The Portuguese wine staple was at Middleburg[1], and Antwerp, as has been shown, was the centre for almost every imaginable commodity. The Portuguese, according to Wheeler, "sailed every year full hungerlie about three parts of the earth almoste for spyces, and when he had brought them home the great fat purses of the Antwerpers . . . engrossed them all into their own hands, yea, oftentimes gave money for them beforehand, making thereof a plain monopolie[2]." Nor did the English buy only spices; cotton, sugar, drugs, and jewels, were among the Portuguese goods they exported from Antwerp; and of English goods the Portuguese took lead, tin, dairy produce, and cloth, though much of this last commodity passed to Portugal through Spain[3].

Direct trade also was increasing; in 1503 the first Portuguese spice ships arrived at London, loaded with pepper[4]; in 1530 the first charter was granted to the merchants trading to Spain and Portugal[5]. The western ports were naturally those most interested in this commerce. Southampton, Lyme, Exeter, Barnstaple, and Chester, were all concerned in it, whilst Wales sent its cloth to Bristol to be there exchanged for Portuguese salt and wine[6]. The bulk of the cloths sent to Portugal, however, consisted of the coloured cloths originally made in Kent and Suffolk, and the market seems to have been largest

[1] Halyburton's *Ledger*, 31.
[2] Wheeler, J., *Treatise of Commerce*, 47.
[3] L. Guicciardini, *Descrittione di lutti in Pæsi Bassi.*
[4] Cunningham, *Industry and Commerce*, II. 478.
[5] *Henry VIII. St. P. Cal.*, 2998, No. 6654, g. 1.
[6] Royal Historical Society's Transactions, N.S., XVII. E. A. Lewis, *Industry and Commerce in Mediæval Wales.*

for the completely finished, dressed, and dyed cloths. The importance of cloth in the direct Portuguese trade, and the probable small value of the total trade itself, appears from certain Custom Accounts of 1567-68. These show that the custom on cloth exported to Portugal amounted in the first year to £219. 9s. 2½d., while the customs on all other goods sent thither were only £44 and 16 pence; and in 1568 the custom on cloth was £389. os. 8¾d., while the remaining customs were £69. 3s. 3½d.[1].

Cloth thus appears, as it long continued, the mainstay of the English trade with Portugal; but, of the articles Portugal sent in return, wine, once of such great importance, seems during the sixteenth century to have descended to an inferior position. In the Customs Accounts of the early years of Henry VIII. it ranks highest amongst Portuguese products; but, in the account above quoted, it appears as paying in 1567 only 27s. tonnage out of a total of £375. 15s. 6½d., on all articles sent from Portugal; and in 1568 only £14. 13s. 6d., out of £281. 4s. od. In the lists of imports from Portugal to London, in 1574, wine is not mentioned[2], and though it appears in the list of goods of Portuguese growth in 1564, no stress is laid upon it; the list being headed by "sawlt in great abondance[3]."

But the principal wealth of Portugal was derived, as has been seen, not from its own products, but from those of the Indies, and of Africa, spices, sugar, drugs, hides, "calicowte cloth." Sugar, especially, was important. The Portuguese first brought it from the Indies, and from Barbary; then themselves cultivated it at St Thomé, and at a later date transported it to Brazil. During the period now under discussion sugar was frequently imported to England from Portugal or the Portuguese dependencies,

[1] *El. Dom. St. P. MSS.*, XLVII. No. 9.
[2] *Cotton MSS.*, Nero, B. 11, fols. 298-99.
[3] *El Dom. St. P. MSS.*, XXXV. No. 37.

the Azores and Barbary—especially the latter. In 1574-75 and 1575-76, sugar (apparently at £10 a chest) was the most important item in the imports from Barbary to England; the total worth of these in the first-named year was £28,639, of which £20,680 was in sugar, and in the second year's account there were £13,480 worth of sugar out of a total of £17,775. Sugar brought from Portugal itself, in the same year, reached barely one-twentieth of the above sum, but even so in 1574-75 it ranked next to pepper in importance, and in 1575-76 was only exceeded by the three great spices, pepper, cloves, and cinnamon[1].

It appears to have shared in the general rise in prices during the latter part of the sixteenth century. Malynes, in contrasting the prices of 1620 with those of 1550, calculates the value of cloth sent to Lisbon in sugar. In 1550, he declares, two chests of sugar could be bought for one London-mingled coloured cloth. In 1620 two cloths could buy only one chest[2]. It would not have been surprising if the calculation had been based on spices. The merchant adventurers, deserting the market of Antwerp, took their cloths direct to Lisbon, and there exchanged them for spices and drugs. In 1574 the value of the pepper alone brought from Portugal to London was £8,383, more than half the total of the Portuguese imports; and a similar proportion appears in 1575[3].

Nor was this the only monopoly to which the Portuguese pretended. The gold and slaves of Guinea, the sugar and hides of Barbary, they also claimed as their exclusive right. But these demands could not be maintained.

The desire of other nations, particularly the English, to share in these new benefits increased yearly, and no remembrance of ancient amity could stay them

1 *Cotton MSS.*, Nero, B. 11, fols. 298-69.
2 Malynes, *Lex Mercatoria*, 65.
3 *Cotton MSS.*, Nero, B. 11, fols. 298-99.

from attempting to gratify it. Still the Charter to the Merchant Adventurers in 1503, showed the influence of the old alliance in the clause which stipulated that no expedition should be made to "such heathen and infidel countries as are already discovered and reduced to the obedience of the King of Portugal or any other prince, our friend and confederate[1]."

Nor did the Portuguese at first rouse themselves to jealousy when, in 1530, William Hawkins sailed to Guinea and then to Brazil[2]. He left the spice countries untouched, and it was these Portugal was most anxious to guard. Two attempts the English made to find their way thither without conflict with the Portuguese. One in 1541, when a dearth in Portugal forced her to apply to England for corn. In their reply Henry VIII. and his Council made it a condition that the corn might go, if the Portuguese government would admit some Englishmen of the king's appointment to adventure for spice in the next Portuguese expedition to Calicut[3]. The concessions seemed small, the need of Portugal great; but she did not comply; and the next attempt of the English was to evade the monopoly by trying to trade through Russia in 1558, with a view to obtaining the treasures of the East by journeying down the Volga to Novgorod and Astrakhan, crossing the Caspian Sea, and so to Persia.[4] A company was founded for this purpose, but it lost heavily on its earlier ventures; and as long as Portugal remained an independent kingdom her spice monopoly, though endangered, was really untouched.

Nearer Europe, however, their power was less effectually maintained. In 1553 the English made

[1] Rymer, O., XII. 37.
[2] Cunningham, *Industry and Commerce*, II. 506.
[3] *Henry VIII. St. P. Cal.*, No. 1257.
[4] Anderson, *Historical and Chronological Deductions of the Origin of Commerce*, II. 105, 128, 137.

an armed raid on Madeira, but the attempt appears to have excited little notice from the English government[1]. The intercourse with Africa was more important. By the middle of the sixteenth century the Portuguese had a line of settlements along the North African coast, where the chief post was Oran, and extending south-west to Guinea with its famous settlement of El Mina. They were in frequent conflict with the Shereef of Morocco, and as time went on they grew exceedingly jealous of the favour shown by that potentate to the English[2]. Beyond Guinea the Portuguese had scattered stations along the coast as far as Mozambique; but with these the other nations had at this time little concern[3].

As early as 1530, however, William Hawkins had touched at Guinea; in 1536 English merchants traded thither for gold dust and ivory[4], and in 1562 John Hawkins made his first slaving voyage to that coast[5]. In Barbary, too, English trade was speedily established; by 1552 there were Bristol merchants trading thither, exchanging linen cloth, amber and jet, for sugars, dates, diamonds and molasses[6].

To this infringement of their monopoly the Portuguese strongly objected; the first important negotiation on the subject appears to have taken place in the reign of Philip and Mary in 1555. The Portuguese ambassador complained that the English had invaded El Mina[7]. Philip, as a near connection of the King of Portugal's, and as the champion of colonial monopoly, supported the Portuguese claims, and the merchants were ordered to suspend the fresh

[1] Rebello da Silva, *Historia de Portugal*, III. 135.
[2] *El. For. St. P. Cal.*, 1577, 94.
[3] For Portuguese possessions in Africa in the sixteenth century, see Anderson's *Historical Deductions*, II., various references.
[4] Anderson, *Historical Deductions*, II. 62.
[5] Ibid. 117.
[6] Ibid. 92.
[7] *Mary For. St. P. MSS.*, 1555, 17th December, Vol. VI., Nos. 441 and 1555, Nos. 448, 449, 450.

expedition which they meditated, till the question was investigated. The merchants, on their side, pleaded that they had been used to traffic "without hindrance to Asia and Africa, as well as Europe; they had resorted about two years before to sundry places in the government of sundry nations," where they had been well received; and they had been on the point of sending again, when they received the orders of the Council, forbidding them to enter any places under the King of Portugal's government. This order they declared they had obeyed; since on this second expedition they had not entered the country, but had waited in their ships for customers. The plea, however ingenious, was unsatisfactory. The English were forbidden to return to Africa, even to reclaim the hostages they had left with the King of Benin. Next came a rumour of French ships trading to Guinea, and the English merchants again prepared an expedition, and were again stopped; whereon they complained bitterly of their loss, and Mary was so far moved as to suggest that the King of Portugal should compensate them; a scheme which did by no means satisfy the English adventurers[1].

The accession of Elizabeth, and the consequent revolt of England from Spanish influence, strengthened the spirit of enterprise which threatened the Portuguese power. During the first ten years of the new reign, English attacks on Africa—especially the raids of John Hawkins and the Winters—were the source of repeated complaints from the Portuguese ambassador. This unlicensed trade often degenerated to mere piracy; as early as 1559, Spain remonstrated on behalf of Portuguese merchant vessels plundered by the English[2]. Elizabeth's attitude with regard both to the piracy and the African raids was characteristic. She gave the Portuguese ambassador good

[1] *Mary For. St. P. MSS.*, 1555, Nos. 448, 449, 450.
[2] *El. For. St. P. Cal.*, 16th August 1559, No. 1203.

words, and plenty of them. She promised to punish offenders where offences could be proved, and repeated the promise frequently, though its performance was deferred. With regard to the trade to Africa, her attitude was that of a person much misused. Why should the King of Portugal complain of her subjects trading to his settlements in Africa, when the Portuguese might trade to any part of England or Ireland? She utterly denied the right of the Portuguese government to prevent foreigners from trading to any part of Africa, which its subjects had not settled; yet, out of her special amity to the Portuguese king, she would issue a proclamation forbidding her subjects to enter Ethiopia[1].

This was in 1561, but somehow the prohibition proved unavailing. The English merchants and navigators maintained that it was only intended to last for a few months, and acted in this faith. Frobisher in the following year explored part of the African Coast, and reported that, excepting Trepont and Castel del Mina, the Portuguese had no forts between Cap de Verde and Benin[2]. The English promptly concluded they might trade to these unsettled regions, and did so; and Elizabeth answered the Portuguese ambassador's complaints by suggesting that his master had better prevent his subjects from trading with England[3]. In fact, wealthy as Portugal was, her produce, consisting wholly in luxuries, was less necessary to England than England's products to her, and the English were not slow to perceive their advantage. The negotiations continued, but Elizabeth kept to her point; she would forbid her subjects to trade to places actually in the Portuguese obedience, but nowhere else; and the English thereon voyaged where they pleased, without observing such nice

[1] *El. For. St. P. Cal.*, 1561, Nos. 96, 97, 98, 136, 137, 138.
[2] Ibid. 1562, No. 102.
[3] Ibid. No. 104.

distinctions. In 1564, Hawkins fitted out fifteen or sixteen ships for Guinea, and the Portuguese ambassador complained loudly and uselessly of the English expeditions to Mina, Minagualte, and other places, where the Portuguese themselves were forbidden to trade[1].

At last, in 1567-68, the patience of the Portuguese gave way; there had been a few reprisals on the English, and these culminated in the seizure of Winter's ship off the coast of Guinea. The vessel was sunk, the goods confiscated, and the crew imprisoned[2]. Some other ships were also taken, and the indignation of the English was profound. That various Portuguese ships and settlements had during the past ten years been seized, raided, and plundered by Hawkins, Winter himself and other captains did not seem, to the English mind, at all germane to the matter. Portuguese ships were seized at Falmouth by way of reprisal[3]. The Portuguese government, now fairly roused, responded by sequestrating the goods of the English in Portugal. Elizabeth thereon seized the goods of the Portuguese in England. All ordinary trade between the two countries was suspended[4]. Matters seemed to be driving fast to war.

There were, however, powerful factors in England on the side of peace. Besides the political situation which made any war a madness, there was the influence of the legitimate traders between England and Portugal. These were a numerous body. In 1569 they were estimated to number a hundred and twenty in London, Bristol, and Southampton[5]. They were also apparently an increasing body. About 1574 application was made to the Queen for a

[1] *El. For. St. P. Cal.*, 1564, Nos. 649, 804, 824.
[2] *El. Dom. St. P. Cal.*, 1569, 318, Nos. 26, 27.
[3] *El. For. St. P. Cal.*, Nos. 90, 91.
[4] Rebello da Silvia, *Historia de Portugal*, III. 137.
[5] *Cotton MSS.*, Nero, B. I., fol. 173.

charter to an exclusive company of merchants trading to Spain and Portugal; which charter was to include only those who had so traded in 1568. Thereon several merchants, with Alderman Pullyson at their head, after vainly protesting against the formation of an exclusive Company at all, prayed that, at least, it should not be limited to those trading in 1568, as many merchants had taken up the trade since who would be ruined by such a regulation[1].

The importance of the direct trade appears in a petition for its re-establishment in 1571, signed by representatives, not only of London, but of most of the great western ports. Further, these traders had English factors and correspondents in Portugal, forming the nucleus of the great Lisbon factory, and enjoying various privileges and immunities, so that, in these men, Portugal held hostages, as it were, for the good behaviour of the English[2].

England, however, possessed no such security over Portugal. Of the 4,631 foreigners in England in 1571, only 7 were Portuguese[3]. Besides, despite Elizabeth's bravado, the Portuguese market was of real importance to the English clothiers; Portugal took more Suffolk and Kent cloths than did Spain, and much of the cloth which Spain did take was "ventyd" in Portugal[4]. As for the Antwerp trade, it was estimated in 1569 that the Portuguese annually took English cloth from that city to the value of 2,050,000 ducats[5], an amount which the English had no desire to lessen. Portugal, too, had her reasons for peace;

[1] *El. Dom. St. P. MSS.*, XCIX. No. 9.
[2] Ibid. LXXXIII. No. 37.
[3] Ibid. LXXXII.
[4] *Cotton MSS.*, Nero, B. I. fol. 162. This was a reversal of the state of things which had existed at the beginning of the century when English goods passed through Spain to Portugal. See p. 133.
[5] Sayes, 700,000 ducats; fustians, 400,000 ducats; "frizadoes," 600,000 ducats; baies, 200,000 ducats; mockadoes, 150,000 ducats. *Cotton MSS.*, Nero, B. I. fol. 152.

England was a good customer for her spices, and, as a memorialist of the time points out, her monopoly was useless, unless she could find a "vent." The chief "vent" was at Antwerp, and as the English commanded the Portuguese passage thither, they could cut off the Portuguese trade to Flanders, Germany, and the Baltic, if not to France and Spain[1].

These facts, as well as the disturbed state of the Low Countries, were all duly urged in support of a scheme put forward by a Portuguese resident in England in 1569, and promoted by various English merchants, for removing the spice staple from Antwerp to London, Bristol, or Southampton. It was stated that Antwerp's prosperity was due chiefly to the exports from England, Portugal, and Italy, "the one most necessary, the seconde of greate profite, the third of pleasure." England, having the "necessarie" commodity, cloth, could induce the other two nations to follow her lead, and the result would be profitable, even if it were needful to grant privileges to the Portuguese. A spice staple in England would draw merchants from all parts thither to the increase both of the wealth and industry of the country. England would get her spices unadulterated, and at first hand; her navy would benefit by distributing them to France and the Eastland towns, and the Portuguese would gain by buying their cloths direct from England. The possible rivalry of the Muscovy Company was also urged as an inducement to the Portuguese to agree to the scheme[2]. The plan found favour with Burleigh, as he admitted to the Portuguese ambassador in 1575[3]; and, futile as it was, it shows the strong current in favour of peace, which checked the irritation both in Portugal and

[1] *El. Dom. St. P. MSS.*, LI. Nos. 18, 19.
[2] Ibid.
[3] Ibid. CV. No. 45 (Letter of Burleigh to Walsingham).

England, and prevented any violent conclusion to the quarrel.

The trading interest, however, did not incline the English to yield to the Portuguese pretensions in Africa, though they wished that the immediate dispute should be settled by compensating Winter, while cancelling his letters of marque[1]. Indeed, many merchants had even a stronger interest in the Portuguese dependencies than in the mother country herself. The English trade with Barbary was said to be worth far more than the English trade with Portugal; in 1574-75 the imports from Barbary to London amounted to £28,639, and in 1575-76 to £17,775, while those from Portugal in the same years were only worth £11,626. 15s. 0d. and £8,758. 5s. 4d.[2]. The merchants whom Burleigh consulted in 1572 as to the places under Portuguese jurisdiction where the English were wont to trade, though enumerating only Portugal, the Algarves, Madeira, and the Azores, maintained that no commands ought to abolish the commerce with Barbary, where they traded for the sale of cloth. South of Cape Blanco such a prohibition might be endured[3]. In fact, they would concede the trade to Guinea, but would not give up that to Barbary.

The negotiations dragged on for years, managed chiefly by Fogaça, a Portuguese merchant, Secretary Wilson, Walsingham, and the Portuguese ambassador, Giraldi. In 1571-72 a treaty was drafted, which left the North Barbary trade open to England[4]. But it does not seem to have been signed; and an article dated the same month as the treaty appears, bearing the significant heading: "The Ambassador of Portyngalle's article, which was denied him[5]," and containing a general prohibition to the English to trade in the

[1] *Cotton MSS.*, Nero, B. I, fol. 173.
[2] Ibid. B. II. fols. 298-99.
[3] *El. For. St. P. Cal.*, No. 689.
[4] Ibid. 1st January 1572, No. I.
[5] *El. For. St. P. MSS.*, CXXII. No. 62.

Portuguese dominions. In 1573, a commission was appointed to consider the claims of the Spanish and Portuguese against one another for ships taken by each. In 1574, according to the account given by the Viscount Santarem, in "A Statement of Fact," a treaty was signed by the English government, acknowledging the Portuguese rights over Africa[1]; but it could not have been effectual, for in 1575-76 negotiations were still going on. A letter from Burleigh to Walsingham[2] (1575) gives an account of an interview which he held with Giraldi on the subject, in which Burleigh seems to have shown his customary mild pertinacity. The crux was, as usual, the question of the trade to Barbary. Burleigh would not consent to its prohibition; then Giraldi offered to allow the English merchants to trade thither, provided that they carried no artillery, and that they touched at Portugal to register their lading, and obtain individual permission for their trade. The first point Burleigh conceded; the second he thought savoured too much of subjection to Portugal, and declined. The final upshot of the various negotiations was the treaty of 1576, by which three years were allowed for the making of a durable peace, and six months for a mutual restitution of goods under a joint commission. As to Africa, the matter was simply ignored. The English might trade to Portugal and the Algarves, Madeira and the Azores, and the Portuguese to England and Ireland, but no mention was made either of Barbary or Guinea[3].

Such a treaty, of course, really settled nothing,

[1] This document appears neither in the *Calendar of Foreign State Papers* nor in the *Treaty Roll.*

[2] *El. Dom. St. P. MSS.*, CV. No. 45.

[3] A Portuguese version of this treaty is printed by Viscount Santarem, in the *Quadro Elementar*, etc., XV. 320-322. The original in Latin appears in *El. St. P. For. Cal.*, CXL. No. 854, 29th October 1576, signed on behalf of Elizabeth by Francis Walsingham, and on behalf of the Portuguese king by Francesco Giraldi.

even if it had been finally ratified—a point which does not appear. The gulf between the two countries steadily widened. The religious zeal of the young Portuguese king—Sebastian—caused much anxiety in England. Lisbon was the resort of discontented Englishmen like Stukeley, and Irish Catholics like Desmond and Fitzmaurice; whilst Sebastian's vast preparations for his African expedition were rumoured to be intended for Ireland[1]. On the other hand, the English pirates were beyond restraint. The very year after the signature of the treaty, Winter, yet mindful of his wrongs, seized a Portuguese ship off the Isle of Wight, laden with oranges[2]. The danger of war increased daily.

But the death of Sebastian, and the subsequent annexation of Portugal by Spain, completely altered the political situation. England, as the opponent of Spain, could carry on her depredations on territory annexed by that country, while at the same time posing as the champion of Portuguese independence; and thus a formal breach between the two countries was averted.

[1] *El. For. St. P. Cal.*, 1578-79, No. 1445.
[2] Ibid. 1577, No. 1552.

CHAPTER II

THE COMPANY OF MERCHANTS TRADING TO SPAIN AND PORTUGAL

(1577-1640)

Union of Spain and Portugal—Philip II. and the English in Portugal—Influence of commercial interests makes for peace, and of colonial interests for war—Expedition of 1589—Renewed disputes about African trade—Trade with the East Indies—Treaty of 1604—It ignores colonial trade—Effect of treaty on home trade—Revival of the Company of Merchants trading to Spain and Portugal—Its previous charters (1530 and 1577) and history—Relative positions of London and provinces in Company—Exclusion of retail traders—Quarrel with Chester (1579 *et seq.*)—Effect of union of Spain and Portugal upon the Company—Trade during war—Commercial stipulations in Treaty of 1604—Grievances of English in Spain and Portugal—Renewal of the Charter of the Spanish Company, 1605—Petitions for and against it—Nullifying Act of 1606—Movements for renewal of Company—Rivalry of mere merchants and manufacturers—Decay of trade—English traders as intermediaries between Portugal and the Eastland cities—Piracy—Cloth trade—Newfoundland fish trade—Decay of Portuguese spice trade—Rise of Brazil trade (sugar and tobacco)—Difference of Anglo-Portuguese relations in 1580 and 1640.

THE immediate effect on Anglo-Portuguese relations of the Spanish annexation of Portugal was, as has been already said, two-fold; it left the English free to pursue their semi-piratical, semi-commercial intercourse with Africa and the East Indies, while at the same time reviving the old amity between England and Portugal.

That this revival of amity was a mere question of opposition to Spain appears, on the whole, probable; Elizabeth's policy was, as usual, the essence of caution. On the death of the Cardinal-King Henry of Portugal, she sent a special envoy, Wootton, to Spain, with directions to address himself, not only to the governors, in whose hands the settlement of the succession was supposed to rest, but to each of the three chief claimants to the throne—Philip II., the Duchess of Braganza, and secretly to the popular candidate, Antonio, the prior of Crato.

To each Wootton was to give general good wishes; but he was to commit England to nothing, and he was to find out which way the wind blew.

But as Philip's success became certain, Elizabeth's hostility to him increased, and therewith her inclination to support Antonio. The commercial interests of England, however, were by no means in favour of the latter. Philip showed no disposition to interfere with the English trade to Portugal. On the contrary, in 1584 he assented to the appointment of an Englishman "João Telart" (probably John Taylor) as consul at Lisbon, and confirmed the English privileges in that city[1]. Certain accounts for the same year show that the English trade with Spain and Portugal was still active. The imports to London, Bristol, and Southampton from Portugal seem, in this year, to have been worth over £14,000. The returns were made chiefly in cloth and corn. Over 1,600 cloths were sent from London to Portugal and its dependencies, Barbary and Madeira. The value of the rest of the returns—chiefly corn, lead, kerseys, bays, Hasbro' webs, hardware, etc.—seem to have amounted to something over £4,000. The trade to Portugal seems, however, to have been a small proportion (very roughly speaking perhaps one-sixth) of

[1] *Add. MSS.*, 11, 682.

that to the whole peninsula. Thus the interest of a large body of traders, both in Spain and Portugal, made against Antonio; and again and again Mendoza (the Spanish ambassador in England) made use of this circumstance to embarrass the English ministers, by instigating the merchants of Bristol and London to protest[1].

On the other hand, Antonio had arrayed on his side the anti-Catholic interest, represented by Walsingham, and the interest of the explorers and adventurers represented by Drake. The wishes of this party were fixed on the trade to the Indies; a paper put forth in 1580 shows the trend of the ideas of the time[2]. Was it lawful, the writer asked, for Christian merchants to traffic with "heathens and infidels?" If a Christian prince conquered a heathen nation, might the subjects of another prince, an ally of its conqueror, "use traffic with the inhabitants of a place so conquered," or could the conqueror lawfully forbid such traffic? What effect will a league between Spain and England have on the relations of England and Spain in South America? And so forth, and so forth, questions all extremely pertinent to the state of affairs, and especially to the relations of England, Spain, and Portugal. It was natural that men whose minds were exercised on these points should see their opportunity in Antonio's necessity.

The first suggestion was of a footing in the Azores, which would give England the command of the passage to the East and West Indies by the route which Drake had so opportunely discovered. In 1581 a double expedition was suggested to be headed by Drake, first to Terceira, and then to Calicut, where the English should establish a trade in spices, "as a party with the King of Portugal" (Antonio)[3].

[1] *Lansd. MSS.*, No. 41.

[2] "Considerations touching the Lawfulness of Trade to the Indies." *Dom. St P. MSS.*, CXLVI. No. 12.

[3] *Dom. St. P. Cal.*, 13, No. 47.

This project, however, was not carried out, and a policy which found yet greater favour was an attack upon Lisbon itself. The Portuguese were reported as profoundly discontented with Spain, and ready and eager to rise if English help was extended to them. Antonio's promises of recompense were as vast as the promises of exiles are wont to be. Freedom of trade, the payment of five millions of gold, licence to the English to fit out English ships in the harbour at Lisbon, leave to place English garrisons in Portuguese towns, were among the inducements he held out[1].

Drake and his comrades were eager for the attempt, which seemed a suitable return stroke for the Armada; and many merchants, to whom Antonio had already granted letters of marque against Spain, were further allured by his magnificent offers. His success promised to unlock the doors of the Indies to them, and place their daring commerce in comparative safety. Thus the expedition of 1589 became a joint stock affair, in which public policy and private interest were so involved, that Queen, captains, and merchants shared the expenses of the undertaking. It proved, however, an absolute failure. The preparations were ill made, the leaders differed, the Spaniards garrisoned Lisbon, the Portuguese failed to rise, sickness decimated the English forces, and the result was one of the worst fiascoes of Elizabeth's reign. Thenceforth Antonio's cause was hopeless, and thenceforth England continued her attacks on the East as the rivals, not the friends, of the Portuguese[2].

In this manner the English adventurers at last obtained the full advantage of the Portuguese discoveries. The question of the African trade, which had been so hotly debated, previous to the death of Sebastian, was now gradually solving itself. As soon as war broke out between Portugal and Spain,

[1] Hume, M. A. S., *The Year after the Armada.*

[2] For details of this attempt see Major Hume's (M.) *The Year after the Armada.*

Elizabeth redoubled her efforts to defer giving any definite answer on the point, in hopes that either she might obtain better terms from Philip, or that to obtain her help the Portuguese would grant what she chose[1]. The question, however, disappeared from prominence in the ensuing clash of interests, and the English adventurers pursued their own way; 1582 saw the incorporation of merchants trading to Barbary, and in the same year the trade with Benin was opened[2]. In 1588 a Company obtained from Antonio an exclusive right to trade to Senegal and Gambia, whither they went by way of the Azores[3]; and though in a paper on trade in 1596, there is a casual observation that if the "Spanyards take yowe trading with them (*i.e.* to Barbary) yowe dye for it[4]; and though in 1620, Malynes considered Guinea a place to which it was not lawful to trade, yet the commerce continued[5]. In 1598 the first patent of the African Company was renewed, and by the end of the reign of James I. the English trade to Africa may be considered as fairly established.

That which dwarfed the question of Africa was the problem of the trade to the Indies. In 1581 the Charter of the Levant Company authorised that body to trade overland with the East Indies; but Drake had already rounded the Cape of Good Hope. The overland route was no longer the only one possible to Englishmen. Their zeal was further stimulated by the war with Spain, which cut them off from the great emporium of spices, especially as the staple for the Indian trade was removed from Lisbon to Cadiz. In 1586 English ships sailed for spices to the Moluccas, guided by a Portuguese Protestant[6]; and the enormous value of the Portuguese spice ships,

[1] *Sim. Trans. Cal.*, 1580, No. 7.
[2] *Dom. St. P. Cal.*, 88, 54, Nos. 85 and 46.
[3] *Sim. Trans. Cal.*, 1588, No. 357.
[4] *Dom. St. P. MSS.*, 1595, CCLIII. No. 56.
[5] Malynes, *Lex Mercatoria*, 114.
[6] *Sim. Trans. Cal.*, April 1586, No. 248.

which the English now captured with a clear conscience, stimulated the wish of establishing a regular trade with the East Indies—a trade which, according to the custom of the time, should be conducted and governed by an exclusive Company. In 1589 the English merchants memorialised the government, enumerating the Portuguese settlements in India, and pointing out that there was ample room for the intervention of another European nation. The agitation continued throughout the ensuing ten years. Captains were commissioned to make discoveries in the Far East; spice ships were captured; trading ventures increased; till at last in 1600 the East India Company was finally established. Roe was sent out by Elizabeth to the Court of the Mogul, where his negotiations proved successful, despite the bitter opposition of the Portuguese and Spanish Jesuits established there[1]. The peace negotiations with Spain produced a momentary suspension of the enterprise. But before they came to any conclusion the first voyage of the East India Company had been made. Its success was so great that in 1604 the spice trade of Lisbon was declared to be entirely destroyed by the English and Dutch East Indian trade: hence the deduction was made that peace, to be serviceable, must include the concession by Spain of free commerce with the Indies[2].

Spain, however, declined to yield to these demands, and the pacific dispositions of the new English sovereign (James I.) prevented them from being pressed. Hence, the final treaty with Spain in 1604 shows a curious resemblance to that with Portugal in 1576. In 1576 the vital question between the two nations had been that of colonial trade; though of less relative importance in 1604, it was exceedingly prominent, and both the earlier and later treaties are

[1] For early history of the East India Company see J. Bruce's *Annals of the East India Company*.

[2] Letter to Sir Robert Cecil, *Cal. Col. St. P.*, 1604, 141, No. 335.

silent on the subject. There is no word of African trade in the treaty of 1576; no word of Indian commerce in that of 1604. Practically, the two nations engaged to keep the peace in Europe; but their quarrels in the Far East remained to be fought out.

From this time onward, therefore, the story of the Anglo-Portuguese conflict in the Indies has but little direct connection with the English commercial relations with Portugal. Gradually the Portuguese power in India waned, while that of England waxed. Before long, despite all the opposition offered by the Viceroy of Goa, Surat proved itself no unsuccessful rival to the old Portuguese centre. The trade of Ormuz was ruined by the combined attacks of English and Persians. The hostility lasted till in 1635-66 the success of the Dutch drove England and Portugal to make common cause against them. But only the sound and rumour of this strife, fierce, vital, unceasing as it was, reached England. Occasionally, a batch of English prisoners would be sent from the East Indies to Lisbon[1]; and the exertions of the English consul at that town, and of the English ambassador at Madrid, to obtain their freedom, would bring the whole question of colonial rights again under discussion. News from the East, arriving at Portugal, was eagerly hailed by the English there, and carefully reported to the Home Government; but the incidents of the struggle had little effect on either the political or the commercial connection of England and Portugal between 1605 and 1640, profoundly though its results modified their subsequent relations. How disconnected were, apparently, their European and Eastern interests is shown by the fact that the peace of 1604, impotent and negligible in India, yet proved a sufficiently practical thing at home. With all its defects, the treaty, at least, made overt trade between England

[1] *E.g.* cases mentioned in 1606, Winwood, II. 221.

and Spain and Portugal practicable after a lapse of twenty years, with the immediate result of the revival of the "Company of Spain and Portugal."

This Company, to which allusion was made in the last chapter, claimed to have derived its first charter from Henry VIII. in 1530. This charter, however, concerned only merchants trading to Spain and Andalusia[1]; not till Elizabeth's reign were merchants trading to Portugal definitely included. The question then raised of the incorporation, or re-incorporation of merchants trading to Spain and Portugal was agitated for some time before the charter was obtained. The opposition seems to have been considerable. In 1574, a petition against the proposed incorporation was presented by Alderman Thomas Pullison, and about seventeen others. Their chief objection was to the article excluding from the proposed Company all who were not traders in 1568, "thereby inhibiting some of the Queen's subjects without cause from their lawful liberty, which never yet was seen or known[2]." Apparently among the merchants thus restrained, there were many who shipped cloth to Flanders, Hamburg, and other Eastland towns, and buying German commodities therewith, shipped the same back to England, and thence in English ships, with English crews to Portugal, where they exchanged these foreign commodities for oil, bullion, and "Iorne." It was suggested that this carrying trade would be usurped by the Flemings, Spaniards, or French, if the English merchants were in any way restrained. In one copy of the petition, there is a notable hint of the rising protest against monopolies in the declaration that such restraint would injure commerce by concentrating trade in few men's hands, "which breedeth enhauncement and dearth of commodities."

[1] *Harl. MSS.*, XXXVI. 19.
[2] *Dom. St. P. MSS.*, XCIX. No. 9; *Cott. MSS.*, Nero, B. I. No. 220.

The view, however, that trade must be governed and restrained in the interests both of the traders and the community, was too prevalent for these protests to avail, and, on 5th June 1577, the suggested charter was granted[1]. By this patent, Leicester, Crofts, Walsingham, Cobham, Sir Thomas Gresham, Sir William Winter, Edward Osborne, Thomas Pullyson, and other merchants of London, a large number of traders from provincial towns such as Bristol, Exeter, Southampton, and Kingston-on-Hull, about thirty English merchants resident in Spain and Portugal, and other persons who had traded to Spain and Portugal before 1568, were formed into a corporation with a common seal and the title of the President and assistants of the Company of Spain and Portugal. The Company was to have exclusive privileges of trade; many evils having arisen, it is stated, from ignorant persons engaging in the trade. No craftsman or retail trader was to be admitted. Persons who had begun to trade in 1568 might be admitted to the Company if they applied during the first year on payment of £5; on payment of £10 if they applied subsequently. The constitution of the Company was somewhat involved. It was ruled by a President, John Mershe, and forty assistants or "consiliarii," who were named in the charter[2]. The President and assistants were to make regulations for the benefit of trade, were to levy fines and impositions, and inflict penalties, and appoint the officers necessary for carrying out their regulations. They might appoint Presidents of the English in Spain and Portugal, who in their turn might appoint deputies to govern the English traders in these countries and their dependencies; and these subordinate Presidents could choose for themselves six consiliarii from among the better and more discreet

[1] *El.* 19, *Pat. Rolls*, Part 8, 45. See Appendix II. 2.
[2] For further details see Appendix II. 2.

merchants. In the hands of the President and his assistants lay the power of admitting or expelling members. Traders violating the privileges of the Company, or disobeying its commands, would be punished by the arrest of their persons or goods.

The rights of provincial towns seem to be somewhat scantily recognised. Of the forty assistants named in the Charter, three were of Bristol, one of Exeter, two of Southampton, one of Ipswich, and two of Kingston-on-Hull; and the predominance of London appears even in the regulation that one-quarter of the consiliarii are to be provincials. Whether the safeguards mentioned above sufficed for the provincial towns does not appear, but if the accounts for 1582-84 are in any way typical, the chief volume of trade appears to have been concentrated in London. The value of the trade done by the capital seems, cloth apart, to have been more than double that of Bristol and Southampton together; and London seems also to have trafficked with many more different places in Portugal, such as Faro, Vianna, Aveiro, than the two provincial cities.[1]

The friction between London and the provincial cities appears in the dispute with Chester which took place a year or so later, and which was further complicated by the question of the right of the retail traders to act as merchants. In Chester a feud, such as was not uncommon at this date, existed between the "mere merchants" and the retailers. The "mere merchants" in certain petitions of 1578-79 alleged that they had received a Charter from Mary for exclusive trade with Spain and Portugal. Hereupon they had requested the Portuguese officers to admit no English wares except from these merchants; and not being able to secure this modest demand they found themselves driven to join the new Spanish Company. On the other hand, the retailers and small traders of Chester, claimed that the Charter

[1] *Lansd. MSS.*, No. 41 *et seq.*

in question had been granted to the whole town, and conveyed a right to the citizens of trading when and where they liked. Hence no patent to the Spanish Company could affect them; a claim, of course, in direct contravention of the clause which forbade any retailer or artisan to deal with Spain or Portugal. The dispute was brought to an issue by a question about the export of 12,000 dickers of calf skins. The citizens claimed that the licence for their exportation should have been granted to the whole town in aid of the restoration of their harbour, and that a few "mere merchants" who had joined themselves to the Spanish Company had unjustly diverted the grant of the licences to themselves.[1]

The Chief Justice and the Master of the Rolls decided on appeal against the Spanish Company that the Charter of Mary to Chester applied to the whole city, and that no subsequent incorporation could prevent the men of Chester from trading when and where they would. The retailers and a committee of merchants, to whom the case was referred, further suggested that the "mere merchants" of Chester should be allowed to deal as retailers, and the retailers as "mere merchants"; thus giving up as impracticable, in this instance, the attempt to draw a hard and fast line between the two classes of traders. The merchants, however, were by no means satisfied with these awards, and the matter was still in dispute in 1589[2].

Despite this apparent defeat, the Company appear to have exercised their powers with vigour, and to have been a body of recognised importance. The commerce already alluded to, which the merchants trading with Spain and Portugal carried on between those countries and Flanders and Germany, may have

[1] *Dom. St. P. MSS.*, CXXIX. Nos 52, 53.
[2] *Dom. St. P. Cal.*, 1589, CCXXIII. 592, No. 53; and CCXXIV. Nos. 4 and 18.

affected the relations of the Spanish Company with the newly incorporated Eastland Company; since in the Charter of the latter, in 1579, the Spanish Company, together with the Merchant Adventurers, are singled out for admittance to the Eastland Company on special terms[1]. In 1579 there was an order for the arrest of all those who refused to obey the rules of the Company[2]; and in 1586 the Company made an Act restraining any merchant from importing any article in exchange for corn except salt, bullion or oranges[3].

The annexation of Portugal by Spain was, however, a heavy blow to English trade with both countries. The virulence of the Inquisition in Spain had caused a tendency toward concentrating English trade at Lisbon, and most English cloth sold in Spain passed through Portugal[4]. Moreover, Spain and Portugal were now England's chief markets, the troubles having greatly depressed trade both with the Low Countries and France[5]. Even after war broke out, commerce with Spain and Portugal occupied an important place in the thoughts of the English ministry. In 1587 a list of suggestions was submitted to Cecil for the better securing of English trade with Portugal[6]; and, in the same year, a pamphlet entitled, "A Note of the Commodities of all the Ports where Merchants trade[7]," dwells on the importance of the exports from the coast round Lisbon. In 1598, Cecil pointed to the reopening of trade with Spain, Portugal, Barbary, the Levant and the Eastland towns as the principal reason for peace[8],

[1] Camden Society, publications, Series III. Vol. X., "Acts and Ordinances of the Eastland Company." Ed. M. Sellers. Introd. xvi.
[2] *Dom. St. P. Cal.*, 626, No. 24.
[3] *Dom. St. P. MSS.*, CXLI. No. 45.
[4] Rebello da Silva, *Historia de Portugal*, IV. 600.
[5] *Sim. Trans. Cal.*, 1586, No. 505.
[6] *Lansd. MSS.*, 53, No. 33.
[7] *Dom. St. P. MSS.*, CCI. No. 14.
[8] *Dom. St. P. Cal.*, 2, No. 3.

and in 1601 a striking proof of the English attitude appeared in the admission by England of Spanish wares, though Spain still confiscated those of English merchants[1].

It is not, however, to be supposed that even after 1589 there was no commercial intercourse between England and Portugal. In 1590 Burleigh was considering the constitution of a proposed trading fleet to Spain and Portugal, to consist of not more than forty vessels, the largest not to exceed 300 tons burden, and none to carry munitions or victuals but for their own use[2]. The very complaint put forward by a Bristol man in 1591 that, though a member of the Spanish Company, he could not trade with Spain and Portugal owing to the troubles[3], shows that the war was looked upon as no impassable barrier. Especially does this appear to be the case with Portugal. For some little time there was an attempt on the part of the English to distinguish between Spain and Portugal, and to exempt the latter country from the treatment usually meted to an enemy. Portuguese goods seized by the English were, on some occasions, restored. Two Portuguese merchants, Peter Freire and Bernardo Luis, were specially exempted from the edict, forbidding Portuguese trade with England (1586), on the score of the help and protection they had given to English merchants at the outbreak of the war[4].

Even after the expulsion of the English merchants from Lisbon in 1589, and the imprisonment of the Consul Taylor and others on the charge of conspiracy, a large amount of intercourse, more or less clandestine, seems to have been kept up with Portugal. The frequency with which the export of cloths to Lisbon, or the import of salt and vinegar

[1] *Dom. St. P. Cal.*, 38, No. 57.
[2] *Dom. St. P. MSS.*, CCXXXV. No. 10.
[3] *Dom. St. P. Cal.*, 58, No. 42.
[4] Ibid. 326.

from that city, or from Aveira and Setubal, or any of the coast towns, was made a cloak for espionage, seems to point to such secret traffic being of fairly common occurrence.

The Portuguese in England assisted in this trade. A ship loaded with black baize sailed for Portugal in 1588 on behalf of Dr Nunez, and returned laden with wine[1]. In the same year ships, purporting to belong to Portuguese Protestants in England, but which were really English property, sailed for Lisbon with cloth, and brought back cochineal, spices, raisins, and wine[2]. In 1589 a cargo of sugar and pepper, loaded at Lisbon for England, was insured for 6,000 crowns[3]. During the ensuing ten years there were many complaints as to the decadence of trade, though it appears to have been fairly active. Disguised as Irishmen, the English carried on their trade with Lisbon and Aveiro, under penalty of imprisonment and torture if discovered[4]. The trade must also have been on a fairly large scale. In 1599 complaints were made of an Englishman who was said to have betrayed various ships trading to Cadiz and Lisbon, and various merchants in Portugal, who traded with the English, whereby many merchants were ruined[5].

As soon as the peace came, all this secret and repressed trade naturally sprang into open and vigorous life. In the petition of the maintenance of the Spanish Company in 1606, the petitioners declare, that since the peace, all sorts of unskilful people have entered into traffic with Spain and Portugal; and by glutting the market have lowered English, and enhanced Spanish, prices till there had been a loss of about £40,000 a year. Apart from the alleged loss there were other disadvantages, connected, or thought to be connected, with the number of small

[1] *Sim. Trans. Cal.*, No. 255. [2] Ibid. No. 229.
[3] Malynes, *Lex Mercatoria*, 114.
[4] *Dom. St. P. Cal.*, 1597, 43.
[5] Ibid. 1599, 243.

capitalists who now entered the field. The difference between the laws and religion of Spain and England made the grant of privileges to merchants trading thither of peculiar importance; and the "mere merchants" pleaded that it was impossible to ensure fair treatment for the English at the hands of the Spanish government, so long as English trade was represented by a crowd of obscure, scattered, and irresponsible individuals[1].

In fact, many of the Spanish exactions appeared sufficiently burdensome, while, on the other hand, the growing weakness of Spain provoked the English merchants to exorbitant demands. In "a note of such matters as the English marchauntes trading Spain and Portugale doe most humbly offer . . . to be considered of in the Treaty of Amity between our Kinges most excellent Majestie and the King of Spain," numerous requests appear. Not only is the confirmation of all privileges demanded, but also freedom of trade to any part of the Spanish dominions, thereby solving the whole disputed colonial question in favour of England. Disputes between foreigners and English were to be remitted to England for settlement; no dues or customs were to be levied on exports or imports from or to Spain, save such as existed before 1589. Englishmen trading in English ships were to be allowed to take the same ships back without interference from Spanish officials. In addition to these, were various demands for the benefit of Englishmen residing in Spain[2]. Naturally all these requests were not acceded to, though some were obtained.

By this treaty of 1604, free trade between the two countries was re-established as it had been before the war. No greater imposts were to be levied on goods imported or exported than in 1589. The new

[1] "Reasons to Mayntayne the Spanish Company." *Dom. St. P. MSS.* XXI. No. 2.

[2] *Cott. MSS. Vesp. C.*, XIII. No. 95.

30 per cent. tax in Spain was not to be levied on any goods exported by the English to English or Spanish territories. Generally speaking, English and Spanish subjects were to be on an equality, in the dominions of both princes, and all old rights and privileges were to be secured[1]. These concessions might have proved satisfactory if adequately carried out, but on this point there was doubt; and this doubt, joined with the revival of trade, gave force to the Spanish Company's demands for a confirmation of its old Charter, which was readily obtained. The confirmation, however, proved insufficient to insure to the Company its former powers. The host of irregular traders who had come into existence under the cover of the war, and the stimulus of the peace, not merely protested against the Company's exclusive powers, but disregarded them on the ingenious plea that they had become void through want of use[2].

The "mere merchants" thereon petitioned for a reconstitution of the Charter, and the matter being referred to Coke and some others, the old Charter was examined, certain technical flaws discovered in it, and a new Charter was granted 31st May 1605[3]. As far as the Company's powers went they were almost precisely similar to those of 1577; the right to exclusive trade; the right to regulate trade; to provide for the government of Englishmen in Spain and Portugal, to levy fines and impositions, and to inflict punishments—all these powers were as full and ample as ever. In the constitution of the Company, however, there were some marked differences. There were to be 61, not 40, assistants, of whom 30 are to be Londoners, thus securing almost as great a predominance as before to the capital; this supremacy, moreover, seems disproportionate,

[1] Rymer, XVI. 585 *et seq.*
[2] *Cott. MSS. Vesp. C.*, XIX. 30.
[3] *Dom. St. P. MSS.*, XIV. No. 21.

since of the 577 merchants named in the Charter, only 237 were of London. On the other hand, many more representatives of provincial towns are named in the new Charter than in the old one; merchants of Bristol, Exeter, Bridgewater, Yarmouth, Chester, Plymouth, Hull, Tiverton, Taunton, Chard, Totness, Lyme, Barnstaple, and Southampton, are all named among those to whom the Charter is granted; and the general constitution was made more democratic than formerly, inasmuch as the assistants, like the President, are to be elected yearly.

All who were free of the old Company, with their children, and all apprentices were to be admitted to the new Company; and all "mere merchants" not belonging to another company might be admitted on paying £10 if they made application during the first year of the Company's existence; on paying £15 if the application occurred during the second year; or £20 if it was deferred till still later. Merchants belonging to other companies might be admitted on making certain payments; but all retailers and craftsmen were to be excluded as rigidly as ever.

It was apparently on this rock that the Company split. The protest which the retailers of Chester had voiced twenty-five years before, was now taken up all over England—especially in the West Country.

Between the western ports and London, there seems at this time to have been considerable jealousy, which may possibly have been heightened by the nature of the trade with Spain and Portugal.

First among the English exports was, of course, cloth, and in the above-mentioned accounts for 1584, London was almost alone exporting it; yet its importance was so great that a little calculation shows that its worth probably balanced the whole import of spices to all three ports, London, Bristol, and Southampton[1]. But, in addition to this, a large and particularly

[1] *Lansd. MSS.*, No. 41.

contraband trade in provisions had existed during the closing years of the sixteenth century. A dearth of corn at Lisbon had been of frequent occurrence, and the English traders had made no scruple of supplying this want[1]. As early as 1580 the exporters of wheat had been a thorn in the side of the Spanish Company. In the ordinance already quoted of that year, the Company declare that many ships not belonging to the Company had repaired "very disorderly" to Spain and Portugal, carrying corn and fish, and bringing back what they chose, thus lowering the price of English, and increasing that of Spanish, goods[2]. In the general disorganisation following on the war this ordinance was probably disregarded. The indignant maintainers of the supremacy of the Company declared that the trade in wheat was injurious to England's marine, affirming that corn was often transported in boats of under 30 tons' burden[3]. Clearly the provision trade was especially suited to the small capitalist, and hence the revolt against the Company was not only a revolt of the western ports against London, but a revolt of the lesser trader, possibly the retail trader against the greater.

The Company, for its part, made a vigorous defence which throws a good deal of light on the state of trade at the time. They exalted the benefit of the cloth trade as furnishing employment for the people of England, while deprecating the traffic in victuals (already shown to be the trade of the small people). They declared that since the peace the English had sent over so much corn that the Spaniards asked if

[1] In 1587 nine Bristol merchants were accused of sending provisions to Spain, *Dom. St. Add. Cal.*, 232, No. 62, and "wheat all the winter" together with butter and other food, is mentioned as a suitable export to Lisbon in 1595. "A special direction for divers trades of merchandise to be used for soundrie places upon advertisement." *Dom. St. P. MSS.*, CCLV. No. 56.

[2] *Dom. St. P. MSS.*, CXLI. No. 45.

[3] *Cott. MSS. Vesp. C.*, XIII. 137.

they brought hogs to eat it; that the Newfoundland fishermen sold fish cheaper by one-half than the merchants would have sold them; "if the fishermen persist in trading themselves, at least they make their homeward lading with money, salt, or oranges, and not in frivolous commodities;" that the dissolution of the Company would damage the king's customs, for the German, Eastland, and Muscovy merchants who traded with Spain and Portugal through the Company would then take their goods direct to the Peninsula, instead of bringing them first to England; that the traders to Spain and Portugal so multiplied that there were now two hundred of them, though one-tenth the number could manage the trade; that these unskilful traders looked to make up the losses resulting from their want of experience by importing the frivolous and perishable commodities of Spain and Portugal, such as "sak, bastard, figges," and that for these a wise merchant could make a much better bargain than was now made by the inexperienced traders, who ought to have arranged that the recent returns should have been made in bullion. Corn, it was declared, should not be allowed to be exported in any ship of less than 100 tons' burden[1].

In short, the whole argument was urged in favour of the great capitalist at the expense of the small one; and it was backed up by the assertion that an organised and responsible body, like the Company of which the Charter had already been recognised in Spain, would be far better able to maintain a consul in that country, and assert the rights and privileges of English merchants in the Peninsula, than a host of disconnected traders would do.

The outcry against the Company was, however, too strong; the long war had effectually broken its power. In 1606, an Act was passed by which

[1] *Cott. MSS. Vesp. C.*, 13, pp. 135 *et seq.*; and *Dom. St. P. MSS.*, 1606, XXI. No. 2.

all subjects of the English crown were left free to trade to Spain and Portugal. At first it seemed doubtful whether the Company was actually dissolved by this Act; but, at any rate, it was a fatal blow.

The protests were numerous and partially justified. The difficulty of securing the privileges guaranteed to the English in Spain, by the Treaty of 1604, had already been experienced; and it was declared that these would be enhanced by the disappearance of a strong and responsible body like the Company[1].

The English ambassadors at Madrid, too, complained that the Spanish government was far from keeping exactly to the Treaty of 1604; especially with regard to the 30 per cent. tax on exports which seems to have been levied on the English, despite all promises[2]. The English envoys conceived that their efforts towards the removal of these grievances would have been of much more effect had there been a company to back them[3].

Several movements occurred for the re-establishment of the Company, originating generally either in the ill-treatment of the English merchants resident in Spain and Portugal, or in the decadence of trade; though the numerous complaints of irregular traders renders it doubtful how far the general depression, which culminated in 1620-22, seriously affected Anglo-Portuguese commerce. There were, however, certain special causes which may have injured it. The increasing power of the Barbary corsairs, whose fleets were far better organised than those of the English merchants, must have seriously affected all South European commerce; and the backwardness of the merchants trading to Spain and Portugal to

[1] *Dom. St. P. MSS.*, XXI. No. 2.

[2] *Cott. MSS. Vesp. C.*, 13, p. 141.

[3] Digby at Madrid declared that though he had brought the merchants' affairs to an issue, yet the merchants fell into many troubles for want of an established company, and "extraordinarily hurt their trade." (1612 (?) *Dom. St. P. MSS.*, LXXII. No. 147.)

contribute to the fund for the suppression of the pirates may be an indirect evidence of the damage they had sustained[1].

A hindrance peculiar to the English trade with the Peninsula appeared in the war between Spain and the Low Countries, and its influence is shown in the Anglo-Spanish treaties of 1604 and 1630. Numerous precautions were taken in these treaties to prevent the English in any way becoming intermediaries between the Dutch and their enemies. No Spanish goods were to be exported to Holland, unless the 30 per cent. tax was paid. No ships built in the Low Countries were to be used by the English in their trade with Spain. All English goods were to be sealed and registered with the name of the place whence they came, in order that Dutch goods might not be introduced under the disguise of English.

These regulations seem to have been specially injurious to the English trade in Eastland and German commodities, such as linen, wax, hemp, cordage, Hamburg cloth, canvas, lock-rams, and so forth. The annoyance was the greater, as these goods, according to a memorial in 1604, formed the staple of the English commerce with Spain and Portugal. English produce, apart from corn and fish, was said not to suffice to furnish forth twenty ships a year[2]. In view of other lists of exports to Spain and Portugal, this statement is probably exaggerated; but the various treaty stipulations, and the excuse they gave the Spanish officials for surveillance and interference, seems to have been very embarrassing[3].

Neither pirates nor custom-house officers, however, were so harmful in the opinion of the merchants trading to Spain and Portugal, as was the lack of

[1] *Dom. St. P. Cal.*, 1621, 558. (Vol. at end of James I.'s reign.)
[2] *Dom. St. P. MSS.*, 1604, XI. No. 17.
[3] See *Cott. MSS.*, *Vesp. C.*, 13, p. 141.

regular "government." Their replies to the enquiries, made by the Privy Council in 1617, all tend towards this point, as do most of their other complaints.

They were oppressed, they declared, by the rivalry of the clothiers of Devonshire and the north, who sent their goods abroad direct; and, having two trades, while the unhappy "mere merchants" had only one, could undersell the latter and ruin them. The same complaint was also brought against the linen-drapers. The tobacco-dealers also were complained of. Tobacco, the merchants explained, was a drug, and should, therefore, be bought with inferior goods, but the English tobacco-dealers frequently took over the bays and perpetuanos—the "best and most vendible" commodities—which they sold cheap, to the ruin of the "mere merchants," in order to get the ready money wherewith to purchase the tobacco. This inconsiderate eagerness raised the price from 2 or 3 ryals to 16, 18, or 20 ryals the lb.[1]; whilst, according to another account, English goods had in a few years fallen 20 per cent. in the Spanish market.

The same system was pursued by the grocers, vintners, salters, sugar bakers, and dyers, who were the natural customers for the wine, fruit, oils, sugars, indigo, and cochineal, which were the chief returns from Spain[2].

In addition to all this, the shopkeepers, retailers, and others now sent over as factors, were incompetent, and injured the business; and, finally, all this individual dealing naturally involved sending single and solitary ships to the Peninsula, which were in far more danger from the pirates than a fleet sent by a company would be. The natural remedy for all these grievances was a charter to the "mere merchants," by which the clothiers and retailers

[1] *Lansd. MSS.*, No. 152. "The Humble remonstrance and informacion of the Merchants trading with Spayn and Portugall."

[2] *Lansd. MSS.*, No. 152.

would be excluded from the direct trade which so enhanced the price of Spanish commodities[1].

Apparently, however, the petition was not granted, and though the "Spanish Company" is again and again alluded to in the Domestic State Papers from 1606 onwards, yet the phrase may be used to mean only the general body of merchants trading to Spain and Portugal, without attributing to them any special organisation; and the next serious attempt at reviving the Company did not take place till 1630.

Possibly the fresh adjustment of relations, incidental to the peace negotiations at that period, may have induced the merchants to make another attempt; and their success seemed so likely that the appointment of a consul in Lisbon after the peace was suspended till the question should be settled[2]. The West Country, however, roused itself vehemently against the proposal. Dartmouth protested that such an Act would ruin thousands[3]. Cornwall stood up in defence of its old right to export cloths free of duty[4].

The controversy continued intermittently for the ensuing ten years. In 1633 the balance of opinion was swaying so decidedly in favour of the merchants that the Council ordered that all ships trading as "interlopers" should be stayed, pending the final decision[5]. In 1635 a fresh petition was presented, pointing out the grievances they suffered at the hands of the vintners, who combined to beat down the price of the wine imported by the Spanish merchants, and again complaining of the intrusion of shopkeepers and other unskilful persons[6]. These reiterated demands so far wrought on the Council, that they referred the consideration of the matter

[1] *Lansd. MSS.*, No. 152.
[2] Chandler's *Petition*, *For. St. P. Portugal*, Bundle 4.
[3] *Dom. St. P. Cal.*, 1631, CXCVIII. No 59.
[4] Ibid. pp. 159, 176, 201.
[5] *Dom. St. P. MSS.*, CCXLV. No. 8.
[6] Ibid. CCCIII. No. 14.

to the Attorney - General, who recommended the granting of a charter to the merchants, incorporating them into a Company, but not granting them privileges of exclusive trade[1]. Even this limited order aroused great opposition. Exeter, Plymouth, Dartmouth, Totnes, Barnstaple, Southampton, Poole, Weymouth, Lyme, all protested[2]; and the suggestion does not seem to have been carried into effect, to judge by a fresh petition of the merchants praying for its execution in 1637[3]. The matter still remained undecided, till the separation of Spain from Portugal in 1640 necessitated a fresh adjustment of commercial relations between the smaller county and England.

All these complaints, however, do not give the idea that trade was really in a hopeless condition. The retailers, craftsmen, and others would hardly have entered so vigorously into the traffic, had it been unprofitable. The zeal of the traders was such that when, in 1624, the merchants were advised not to trade to Spain, in view of the probable war, twenty of them did set sail, in defiance of all danger[4]. On the whole, it seems probable that trade was so far depressed as no longer to afford a profit to the middleman as well as to the producer in either country. Thereon the producer endeavoured to dispense with the middleman's services, and hence the whole trouble arose.

Conspicuous among various branches of commerce, said to be ill affected by the general depression, was the cloth trade. In this case, too, lack of good order and government were alleged as the cause of its decay, at least, as far as Spain and Portugal were concerned[5]. But in 1607 an Englishman at Viana, while lamenting that where 1,000 cloths had formerly

[1] *Dom. St. P. Cal.*, 2nd June 1636, 529, No. 28.
[2] *Dom. St. P. Add. Cal.*, 1636, 534, No. 52.
[3] *Dom. St. P. Cal.*, 103.
[4] Ibid. 170, No. 2.
[5] Paper by Misselden, *Dom. St. P. MSS.*, XX. No. 4.

been sold in Galicia and Bayonne, now only 200 could be disposed of, and those on credit, yet attributed this decay, not to the lack of governance, but to the fact that the long war had stimulated the manufacture of cloth in Spain itself[1]. Foreign cloth manufacture appears to have continued to increase, and in 1620 and subsequently the export of materials for cloth was forbidden, without apparently very much effect as regarded the depression in the English manufacture. The decay in the trade appears to have affected both the quality and the price[2]. According to Misselden, cloths which in 1606 were sold for 25 ducats the piece, now fetched only 13, 12, or 11 ducats. Despite this, however, cloth of various kinds continued to be the chief export from England to Spain and Portugal. Scotch cloth was said in 1598 to be the common wear of the poorer Portuguese[3]. On the whole, dyed and wrought cloths were said to find a most favourable market there, and also West Country cloths, and such special manufactures as Devonshire cloths, kerseys, perpetuanos, and bays[4].

The Colchester bays, indeed, were of such importance that in 1635 the merchants trading to Spain and Portugal alleged that the chief part of their trade consisted in the transport of these cloths, and entered into a fierce controversy with the town of Colchester with regard to various alleged defects in the making of these important goods[5]. A rival to

[1] *For. St. P. MSS. Portugal*, Bundle 3, 24th December 1607. John Donnington to Mr Thomas Wilson.

[2] Rebello da Silva, *Historia de Portugal*, III. 200.

[3] *Dom. St. P. Add. Cal.*, 401-2, No. 23.

[4] Dressed and dyed cloths occur first in the list of the Spanish Company's exports in 1605 (*Dom. St. P. MSS.*, VIII. No. 35), Devonshire cloths, kerseys, bays, and perpetuanos arementioned in the petition of 1617. An undated list of exports to the Peninsula begins with Western cloths, bays, Devonshire Dozens, etc., and in a merchant's "waste book" for 1633, 100 double says, 896 Colchester bays are stated to be shipped to Lisbon. *Dom. St. P. MSS.*, CCLXXII. No. 30.

[5] *Dom. St. P. Cal.*, 306, No. 89.

the bays might, however, be found in the newly devised Spanish cloth, which was chiefly manufactured in the West Country, and the importance of which appears in the endeavour of the London merchants in 1638 to get its whole transport into their hands, to the intense indignation of the western clothiers[1]. If the cloth trade diminished, other exports rose in importance, such as that of fish from Newfoundland to Spain. This appears to have been so valuable that, in 1625, the government were recommended still to permit it, lest Spain should retaliate by forbidding the transport of wool to England[2].

These changes seem to be the only noticeable alterations in the export trade to Spain and Portugal from 1580 to 1640, which, as before, was mainly confined to the export of necessaries: cloth, linen, provisions, lead, tin, hardware, haberdashery, forming the staples of trade on the English side.

In the imports to England from Spain and Portugal, there was, however, considerable modification. In 1584-85 these, as far as Portugal was concerned, had consisted mainly in spices and other East Indian produce, salt, green woad (especially from the Azores), fruit and sugar (largely from Barbary and the Azores), and Brazil wood; and of these spices and the East India produce form by far the largest part[3].

During the next twenty years there seems to have been little change, to judge by the list of imports by the Spanish Company in 1605[4]. But during the

[1] *Dom. St. P. Cal.*, 1638, 185 and 218.

[2] Ibid. 474, No. 49.

[3] *Lansd. MSS.*, No. 41 *et seq.*

[4] *Dom. St. P. MSS.*, VIII. No. 36. These include "felte, woole, oil, sawlte, figges," Spanish soap, sumach, silk manufactures, almonds, aniseed, sugars, olives, oranges, green woad, spices, drugs, dyes, etc. The exports of Spain and Portugal are not distinguished; but it may fairly be inferred that commodities previously mentioned as the products of Portugal and its dependencies continued to be brought from those countries.

next forty years there was a considerable alteration. The tendency of English industry and commerce at this time seems to have been to enable England to do without the commodities supplied by the Peninsula; a fact which may partly account for the economic perplexities of the time.

By the end of the reign of James I., a change was already appearing; the list of goods imported by the merchants trading to Spain and Portugal includes only sack and bastard, raisins, figs, oil, sumach, iron, wool, almonds, and cork[1]. This list, however, is probably incomplete. At any rate, it would have become so in a few years, as it omits two articles which certainly formed a great part of English trade with Spain and Portugal—sugar and tobacco.

The most marked omission, however — that of spices—probably represents something like the fact. The English and Dutch East India Companies were rapidly crushing the Portuguese. By 1640 Charles I. was able to obtain £120,000 worth of spices from the English East India Company[2], and the days of English dependence on Portugal for Eastern luxuries were at an end.

With regard to another great Portuguese export, which does not appear in the above list, to wit, salt, its omission may have been due to accident or some special cause. Certainly, salt was still imported from Spain and Portugal. The English salt industry, which had developed considerably during Elizabeth's reign, had now reached the point at which it began to demand protection; hence, through the reigns of James I. and Charles I., there was a perpetual contest between the fishing towns, like Yarmouth, which desired to import foreign salt, and the great English salt works at North Shields.

Thus two of what had been staple commodities of Portugal in its commerce with England, were

[1] *Dom. St. P. MSS.*, CLXXXIX. No. 34.
[2] *Dom. St. P. Cal.*, 1640, 654, No. 64.

much diminished in importance. Of the others, fruit, wine, and oil, appear to be the most constant; but here, too, trade was temporarily hindered by the duty levied on the export of wine and oil from Portugal in 1605, which Salisbury said indignantly, would destroy all the benefit the English looked for from the peace. Oil, however, continued to be a staple of the trade; and a futile effort was made to encourage its further import from Spain and Portugal in 1618, by forbidding the use of any but olive oil[1]. Wine seems to have increased in importance in the list of imports, though what came from Spain, and what from Portugal, it is difficult to distinguish.

The two articles, however, which to some extent seem to have taken the place occupied by spices, were sugar and tobacco. The tobacco, usually called Spanish tobacco, seems to have come in part from Brazil; and its chief rival was the tobacco from Virginia. At first the Spanish tobacco was the most important of the two; in 1619 that imported from Spain seems to have been nearly three times as much as that from Virginia[2]. In 1622, £60,000 worth were said to be imported annually from Spain, and a suggestion was made for the prohibition of this trade in the interests of the English colonies[3]. In 1623 it was said to have replaced silver in the Spanish trade[4]; but its prohibition was re-urged in 1626, and, finally, in 1627 the import of all but Virginian tobacco was forbidden, saving only a supply of 50,000 lb. for the king's household[5].

The prohibition, however, was not altogether effective, for in 1631 complaints were made that a

[1] Latimer, *Bristol*, 67.

[2] Customs Account $\frac{91}{10}$.

[3] *Dom. St. P. Cal.*, 1622, 447.

[4] Ibid. 1623, 254, No. 24.

[5] Ibid. 1627, 289, No. 61.

large amount of Spanish and Brazil tobacco was smuggled into the country[1]. Licences, too, were as usual granted to special persons to import the forbidden articles to such an extent, that, in 1636, the Spanish merchants offered £12,000 a year for their farm[2], which contrasts curiously with the fact that, in 1638, tobacco was imported from England to Spain. Obviously the colonial rivalry must have greatly embarrassed the Spanish trade, and the prohibition of 1627 seems to have left sugar and fruit as almost the only Spanish and Portuguese exports of importance, which were comparatively unhampered by legal restrictions.

The sugar trade had long been important; in 1584 over 1,000 sugar chests had been brought from Barbary[3]; in 1595 the value of sugar brought into London far exceeded that of the spices.[4] This, however, must have included the sugars from Barbary, which were an important item in the trade there; and the direct trade of England with Barbary had been so far established that Barbary sugars may now be considered as rather a rival to Portuguese produce, than part of it. Apart from Barbary, however, the Portuguese and Spanish sugars were obtained from St Thomé, from the Azores, from Madeira, and from Brazil. On the whole, the trade was looked on favourably by the English authorities; it did not as yet interfere with their own colonial produce, and as the sugar was imported from Portugal raw, the interest of the London sugar bakers weighed in its favour. In 1598, in a paper on the question of the import of refined sugar, it was declared unnecessary to interfere with the sugar import from Spain, Portugal, Barbary, the Islands, Madeira, and Brazil, as none of these

[1] *Dom. St. P. Cal.*, 1631, 475, No. 11.
[2] Ibid. 1636, 551, No. 7.
[3] Ibid. 1638, 436, No. 84.
[4] *Lansd. MSS.*, 81, No. 46.

countries made refined sugars[1]. The sugar duties were among those reduced in 1609-10[2], and on the whole the trade continued peacefully and prosperously.

In the various controversies between the merchants and the retailers, sugar is again and again mentioned as an important import. In the "waste book," already quoted[3], the returns from Lisbon are wholly in sugar and fruit. The ships casually mentioned as trading with the Azores, or with Portugal itself, are, on the whole, more often laden with sugar than with anything else; and, though the assertion is somewhat sweeping, there may have been good grounds for the declaration in 1640 or thereabouts in "Breefe considerations concerning the trade, that may be expected hereafter, between England and Portugal," that "all our trade consists in the bringing of sugars to England[4]."

That such an assertion was possible at this date shows how changed a world the Portuguese government had to face, when, in 1640, Portugal at last disentangled itself from the yoke of Spain.

In 1580 the Portuguese empire was equalled only by that of Spain itself; now in the east, it was rivalled and out-rivalled by the Dutch and English. Then Portugal had had the monopoly of one of the most valuable of commodities, spice; now its chief asset was the trade in sugar, in which the English colonies were soon to prove dangerous rivals. Then England, if anything, was the inferior. Now, the natural advantage which the trade in necessaries gave her, was enhanced by the improvement in her position in the east. Henceforth, if the old alliance was renewed, its political advantage

[1] *Lansd. MSS.*, 81, No. 42.

[2] Twelvepence per cwt. was levied on muscovado, and tenpence on St Thomé sugars.

[3] P. 170, n. 4.

[4] *For. St. P. Portugal*, Bundle 4.

would fall mainly to Portugal, and England would try to buy commercial privileges as the price of political support. Thus it was on a new stage, not only of her own history, but of her relation with England, that Portugal entered after the revolution of 1640.

CHAPTER III

THE LISBON FACTORY AND THE TREATY OF 1654

(1640-1654).

Revolt of Portugal from Spain—Effects on Anglo-Portuguese relations—Treaty of 1642—Colonial Articles—Africa, India—Brazil trade during the past sixty years—Brazil Article in Treaty of 1642.—English in Portugal—Their privileges—Consuls—Account of their establishment in Spain and Portugal—Articles in Treaty of 1604 concerning English subjects in Spanish territory—Complaints of English in Spain—Difficulties concerning the powers and payment of consul—Attitude of English merchants towards consuls—Early patents—Articles concerning consuls in Treaty of 1642—Position of English factories in Portugal—English Civil War—Its effect on Anglo-Portuguese relations—Rupert at Lisbon—Attitude of English factory—War between England and Portugal—Negotiations for peace—Exaggerated demands of England—Treaty of 1654—Articles concerning Brazil trade—Brazil Company—Articles concerning English in Portugal—The Religious Question—General commercial stipulations—Secret Article—Results of Treaty.

FEW revolutions have been accomplished with greater ease and speed than that which in 1640 freed Portugal from the yoke of Spain; the seizure of the Spanish governors at Lisbon resulted not only in the emancipation of Portugal itself, but in that of its colonies from Spanish rule. With the exception of Ceuta, such of the Portuguese settlements in Africa, India, and America, as remained at the end of a sixty years' struggle with England and Holland, returned at once to the possession of the mother country. They were sadly diminished in number; but this Portugal could not at present afford to resent; she was involved in a life and death struggle with Spain, and was driven by all means to seek the friendship and assistance of the other powers of Europe. Of these, England, formerly the most constant of Portugal's allies, was already on the verge of civil war, and the English government hesitated somewhat before receiving the Portuguese ambassador. Charles I. desired some reassurance as to the position of John IV., and above all he wished to be clear that alliance with Portugal would not involve a war with Spain. The Portuguese ambassador hastened to give historical proofs of John's right to the throne, while reiterating that all his master sought was England's friendship; he by no means hoped nor desired that she should attack Spain. These declarations were satisfactory, and a treaty was signed in 1642, which marks the renewal of direct relations, both political and commercial, with Portugal[1].

In the General Articles this treaty resembled those of 1576, 1604, and 1630; friendship and alliance "in perpetuum" between the two nations; mutual commerce within each other's boundaries, restricted only by the ordinary laws and customs of each nation; and the just treatment of the subjects of each king in the territories of the other (Articles 1, 2, and 3). One novel stipulation the enmity between Spain and Portugal rendered necessary: by Article 2 English ships might not trade direct from Portugal to Spain; but this was the only allusion in the treaty to the quarrel between these two nations.

In the Colonial Articles, however, there were important changes. The fourth Article, indeed, only stated generally that the English might trade to the Portuguese dependencies as freely as men of other countries; and might enjoy all the privileges which

[1] G. Chalmers, *Collection of European Treaties*, II. 257-67.

were theirs before the Spanish annexation of Portugal. The question of Africa, however, which had been so acute in 1576, was at length dealt with; wherever the British had hitherto been wont to trade in Africa they might now trade, paying duties no higher than were imposed on other friendly nations; further, if foreign ships were needed for Portuguese African commerce, those of the English might be employed, and commissioners were to be appointed on both sides to settle "a free commerce[1]." As to the two questions that had risen into prominence during the last sixty years—the questions of India and of Brazil—these presented more points of difficulty.

The East India Company had already, in 1635-36, been driven by the rivalry of the Dutch to make a treaty with the Portuguese viceroy of Goa, and this treaty they desired to see maintained. By this compact four English ships were to go yearly to the East Indies, of which two might trade at the Portuguese ports[2]. These provisions were confirmed by Article 12 of the Treaty of 1642, which extended their scope so as to affect all places beyond the Cape of Good Hope.

The question of Brazil was more difficult; English trade there had existed as long ago as 1540[3]; early in Elizabeth's reign the Portuguese ambassador had protested—of course, in vain—against the English traffic with that country. The Spanish annexation of Portugal does not seem to have seriously affected this growing trade. Rebello da Silva explains that the Portuguese governor, having no orders from Spain, did not interfere with the English[4]. It was true that Mendoza in 1582 advised that English ships trading thither should be sent to the bottom[5]; but

[1] Article 13.
[2] Bruce, J., *Annals of the East India Company*, I. 334.
[3] Anderson, *Historical Deductions*, etc., II. 71.
[4] Rebello da Silva, *Historia de Portugal*, V. 160.
[5] *Sim. Trans. Cal.*, 1582, No. 58.

the advice was more easy to give than to carry out, and the chief interference the English suffered arose from the Inquisition, with which they more than once came into serious conflict; the check, however, was not enough to prevent trade. The merchants trading to Spain and Portugal complained bitterly of the Brazil traders as of persons endangering their commerce, but the English Council declared on appeal that English merchants might freely trade thither (1582)[1]. An elaborate attempt was made in the following year to prove that the Brazil commerce could not be profitable, as the ships required were so large (at least 1,000 tons), and the victuals needed for the voyage left so small a space for the cargo[2]. Cogent as these reasons appeared, however, the blinded English merchants persisted in their traffic; fifteen ships set out in 1587[3]. The goods chiefly exported thither were coarse linen and woollen goods, looking-glasses, hardware, haberdashery, and all kinds of small wares. The returns were in coarse sugar, molasses, and dye woods[4].

The question of Brazil, like other colonial matters, was judiciously ignored in the Treaty of 1604, but it was covered by the Spanish enactment of the following year, which forbade all foreign trade to the Portuguese dependencies (except Madeira and Azores) under pain of death[5]. The regulation proved ineffectual to protect Brazil. At times the attention of the English may have been diverted by the needs of their own colonies in North America; but the desire to get a footing in the southern half of the hemisphere continued and revived whenever Spanish weakness or hostility gave the opportunity[6].

1 *Sim. Trans. Cal.*, 1582, No. 275.

2 Ibid. 1583, No. 352. 3 Ibid. 1587, No. 48.

4 *Dom. St. P. MSS.*, 1595, CCLV. No. 56.

5 *Collecção de legislação antiga et moderna do reino de Portugal Leis Extravagantes*, I. 3.

6 See Guiana Expeditions of 1626 and 1640. (*Cal. Col. St. P.*, America and West Indies, 85; No. 28; 316, No. 81, etc.)

The success of the Dutch, who were thought to intend supplanting the Spaniards as colonial monopolists, was another spur to English ambition[1]; and English jealousy of these rivals appears in a pamphlet entitled, "A Brief Consideration, etc.," issued presumably about 1641. The writer's alarm is particularly excited by the fact that the Dutch have already agreed with Portugal that each nation should keep what it at present possesses in Brazil[2], so that the Dutch can trade there direct, whereas the English have to "fetch the compass." The matter must have been of considerable importance, if, as is here stated, "all our trade" (presumably with Portugal) "consists in the bringing of sugars to England." The difficulties confronting the English were great. First, they must carry their goods to Portugal, where they pay 23 per cent. import duty, and 3 per cent. on re-exportation. Then, having taken the aforesaid goods, or their proceeds to Brazil, and there exchanged them for sugars, a duty of 10 per cent. has to be paid before the sugar can be taken from Brazil; 23 per cent. before it can be entered at Lisbon, and 3 per cent. before it can be re-exported to England. Sugar must, indeed, have been valuable, if under these circumstances the Brazil trade was a profitable speculation[3]. The writer is eager that the treaty should work a reformation in this particular. But the only Article of the Treaty of 1642 which touched on Brazil (Article 16) merely arranged for the appointment of commissioners to settle within two years the question of the freighting of English ships for Brazil by the

[1] *Dom. St. P. Cal.*, 1637, CCCLXIX. 459, No. 4.

[2] In 1637 the Dutch took Todos Santos; and in the same year a plan (which came to nothing) was propounded in England for forming a Company to force a trade with the West Indies and Brazil. The Company was to have a capital of £50,000 "per annum," and was to have an agent, not only for trade, but for conquest and colonisation. (*Dom. St. P. Cal.* CCCLXVIII. No. 114.)

[3] *For. St. P. Portugal*, Bundle 4.

Portuguese; another proof, if one was needed, of the great and growing importance of the English shipping.

The remaining Articles chiefly concern the English in Portugal. That this should be the case is a proof of the growing importance of the colony of English merchants and factors now settled in the various towns of Portugal. From this time onwards the "factories," especially that at Lisbon, play an increasingly prominent part in the relations of England and Portugal.

To appreciate duly their importance and their requirements, it is necessary to glance at their history. The settlement at Lisbon was an old one. Some of the privileges of the English dated back to the fifteenth century, and they had since been confirmed and increased. The merchants and others had not only the elementary privileges of immunity from private theft and violence; they were not to be forced into the service of Portugal. In the event of war between England and Portugal, their goods were not to be seized nor themselves imprisoned. They might carry arms for defence, might wear silk, might own and ride horses. Above all, they had their own judge or Conservador, whose jurisdiction had at first extended only over causes which touched trade or "merchandises"; but to whom the English had gradually referred other causes, till they claimed that they could only be arrested by his warrant, except in criminal cases where the offender was taken red-handed[1]. The general desire of the English, in fact, was to escape from the ordinary Portuguese courts. The administration in Portugal seems to have been both corrupt and arbitrary, and strangers, ill-acquainted with the customs and language of the country, suffered considerably. Their difficulties increased when the spread of the Reformation put the barrier of religious difference

[1] *Os Privilegios.*

between them and the native Portuguese; and the annexation of Portugal by Spain emphasised this difference. The appointment of a consul to govern the English merchants abroad, and to defend their cause when needful, was a natural remedy for these evils: hence the power of appointing (and paying) such consuls was among the rights conferred on the Company of Merchants trading to Spain and Portugal by their Charter of 1577[1]. They appear to have exercised this right for, in 1584, Philip II. confirmed all the old privileges of English factors in Portugal, and further appointed John "Telart" (? Taylor) as consul[2].

In 1587 the needs of the English in Portugal appear in the request of Burleigh that the King of Portugal should allow "our nation" a house "to be theyr free hoast and lodging," and the governor thereof "to have Auctorytye to determine all controversies between our nation without daunger of the law of the countrey"; also that no merchant should forfeit his goods for offences committed by his servants; and that no duties, except those already customary, should be imposed on goods imported by the English[3].

These requests were, of course, of no effect at the time, and the expulsion of the English merchants in 1589, and imprisonment of John Taylor, must have been a paralysing blow to the growing factory. It soon revived, however, and the prospect of peace in 1603-4 was the signal for a shower of demands for safeguards for the English traders in Spain and Portugal. One of the hardest fought points of the

[1] The same right of appointing consuls had been conferred in 1530 by the old Charter to merchants trading to Andalusia, which had been confirmed by Charles V., and it was on this probably that the merchants in 1605 founded their declaration that they had had consuls for a hundred years past; but it seems questionable if there were consuls in Portugal before 1577.

[2] *Add. MSS.*, 11682. See chap. ii.

[3] *Lansd. MSS.*, 152, No. 33.

treaty was the question of the toleration of the English religion in the Spanish dominions, and the immunity of the English from the jurisdiction of the Inquisition[1]. The English petitioned that they should be allowed to use English prayer privately in their own houses, and that they should not be compelled to go to the Spanish service or to any Catholic rites; in especial, they desired that if they chanced to meet the Host in the street they may be permitted to turn aside so as not to do it homage. They desire to be protected by the magistrate so long as they do not wilfully offend against the Catholic religion; and, when such offence occurs, they desire that the case may be dealt with by the English consul, and not by the Inquisition. In regard to temporal matters, besides asking for the confirmation of all their former privileges, they prefer what becomes a very constant request, that the goods of merchants dying in Spain may be administered by the English consul, with the assistance of other English merchants. They also desire that their books and warehouses may not be liable to search or confiscation; that they may elect consuls for their government; and that no officers of the King of Spain shall intermeddle with the private government of His Majesty's subjects, according as it was granted by King Henry VIII., and confirmed by Charles V.

These demands were far more definite than were the actual clauses of the Treaty of 1604[2]. There was a general clause, stipulating that subjects of the one king in the dominions of the other should be as well used as were the native born lieges; there was another vague clause, that the goods of Englishmen dying in Spain were to go to their heirs; all privileges were confirmed, but no definite statement was made on the question of the appoint-

[1] *Cott. MSS.*, *Vesp. C.*, 13. 95.
[2] Treaty of 1604, Rymer, O., XVI. 58 *et seq.*

ment of consuls. By the three secret Articles, however, freedom of conscience was to be assured to the English merchants; a privilege to which the chiefs of the Inquisition strongly objected. The result of their objections, and of the natural jealousy which the Portuguese and Spaniards entertained of the favoured strangers, was that the early years of the seventeenth century were marked by a series of complaints from the English traders and factors resident in Portugal. The insistence of these complaints is the more striking, since they could hardly at this time have formed a very large body. In 1577 the Spanish Company included less than forty merchants resident in Spain and Portugal. The effect of the war would probably be to diminish their numbers; so that, even allowing for their servants, apprentices, and families, and for the various English retailers, craftsmen, and others, who might be found in the Peninsula, the whole body of English may well have been too small, and of too little importance to be able to bring any effective pressure to bear on the Spanish officials for their own convenience.

How little power they had of securing their privileges, appears in a couple of petitions sent up to the English government, apparently, in 1605 and 1606, just after the peace. One of these petitions[1], begins by the declaration that the condition of the merchants is so miserable that if the English government cannot secure them better treatment, they beg that they may be assisted to leave the country. They declare that they are forced to find securities that the goods they export without paying the 30 per cent. duty shall go only to England or to the Archduke's dominions. Among other grievances, they complain that the estates of Englishmen dying in Spanish territory are seized by the officials, and their bodies denied Christian burial; that an extra

[1] *Cott. MSS.*, *Vesp. C.*, 13, p. 40.

tax of a quarter per cent. on all English goods was imposed for the benefit of the Chapel of St George at Lisbon, and for the maintenance of English priests and fugitives; that the officers of the Inquisition insist on searching English ships; that their goods are so arbitrarily rated that a nominal tax of 15 per cent. is sometimes doubled; and that the landing of goods was often unreasonably delayed. The other petition[1] is less tragic in tone, but the complaints are numerous; the Inquisition have seized an Englishman at Faro for heresy; the English Anglican prayer-books are not allowed to be circulated privately among the English; their right of choosing consuls is invaded, the Spanish government restricting their choice to Spaniards and Catholics; they may not freight their ships if any Spaniard demands the freight, and they have to pay a higher freight on English than on Spanish ships. English woollen goods were seized on the suspicion of being Dutch; captains of ships and other Englishmen were frequently arrested on one pretext or another (often under colour of the 11th Article), and the old complaint, with regard to the goods of English dying in Spain, was brought up. These grievances, of course, referred generally to all places under the Spanish dominion, but there is no evidence that the condition of the English in Portugal was better than elsewhere[2].

Meantime, the question of the consuls was rendered more difficult by the collapse of the Spanish Company just after they had appointed their first consul under their new Charter. This consul, Hugh Lee by name, clung to his post in the face of difficulties raised less by the Spanish government than by the recalcitrant

[1] *Dom. St. P. MSS.*, 1605, XVI. No. 18.

[2] Arrests of various pretexts of English goods in Lisbon were frequent. In 1607 the merchants begged for letters of marque, as they could not get "redress by peaceful means." In the following year several English were imprisoned by the Inquisition for having given scandal to religion. Winwood, II. 353 and 397.

English themselves, who manifested the strongest possible objection to paying consulage (a quarter per cent. tax on imports and exports[1]). The business was complicated by the presence in Lisbon of many English and Irish Catholics and political refugees; further, the English merchants had a habit of sending their sons and servants to Lisbon to learn the language, and these inexperienced youths frequently fell into temporal difficulties as well as becoming easy converts to Catholicism, much to Lee's distress[2]. His main difficulty, however, lay in the enforcement of his authority at all after the collapse of the Company. "Every one," he wrote distressfully, "followeth his own ways." He had spent about £200, and spared no trouble in removing abuses; but his fellow-countrymen, mostly "youths and disgoverned people," showed themselves stolidly disinclined to reimburse him. Even the tax on the incoming ships which the merchants did continue to pay, did not go entirely into the consul's pockets; a considerable portion was intercepted by an official appointed by the Viceroy, so that only about £60 a year came to Lee[3]. Still, he stuck to his post, despite these discouragements, and kept up a pretty brisk correspondence with the home government, and with the English ambassador in Spain. Cornwallis wrote (1607) that he heard weekly from Lee, who, "according to the measure of his understanding advertiseth diligently" the various passing events.

Lee's function, however, could not, in his own opinion, be limited to that of a newsmonger; and he was most urgent to have his patent confirmed by the English government. In 1608 he wrote that the Spanish king, in addition to confirming all previous privileges, had issued a warrant for the consul to fulfil his functions in any court of justice. But, unless Lee had a further confirmation from the

[1] *For. St. P. Portugal*, Bundle 3.
[2] Ibid. [3] Ibid.

English king, his authority would be disregarded particularly by the Scotchmen and Irishmen in Portugal. Further, he desired that his authority might extend over all the Portuguese dominions, including Madeira and the Azores[1].

Lee's request was backed by the English ambassadors, especially Digby. The latter desired that consuls should be appointed all over Spain. To this, however, the Spanish ministry objected, declining to allow Protestant officials; but, as far as Lisbon was concerned, they presently permitted the English government to grant a formal patent to Lee, who had apparently hitherto been acting on the appointment of the defunct Spanish Company. His patent (8th November 1611) gave him the right to act as consul, and the power of levying a quarter per cent. on imported goods to supply his expenses[2].

This definite appointment probably marked a stage in the history of the English residents in Portugal. They had now an acknowledged referee in cases of difficulty, and an acknowledged representative to take up their cause against the possible oppressions of the government, under which they lived. Moreover, they bore the common burden of his support, and a common interest in seeing that he was efficient: all which circumstances must have tended to draw them into a more coherent and compact body than formerly.

The arrangement, however, was far from flawless; and after the temporary disorganisation of trade, caused by the war of 1625, the merchants took the opportunity afforded them by the renewal of arrangements in 1630, and put forward their grievances. The question was complicated by the facts that there were two claimants to the consulship, of whom one

[1] *For. St. P. Portugal*, Bundle 3.
[2] *Dom. St. P. Docquets*, X. See Appendix II. 3.

Chandler seems to have been supported by a large number of merchants[1].

The merchants' view of a consul's functions was well expressed by Coke, to whom the matter was referred. He reported that the duties of a consul were to assist and to govern the English in Portugal, adding, "How far the word 'govern' may extend, the merchants doubt; for the rest, they find it reasonable[2]." Another point raised by the merchants was the question of the consul's right of appointing deputy consuls; in this they conceived they ought to have a voice, and, in the time of Consul Stone, the question had caused such friction between him and the factory that "he was forced to flee[3]."

The old question concerning the goods of Englishmen dying in Portugal was also revived. The laws of Spain did not permit the consul to administer them, as by his patent he had a right to do; and the English merchants did not appear anxious that this power should be conferred on him, unless two of their number were associated with him in his capacity of executor. The vexed question of consulage came up again; the merchants already had to pay 23 per cent. on imports, and it was doubtful if the King of Spain would permit any imposition save that levied by his own government. Even if he did, the manner of levying the quarter per cent. consulage had given great offence. For the purpose of exacting his due, the consul had apparently demanded to see the merchants' books; a demand made "by no prince in the world, nor by the Inquisition itself," as the merchants indignantly declared. Further, they

1 The former Consul Stone (Lee's successor) demanded the post; but even before the war he had become infirm, and had appointed Chandler as his substitute. However, as the Spanish government objected to this plan, Chandler, according to his own account, became actual consul, and now wished to have the office again. (*For. St. P. Portugal*, 4. Chandler's *Petition*, 1606.)

2 *Dom. St. P. MSS.*, CLXXXIII. No. 32.

3 Ibid.

pointed out that the Inquisition was needless, since the consulage could be levied on the custom-house valuation of the goods. As for the quarter per cent. levied by the consul on the sale of ships, to that the merchants objected altogether, as they did to the consul's pretension to appoint an interpreter, which they thought needless. Finally, several of the oldest merchants in Spain and Portugal declared that they did not see any use at all in a consul, especially if his patent had not been confirmed by the King of Spain. During the various periods when no consul had been appointed, they had managed the business easily by the help of the Portuguese themselves, and they had never received any benefit whatever from the consuls[1]!

Despite this disparaging view of consuls, as useless luxuries, they continued to be appointed, and during the next ten years the continued disputes between the English and Spanish governments must have afforded them plenty of scope for activity. With a view of preventing the introduction of Dutch cloth as English, it was ordered that all English cloth imported to Spain should be sealed with the name of the place where it was made (15th March 1638-39)[2]. Several Englishmen were arrested on the accusation of fraudulently importing Dutch goods, and cases of arbitrary imprisonment, possibly on a charge of an attempt to evade the customs, also occurred. Again, there were perpetual complaints of unnecessary delay in the unloading of ships; and another disturbance was caused in 1635-36 by the imprisonment of some English sailors at Lisbon on the charge of exporting plate[3].

Cases such as these showed the expediency of

[1] *Dom. St. P. MSS.*, CLXXXIII. No. 132.

[2] *For. St. P. Portugal*, Bundle 4. This decision greatly annoyed the merchants importing Eastland commodities to the Peninsula. They declared that their market would be spoiled should they be forced to reveal where their goods were made.

[3] *Dom. St. P. Cal.*, CCCVII. No. 81.

having some authoritative person to whom to appeal; nor was the consul's duty only that of a judge. His functions are pretty clearly defined in the patents of Chandler and Howe (1634). He was to be consul of the English in Portugal, the Algarves, Porto Santo, Madeira, and Barbary. Despite all protests, he was still to appoint deputy consuls and interpreters. His business was to protect traders, and to compose quarrels between the English themselves. In concert with two or three of the more important merchants, he was to act as executor of those Englishmen who died intestate or, if their wishes had been expressed, he was to see that they were duly carried out. If any factor in Portugal was suspected of dishonesty, the consul was to seize his goods in the interests of his employer, and ship the accused man himself back to England. For the benefit of poor or shipwrecked English, the consul and his associates were to raise a rate on the English inhabitants of Portugal, to aid these unfortunates, and send them back to their own country. Finally, the question of consulage was to be settled by the consul receiving one ducat on every English ship coming to Portugal, and one-quarter per cent. on all goods imported by Englishmen. The vexed question of the consular inspection of the books was settled by an order that the consul should see the ship's bill of lading for the purpose of levying his tax, while the valuation of the goods was to be that made at the port custom house[1].

These provisions were in part confirmed by the Treaty of 1642. The consuls, not mentioned in any previous compact were here recognised as an established institution; even though Protestants they might exercise full powers; and Article 9 placed the administration of the goods of Englishmen dying in Portugal in the hands of the consul and two merchants named by the Conservador. The treaty dealt also with the religious difficulty and the question

[1] *For. St. P. Portugal*, Bundle 4.

of the Inquisition: Article 17 provided for the toleration of English Protestantism, while, on the other hand, English converts to Catholicism taking service in Portugal were not to be molested on that account by their Protestant fellow-countrymen (Article 7), and debts due to the English by prisoners of the Inquisition were to be paid out of the proceeds of the latter's goods (Article 6). In a general way, the English in Portugal were to have as great privileges as any other nation.

The inclusion of such Articles in a national treaty marks the importance to England of the English colony in Portugal: and, for at least the next hundred years, the relations both general and commercial of Portugal and England were largely swayed by the interest of the English factories.

For some reason or other, the privileges of the English do not seem to have been touched after the Portuguese revolution until 1645[1], when John IV. issued a decree confirming them, on the special petition of one Thomas Bostock and the English merchants in Portugal[2]. This petition gives a doleful picture of the distresses of the English in Portugal at the time. In defiance of their privileges they are not allowed to carry arms; heavy exactions are wrung from them if they lade English ships in preference to Portuguese; and they are arrested on the warrants of different judges, and tried in various courts, instead of being relegated to their Conservator, as by a fifteenth century grant they maintained should be the case. John IV. thereon granted a confirmation of all privileges, and two years later strengthened the confirmation, inflicting heavy penalties upon all who violated them.

So far, the attitude of the king was exceedingly favourable, and the English community in Portugal probably flourished during these disturbed

[1] Santarem, etc., *Quadro Elementar, etc.*, XVII. 53.
[2] *Os Privilegios do Inglez nos reynos e dominio de Portugal.*

years. The establishment of the Brazil Company in 1648 with its right of exclusive trade to Brazil may have somewhat circumscribed their efforts; but even this cannot greatly have affected them, as in 1650 Blake found nine English manned ships in the Brazil fleet[1], while a considerable part of their freight was of English ownership. The importance of English shipping and English capital to Portugal was openly acknowledged in 1649, when the Portuguese ministers told Rupert that English vessels were necessary for their Brazil trade, as the war with Castile and Holland caused them to need more ships than they could build[2].

The sums claimed by the English after the seizure of the merchants' goods by the King of Portugal in 1650 show the extent of their trade. £10,000 were claimed for seizures in Lisbon, and £12,500 for those in Oporto and the Western Isles; £3,000 were owing by the king for provisions supplied by English traders to his fleet. One English firm alone (Bushell and Company), had had a venture worth £5,000 in the Brazil fleet. English ships in the Portuguese service seized in Brazil were estimated at £23,614; and the final total of the debt was estimated at £140,839[3]. Even allowing for the exaggeration of claims made by members of an injured and victorious nation, these figures bear witness to the importance of the English factories in Portugal.

With regard to the direct trade between England and Portugal, it was necessarily checked by the civil war; but there was no intervention on the part of either government, save that the English Parliament in 1644 passed a resolution in favour of a "free trade" with Portugal. How largely that trade also must have been conducted by English capital, and

[1] *Dom. St. P. Cal.*, 395-96, 428, 444.
[2] "Prince Rupert at Lisbon" (Ed. S. Gardiner), *Roy. Hist. Soc. Camden Miscellany*, X.
[3] *Add. MSS.*, 4192, pp. 85-6.

English shipping appears by the acknowledgment of the Portuguese ambassador in 1644, that Portuguese merchant ships do not ordinarily come over sea to this coast, nor Portuguese merchants send merchandise for their account[1].

As time went on, however, and the ultimate victory of Parliament became assured, signs appeared which pointed to a probable breach between England and Portugal. John IV. sympathised strongly with Charles I. The Portuguese resident in London, Dr Antonio Sousa de Macedo, gave the Royalists all the assistance in his power. The order of the Parliament in 1644, forbidding all trade with ports in Royalist hands, provoked a vigorous outcry from Portugal, which, though presumably made in the interest of its own trade, was, of course, favourable to the Royalists. The line of argument shows the Portuguese bias. By the eleventh Article of the Treaty of 1642, Sousa de Macedo points out that the English might trade with the enemies of Portugal, and *vice versâ*; granting then, that the Royalists were the enemies of England, what right had the Parliament to prohibit the trade[2]? In addition to this testimony of friendship for the English king, a marriage was suggested in 1644 between the Prince of Wales and the Portuguese Infanta, whose dowry, together with some naval assistance from Portugal, would, it was thought, enable Charles I. to crush the rebels[3]. The religious interest undoubtedly influenced Portugal, and, in 1645, it is reported that John IV. was anxious that Charles should be supported by all the Catholics in Great Britain and Ireland.

These various schemes were revealed to Parliament in the letters captured at Naseby and Sherborne. The result was the departure of the Portuguese

[1] *Add. MSS.*, 4155, fol. 250. [2] Ibid.
[3] Santarem, *Quadro Elementar, etc.*, XVII. 54; and *For. St. P. Portugal*, Nos. 4, 143.

ambassador from England, and a deepening sense of hostility between Portugal and the dominant party in England.

Still, neither England nor Portugal seems to have been desirous of war. In 1649 the Commonwealth had proclaimed its readiness to renew the English alliances with other nations; and Portugal, engaged with the Spaniards at home, and the Dutch in Brazil, might be thought to have its warlike energies sufficiently occupied.

But the necessities of the cavaliers brought matters to a crisis. Rupert had recently entered on his piratic career, with the assistance of certain ships which had revolted from allegiance to the Commonwealth; and, as a first requisite for defence, he needed a harbour where he could refit his own ships and dispose of his prizes. For this purpose Lisbon appeared extremely suitable; so, towards the end of 1649, Rupert anchored his ships there, and requested the "libertie and protection" of the Portuguese ports; the said liberty to cover the detention of the enemies of the Royalists in Portuguese harbours for three days after the fleet had left, and the right of selling prizes in Lisbon[1]. These requests John IV. could not quite admit; but entrance to his harbours was, he conceived, guaranteed by the Treaty of 1642; and he finally agreed to give certain facilities to English captains selling goods in Portugal. That Rupert took prompt advantage of this last concession to dispose of his prizes[1] was a source of dismay, not only to the Commonwealth, but to Portugal. The Portuguese government, at least, had no wish to see Portugal made a fighting base for the cavaliers; it would be contrary to the "amitye," which that country had always maintained with the English nation. It would destroy Portuguese trade with England, and would cause the departure of many

[1] "Prince Rupert at Lisbon" (Ed. S. R. Gardiner.). See for details of whole affair, *Roy. Hist. Soc. Camden Miscellany*, X.

English then in Portugal. Finally, when Rupert took an English ship conveying Portuguese emigrants to Brazil, the Portuguese government advised him to leave at once if he wished to avoid the sequestration of all his goods; but the Portuguese merchants themselves foiled the government's measures by keeping the prize goods they had bought of Rupert, and declining to pay. The Prince naturally lingered to gather in his debts.

Meanwhile, the Commonwealth had decided on sending an agent, Charles Vane, to negotiate with Portugal, and what was more important, a fleet was despatched under Blake and Popham to lie off the Portuguese coast. The instructions to fleet and agent both were to negotiate rather than to fight; but a fresh act of the Portuguese government made peace still more difficult. In their desire to avoid a bloody battle in Lisbon harbour they had declared that, though the English Royalists might come to sell their goods, not more than four English ships of war might enter the harbour of Lisbon, nor might they remain there longer than twenty days[1].

Rupert, who was already in the harbour, could not be got rid of, but the prohibition was, of course, obstructive to the Commonwealth fleet. At first the latter did not prevent the trade of the English factory at Lisbon. "I come not to hinder, but to further trade," said Blake, in permitting ships to pass to the Western Isles[2]. But the Parliamentarians very decidedly did hinder trade, when they persisted in searching the French ships coming to Portugal, and even in detaining them, lest they should join Rupert.

Meantime, Vane was pleading for a "firm amity," demanding the restoration of the English ships taken by Rupert, trying to raise a Puritan party in

[1] "Prince Rupert at Lisbon."

[2] The Western Isles was the regular name for the Azores. *Dom. St. P. Cal.*, 1653, 206, No. 24 (VI.).

the English factory, and attempting to induce the merchants to accept a consul appointed by the Parliament. But the factory, which, like the nation, was split into two parties, refused on the very sound ground that their present consul's patent had been confirmed by the Portuguese king, which might not be the case with the patent of the Parliamentary nominee[1]. Nor were the generals much more successful in their demands either to be allowed entrance to the harbour, or to have Rupert expelled that they might fight him on the high seas; and Parliament in high indignation bade Blake, if he was still denied entrance, to seize on any Portuguese ships leaving the harbour[2]. Things went from bad to worse; two affrays took place on shore between Puritan and Cavalier seamen, in which the former had the worst. A Royalist fire-ship was launched against the Puritan vice-admiral. Thirteen English merchants, at Vane's instigation, signed a petition to the King of Portugal, protesting that the state of things was ruinous to trade, and begging him to free the harbour from both fleets—naturally without result[3]. Had it been in his power the King of Portugal would have been only too happy to have complied. The very day of the petition, a fresh assault on the Commonwealth's men by Rupert's followers fairly broke down the patience of the English government. Little more than a fortnight after Vane was recalled[4], and in less than another month war was declared between England and Portugal. The first blow fell on the Lisbon factory. Such of the merchants as were leaders of the Commonwealth party were seized and imprisoned[5], and their release and compensation was one of the

[1] "Prince Rupert at Lisbon."
[2] *Thurloe*, I. 147.
[3] Ibid. 142.
[4] *Dom. St. P. Cal.*, IX. 212, No. 84. (Proceedings of Council of State, No. 14.)
[5] *Cal. Clar. St. P.*, No. 350.

points most insisted on by the English Parliament in the subsequent negotiations.

The ensuing war was itself of comparatively slight importance; its chief interest is that it led up to the Treaty of 1654. In this treaty, for the first time, England assumed a position of superiority—of one able to exact her own terms.

It was impossible for Portugal to engage in a vigorous war with England, when all her forces were needed to enable her to continue the struggle against Spain. The English, on the other hand, found the war seriously damaging to their trade[1]. But their sufferings served chiefly to irritate them; they desired to exact the most satisfactory terms possible as compensation, and the Treaty of 1654 bears witness to that wish[2].

The first struggle, however, was over the preliminary Articles—the questions of the release of the imprisoned English merchants, and of the compensation to be paid by Portugal; of the restoration of goods and ships seized by Rupert and left in Lisbon; and other points of temporary interest. Over these the discussion was fierce, but the English demands were on the whole gratified. Of the money exacted from the Portuguese government, half was to be paid at once, and the remainder by an assignment to the English government of half the custom paid on English goods exported to Portugal[3]. Over the treaty itself discussion was cooler and more prolonged. One or two slightly exaggerated demands of the English were dropped, such, for instance, as the suggestion that they should have the exclusive export of Portuguese salt for ten years. The chief political

[1] The Essex clothiers instanced the seizure of the merchants' goods in Portugal as showing that uncertainty in commerce, which caused men to desert trade and invest their capital in land (8th November 1652, *Dom. St. P. Cal.*, 481, No. 52.)

[2] Chalmers' *Collection of Treaties*, II.

[3] The collection of these half customs proved to be a source of annoyance and of friction for many years following.

difficulty concerned the admission of warships to Portuguese harbours[1], which was settled to the satisfaction of the English. The latter had reason also to be pleased with the colonial clauses which marked a distinct advance on the Treaty of 1642.

The first suggestion of the Portuguese ambassador was simply for a renewal of the Article of 1642[2]. But the English Council exacted far more. They would not even consent that only those Englishmen should trade to Brazil who were licensed by the Portuguese king. The English were to trade to the East Indies, Portuguese Africa, and St Thomé, on payment of the usual customs. As regarded Brazil, so long as the English ships sailed in the Portuguese fleet for Brazil, the goods with which they were laden were to pay no more than the ordinary duties. English merchants were to be allowed to trade freely with Brazil in all goods except fish, wine, oil, and Brazil wood, traffic in which was the exclusive right of the Brazil Company[3]. On the other hand, the Brazil Company itself, and the Portuguese nation generally, were bound, if extra ships were required, to hire only English vessels as long as these could be obtained. Nor was this the only clause which marked that regard of the Commonwealth for the shipping which had culminated in the Navigation Act a year or two earlier. By Clause 23 of this treaty, free ships were to make free goods, so far as the English and Portuguese were concerned.

The establishment of the Brazil Company had been a great grievance to the English merchants, who protested that their trade was not free if they were hampered by the presence of monopolists and engrossers. Their complaints may have given rise to the clauses (not found in the corresponding Articles in 1642, 5 and 11) of Articles 3 and 10,

[1] Article 18.
[2] *Birch MSS.*, 4192, No. 3.
[3] Article 11.

by which the English were to import what they pleased to Portugal, and trade as they chose, unthwarted by monopolists, and not bound down to a set price.

These clauses all tended to show the ascendancy England had now gained over her old ally; but it appeared nowhere more plainly than in the Articles concerning the privileges of the English resident in Portugal. In place of the various general stipulations of the Treaty of 1642, special detailed regulations were mentioned; thus by both treaties the English consuls were to be unmolested on account of their religion, and in addition to this, a clause in the Treaty of 1654 stipulated that they should be appointed by the Protector[1]. The question of the administration of the goods of the English dying in Portugal was, as before, to be left to two English merchants, in whose hands the Conservador might put the business; but they were to be chosen by the other merchants, and approved by the consul[2]. The general clause that English merchants should be as well treated as those of any other nation, was crystallised into various very definite stipulations, embodying the privileges that had been granted them from time to time. Thus, the existence of a Judge Conservador, from whom an appeal should lie only to the highest Portuguese court (which appeals should be settled in four months) was especially stipulated for by the English Council (Article 7.)

Special Articles (3, 20, 21) also asserted the English right to employ brokers under the same regulations as the Portuguese, to wear arms, to live where they chose, and to pay no dues but to the king or the chamber at Lisbon; all points untouched, in 1642, as was also the question of the arrest of Englishmen. In the negotiations previous to the Treaty of 1654,

[1] 1642, Article 8; 1654, Article 7.
[2] 1642, Article 9; 1654, Article 7.

the ambassador offered that they should be as free from arrest as any other foreigners[1]. The Council, again practically adopting an old privilege, stipulated that no Englishman should be arrested, save by the warrant of the Judge Conservador, except in criminal cases where the offenders were taken red-handed (Article 13). On the other hand, the aggressive attitude of the Council appeared in their stipulation in the same article that the English might sue any Portuguese, were he an official or not, for debt, and that no protection should avail against English claims. All through, indeed, the somewhat arrogant and lordly tone of the English government appears together with the determination to have such definite statements as should render the English privileges real and actual.

As regards the vexed religious question, there were several Articles. In Article 6 it was stipulated that no English sailor should trouble any one on account of his religion; and the Portuguese ambassador further offered that English sailors converted to Catholicism, and entering the Portuguese service, should give no trouble to their former employers on account of wages, etc., due to them[2]. But the Council insisted that they should not enter the Portuguese service, and that the Portuguese magistrates should join in compelling English deserters to return to their duty. The most important Article, however (Article 14), was moderate, stipulating only that the English should have freedom of religion, and the right to exercise it in their ships and houses. Even this, however, was an advance on what the Portuguese ambassador offered—a vague promise to protect the English in their religion as far as possible, so long as they gave no scandal[3].

The general commercial stipulations bear the same character. Debts due to the English by persons

[1] *Birch MSS.*, 4192, No. 3.
[2] Ibid. [3] Ibid.

arrested by the Inquisition were to be paid from the prisoners' estates within six months[1]; and a similar provision was for the first time made concerning the debts of persons arrested at the king's command. By the Council's demand, goods no more than ships or persons were to be impressed into the Portuguese service. Only two officers were to be appointed to oversee the lading and unlading of the vessels, and if such lading was delayed longer than ten days for dry goods, and fifteen for wet ones, no pay was to be demanded of the English for the extra time[2].

Another point, proposed and carried by the Council, concerned the provision trade, of which so much has been said. Its importance is marked by Article 17, by which any question concerning the goodness of the provisions was to be referred to arbiters, not of Portuguese nationality, to be chosen by the English consul and the Portuguese magistrate.

But the most marked stipulations were those referring to the customs on goods imported by the English to Portugal. The general stipulation that only the usual customs should be paid, was first defined by the Council to mean only those levied in 1642[3]; and when this was not admitted, they insisted on defining them (Article 2) as those paid on 10th March 1653. This, though a more definite statement than had ever previously been made on the subject, was nothing beside the secret Article, which provided that no more than 23 per cent. should ever be levied on English imports to Portugal; that the valuation of the goods, if disputed, should be decided by arbiters chosen by the English consul and the Custom House officers; and that no alteration of the customs should be made without the presence

[1] The ambassador at first suggested a year, and the Council two months. (Ibid.)

[2] Articles 5, 9, 4.

[3] *Birch MSS.*, 4192, No. 3.

and consent of two English merchants residing in Portugal, chosen by the English consul. About this Article, as may be imagined, a great controversy raged. The English alleged in its support that the Portuguese book of rates, which was declared to rule the valuation of goods, was exceedingly arbitrary. Bays, for instance, formerly valued at 12 milreis, were now valued at 15. The suggestion that the price of goods rose when the custom did, was unsound;—"The custome is not the rule of the market but the quantitie of the commodites." When there was a glut, prices fell, and the high custom dues came out of the merchant's own pocket; the uncertainty of the valuation discouraged traders; besides, the customs ought not to be governed by the price of commodities: in England, sugar varied from £9 to £3 in price, yet the custom was unaltered[1].

Such, and such like were the arguments that the English put forward in favour of their demand. The Council declared they had propounded it by the advice of the English merchants, and maintained it stoutly. The Portuguese ambassador did his best to escape from it, alleging that he was unauthorised to accept it, though he was prepared to pledge himself privately that the customs would not be raised. The negotiations over this and other points of the treaty lasted over two years, and the final rather sudden acquiescence of the Portuguese ambassador was said to be owing to his desire to escape from England without witnessing the execution of his brother, the unhappy Don Pantaleon Sa[2].

The ratification of the treaty was another matter. The advantages the English gained were too great to be readily granted, and the Portuguese king hung back for two years more, till the appearance of Blake

[1] *Birch MSS.*, 4192, p. 278.

[2] Gardiner, *History of the Commonwealth and Protectorate*, II. chap. xxxi. 383-88.

off the coast of Portugal settled the matter, and the treaty was ratified.

The Treaty of 1654 may be considered as marking the zenith of the English ascendancy over Portugal. The English trading with Portugal, or residing there, were thenceforth in a situation more advantageous than that of the Portuguese themselves; and this position may have contributed to the extraordinary predominance which the English exercised over Portuguese trade during the early eighteenth century. On the other hand, it certainly greatly increased Portuguese jealousy and hatred of England. Hence the next hundred and fifty years are occupied, first, by a series of disputes between England and Portugal, and secondly, by a vigorous effort of the smaller power against the influence of the greater: both of which results may be largely due to the efforts of the English to maintain the position guaranteed to them by the Treaty of 1654.

CHAPTER IV

THE METHUEN TREATY

(1654-1703)

Marriage of Charles II. and Catherine of Braganza—Reasons for marriage—English support of Portugal against Spain—English mediation between Portugal and Holland—Anglo-Portuguese Treaty of 1661—Cession of Bombay and of Tangiers — Anglo-Portuguese trade — Carrying trade—Brazil provisions—Wine and Brazil trades—Amount of Portuguese imports to England—Sugar trade—Portuguese currency—Competition of Brazil and plantation sugars—Clandestine export of bullion from Portugal—Portuguese prohibitions of foreign goods—Cloth trade in Portugal—Seeming separation of English and Portuguese commercial interests—England needs the political assistance of Portugal—Effect of Anglo-French wars on Anglo-Portuguese wine trade—Decadence of cloth trade—Negotiations for Methuen Treaty—Result of treaty—In what respect was it a bribe to Portugal?

THE fifty years that succeeded the Treaty of 1654 were years of close alliance, both political and commercial, between England and Portugal, in which the chief causes of friction were due to the provisions of that treaty itself. The treaty exacted too much from Portugal, and gave too little for its steady maintenance to be possible. The payment of the sums exacted by the English government as compensation, the maintenance of the English privileges, the limitation of the amount of the customs imposed on English traders, were all points on which the stronger country held the conduct of the weaker to be unsatisfactory. Even before Cromwell's death the English government had complained of the failure of the Portuguese king to pay the sums demanded of him. Moreover, it had objected that the assignment of the customs agreed on for this purpose had been made only on the customs of Lisbon, instead of extending, as it should have done, all over Portugal. The Portuguese king retorted, truly enough, that he had yielded more than ever was yielded before. But the English Council in their usual high-handed way, declined to listen to his excuses or to admit the ratification of the treaty till they were satisfied[1].

The fear of fresh war brought ample promises of satisfaction from the Portuguese government; and peace continued until the Restoration changed England from a somewhat domineering and suspicious ally into one showing, at least for the moment, something like genuine friendliness.

For the first time for nearly three hundred years the alliance of the two nations was cemented by a marriage—that of Charles II. with the Infanta Catherine of Braganza. The inducements to the match were numerous.

Of all the royal houses of Europe, that of Braganza had perhaps shown, in proportion to its means, most sympathy, and had made the greatest efforts on behalf of the Stuarts; the new Minister, Clarendon, was a man with whom gratitude for past services had real weight. Moreover, England was already at war with Spain, and the whole influence of Spain's great rival, France, was given to the support of the Portuguese cause.

Commercial interests, too, made for the Portuguese alliance. Two hundred merchants trading to Portugal petitioned Charles II. to preserve their commerce[2].

[1] Barros e Sousa etc., Viscount de Santarem, *Quadro Elementar das relações politicas e diplomaticas de Portugal com as diversas potencias do Mundo*, XVII. 106-10.

[2] Santarem, *Quadro Elementar das relações . . . de Portugal*, XVII. 115.

It was boldly asserted that the trade with Portugal was far more valuable than that with Spain[1]. Finally, the dower offered was a considerable temptation. In Portugal itself the marriage was extremely popular. "The welcomest news that ever came to Portugal," wrote Consul Maynard[2]; nor was it less popular because its direct significance was almost wholly political. England bound herself to assist Portugal against the power of Spain; not indeed by engaging strenuously in war with that power, but by the despatch of two regiments of horse and two of foot at her own expense, for the Portuguese service; by the promise of naval support, if Portugal was invaded, and by the pledge to make no peace with Spain which would endanger Portugal[3].

These promises, however, though fairly carried out, were of less importance to Portuguese interests than the negotiations with Spain, which England conducted on her behalf. A successful issue to these negotiations was indeed essential to the interests of England; the sort of half-and-half policy which she pursued became in the course of a year or two impossible. As the English envoy, Sir Richard Fanshawe, declared, if she would have that peace with Spain, which was necessary for the prosperity of her commerce, she must either abandon Portugal altogether, or support her so vigorously as to force Spain herself to beg for peace[4]. Fanshawe also warned the home government in 1694 that, if the English wished to continue their trade with Portugal, they must either send their ships under convoy to protect them from the Spanish cruisers, or avenge themselves on Spain by capturing the Spanish ships trading with the Dutch[5].

[1] Fanshawe's *Letters*, 69 (Ed. 1724).

[2] July $\frac{9}{19}$, 1661, *For. St. P. Portugal*, Bundle 5.

[3] Articles, 15, 16, 17, and 18, Treaty of 1661, Chalmers' *Collection of Treaties*.

[4] In Fanshawe's *Letters*, 441 (Ed. 1702).

[5] Ibid. 449.

Spain, still regarding Portugal as a rebel, threatened to seize all English merchants on the Spanish coast who were suspected of trade with the Portuguese, and did seize cargoes of wheat, fish, etc., bound for that country[1]. Thus, both from a commercial and political point of view, the peace between Portugal and Spain, which the negotiations of Fanshawe and Sandwich brought about in 1667, was of the greatest advantage alike to Portugal and to England.

Spain, however, was not the only power whose enmity Portugal dreaded. As far as colonial interests were concerned, the Dutch were far more dangerous opponents; and the struggle between Holland and Portugal had now reached a stage, in which Dutch success threatened English as well as Portuguese interests. In the East Indies, the Dutch were pressing on Goa, and the English conceived that the success of their venture would ruin their own trade on the Malabar coast. In Brazil, English and Dutch rivalry was of old standing; hence the English were pursuing their own interest very directly in the secret Article of the Treaty of 1661, by which they pledged themselves to protect the Portuguese conquests, and to mediate between Holland and Portugal.

Nor was it only from the colonial point of view that the amity of the Dutch was desirable. During the last few years, England's trade with Portugal had been much hampered by Dutch cruisers, who seized on the English merchant ships wherever they found them unprotected; till, in the opinion of an English captain, it would be necessary to have English frigates perpetually guarding the Portuguese coast, unless the trade was to be ruined[2]. Hence the English conducted their mediation entirely from the point of view of their own welfare; and the chief efforts of their envoy, Downing, were directed towards

[1] Fanshawe's *Letters*, 434-35 (Ed. 1702).
[2] *Dom. St. P. Cal.*, 1657, 466.

frustrating all clauses in the Dutch-Portuguese Treaty, by which the commerce of Holland should receive advantage as great, or greater, than did that of England. The absolute disbelief of the English in their own powers of competing with the Dutch, appears in his statement that, if the Dutch had equal privileges with the English, they would obtain all the Portuguese trade; to which Clarendon, assenting, replied that such an equality of privileges would be a great breach of the Anglo-Portuguese Treaty[1]. Downing's efforts were so far successful, that the Dutch-Portuguese Treaty of 1661 contained nothing contrary to the treaty with England[2]; though the English had perforce to give way to an extension of Dutch privileges.

The English, however, obtained a better security against Dutch encroachments in the East Indies, than could be afforded by a treaty, in the cession of Bombay[3], as part of Catherine of Braganza's dower. This port had long been desired by the East India Company, which considered that its possession would secure their trade on that coast.

The waning power of the Portuguese in the East Indies was so marked that a suggestion was made that the English should be allowed to trade to the Portuguese East Indies, since the Portuguese themselves could not do so. There was even some idea that Goa might be ceded to them[4]. This suggestion, however, came only from England, and the grant actually made of Bombay was by no means popular in Portugal, and still less so in the East Indies. Every possible difficulty was made by the Portuguese governor about giving it up to the English, and the claims of the latter to have Salsette and Tana included in the cession were for long disputed. In 1665 the English commander at Bombay made a

[1] *Clar. Corr.*, III. 163, 166.
[2] Ibid. 162. [3] Article 11.
[4] *For. St. P. Portugal*, Bundle 4.

convention with the Portuguese, by which the Bombay dependencies remained to the latter, and they were exempted from all payment of customs in Bombay; a favour they requited by levying great imposts on all ships passing Tana and Salsette. The convention, above mentioned, was repudiated by the English home government; and the question of the dependencies was still in dispute, when in 1668 the English crown handed over the government of this troublesome possession to the East India Company, by whom its importance and value were gradually developed[1].

One other advantage the English also gained in their colonial relations with Portugal. By Articles 12 and 13, in addition to the trade rights already guaranteed by the Treaty of 1654, they were permitted to reside in the Portuguese settlements of Goa, Cochin and Diu, Bahia, Pernambuco and Rio de Janeiro, on the understanding that not more than four English families resided in each place. This concession was thought to be of much importance, particularly as regarded the Brazil trade, and it became the ground of many disputes.

A source of equal embarrassment with Bombay at the time of its cession, and with no compensating future development, was Tangiers. The possession of this settlement had been anticipated by the English as a great commercial advantage. As early as 1657, Monk had suggested its cession. The Portuguese, he said, only wanted it for the slave trade, and it would give the English the command of the Straits[2]. Maynard, in 1661, suggested that it might be made a magazine for the Levant trade[3]. But the hostility of Spain, who refused to recognise the cession to England as lawful, the constant attacks of the Moors, and the sick-

[1] Bruce, J., *Annals of the East India Company*, II. chap. ii. 198.
[2] Anderson, *Historical Deduction, etc.*, II. 441.
[3] *For. St. P. MSS. Portugal*, Bundle 5, December $\frac{8}{18}$, 1661.

ness which decimated the English garrison, all served to prevent these anticipations from being realised. In 1684 the English abandoned Tangiers, and destroyed its fortifications, much to the disgust of the Portuguese, who loudly declared that England might, at least, have given them the opportunity of redeeming their old settlement[1].

The various grants and stipulations of the Treaty of 1661, though stimulated by, and concerning the various commercial interests of the time, had but little effect on the direct trade of England and Portugal during the ensuing forty years.

The one Article of the Treaty of 1661, of real importance from the economic point of view, was the first, by which all treaties from 1641 onward were confirmed, including, of course, the all-important compact of 1654. The provisions of the latter treaty, especially the secret Article, were the chief sources of friction during the ensuing period, and the Methuen Treaty, with which this epoch closed, showed that the English realised that it was impossible to take all and give nothing. It showed also a more obvious and more important change in the commerce of the two countries; to wit, the decline of the Portuguese trade in sugar, and the rise of her trade in wines. In other words, during the forty years from 1661 onwards, Portugal gradually ceases to rely on the produce of her colonies as the main support of her commerce; and reverts to her own home productions, where she had comparatively little to fear from rivalry.

Within a year after the Restoration, English trade with Portugal, despite the strong assertions as to its value, was said to be in so depressed a condition that the English factors at Lisbon were compelled to adventure their whole capital to enable it to continue

[1] For a full account of the English occupation of Tangier, see Miss E. Routh, "The English Occupation of Tangier." *Transactions of the Roy. Hist. Soc.*, New Series, XIX. 1905.

at all[1]. In this statement there was probably some exaggeration. But the exceeding poverty of Portugal must have been injurious to trade, which was, moreover, depressed by the wars in which Europe was, at this time, involved. These wars must have particularly affected the carrying trade, which was so largely in English hands that, according to Maynard, if the Dutch right to search vessels trading to the Portuguese dependencies was abolished, England would soon monopolise all the Portuguese "navigation[2]." English ships, too, absorbed a large part of the Mediterranean trade; and when in 1661-62 a six months' truce with Algiers gave that pirate state the right to search English ships for non-English goods, the compact aroused energetic protests from the English merchants and shipowners in Lisbon[3].

In addition to the carrying trade, the English commerce in various sorts of woollen goods and in provisions continued. The latter was the more prosperous, because no duties were levied in Portugal on the import of corn, cheese, and butter[4]. Arms and ammunition, in which some trade was done, were also exempt. All other goods paid 10 per cent. "decima," and 10 per cent. "ciza" at Lisbon[5]. The Newfoundland fish trade, chiefly carried on through the western ports of England, was flourishing. The commerce of Bristol, with both Portugal and Spain, was chiefly in fish, in exchange for which the merchants of that port brought back wine, oil, and fruit to so large an extent that in 1667 the duties on these goods amounted to £40,000[6]. The wine trade of Portugal was again increasing in importance. The government of the Commonwealth had invested frequently in Portuguese and Madeira "beverage"

[1] *Petition of Merchants*, 2nd September 1661. *For. St. P. Portugal*, Bundle 5.

[2] *For. St. P. Portugal*, 5.

[3] Ibid.

[4] *Os Privilegios.*

[5] Ibid.

[6] Latimer's *Bristol*, 345.

wines, which were held to be a cheap variety. Besides this, figs and other fruit and oil came as usual from Oporto, Aveiro, and other coast towns. But the trade in these commodities may have been hindered by the 10 per cent. tax on their exportation, which the English merchants complained had been levied in defiance of the secret Articles in 1654[1]. The bulk of the returns, however, seem to have come through Lisbon, and to have been made in sugar. The Brazil Company (1661) protested that sugar was the only staple commodity which the Portuguese possessed wherewith to make returns, and the jealousy lest any English ship should trade direct from Brazil to England was extreme. In 1661 four English ships from Brazil actually did unload in London. A furious outcry was at once raised. The English merchants in Lisbon protested that, if this was permitted, no Portuguese trader would lade his goods on an English ship. As a matter of fact, the discharge of the ships appeared to have taken place at the instance of the Portuguese king's agent in England, and the aggrieved party was rather the Brazil Company than the Portuguese government; but the protest clearly showed the Portuguese view of the importance of their sugar trade. They maintained that if the sugar was brought straight to England, Portugal could make no direct returns to that country, and would be compelled to carry on her trade through Italy or Holland[2]. Even with the assistance of the sugar trade, the imports to England from Portugal were very far from balancing the exports, as appears from a customs account of 1662-63, in which the exports from England to Portugal amount to £145,061, as against £86,691 worth of imports. Five years later the imports were lower still, only amounting to £67,692, against £167,178 worth of exports[3]. Of this last quantity

[1] *For. St. P. Portugal*, 4. [2] Ibid. 5.
[3] *Board of Trade Com. MSS. Customs*, Series I. E. 31.

of imports, if a pamphlet written some years later may be trusted, somewhat over half was sent in white sugars[1].

From the English standpoint, such a trade was exceedingly profitable. The exports to Portugal were said to have trebled in the thirty years previous to 1670, though in their woollen trade the English were beginning to be hampered by the French competition[2]. The Anglo-Dutch Treaty of 1674, in which the principle that "free ships make free goods" was asserted, released the English shipping trade from one great danger.

But to the Portuguese the trade was by no means so satisfactory from the point of view of the time, which regarded imports as impoverishing, and exports as enriching. The poverty of Portugal was, indeed, extreme enough to justify the anxiety of her statesmen; nor was her commerce improved by the energy which the Inquisition showed in persecuting her most active traders—the Jews. The Inquisition, Maynard declared, would drive away what little trade and navigation the Portuguese had left.

The exceedingly bad state of the Portuguese currency added to the evil. Continual clipping of the money had so injured it that pieces of eight, which were among the coins most in use, were worth barely half their nominal value. In 1686, the Portuguese government resolved on a reform in the coinage, and recalled the pieces of eight, offering two-thirds their value in exchange, to the great dismay of the merchants; nor were they conciliated by being compelled to exchange the coins thus called in for royal notes, which, it was ordered, should pass current. "Few trust the king, and none dare take

[1] 816 m. $\frac{13}{166}$. Case of the English Sugar Refiners.

[2] Anderson, *Historical and Chronological Deduction of the Origin of Commerce*, II. 494 (Combe's edition).

his money," wrote Scarburgh in 1686-87—a striking testimony to the poverty of Portugal[1].

Other measures adopted by the Portuguese government were likewise ineffectual. Their very exclusive policy, in respect of the Brazil sugar trade, was said to have done much to stimulate the English production of sugar in the Barbadoes. This had developed to a considerable extent under the Commonwealth; but, according to a pamphlet probably issued in the late seventeenth century, Brazil had an advantage over these islands, in the use of water-power to drive the sugar-mills, while no such force was available in the Barbadoes. Moreover, the Brazilians excelled in the production of fine sugars, a point wherein the English planters could not rival them[2]. However, as early as 1661, the English sugar trade was sufficiently developed to make it possible for merchants to smuggle Brazil sugar into England on the pretence that it came from Barbadoes. By 1670, the plantation-grown sugars were said to have beaten the Portuguese muscovados and panel sugars (*i.e.* the inferior unpurified commodity) out of England, and to be reducing the price throughout Europe. The result was that only about 705 tons of white sugar, worth £39,480, were said to be imported from Portugal in 1669, whereas it was roundly asserted that, previous to the rise of the English plantations, the import of Portuguese sugar had been worth ten times as much[3]. Such a statement may well have been exaggerated. Still, English competition must have considerably affected Portuguese trade[4].

[1] *For. St. P. Portugal*, 16.

[2] A somewhat curious contrast to the period sixty years or so before, when England had competed with the Dutch in refining the raw Portuguese and Spanish sugars.

[3] The State of the Case of the Sugar Plantations in America, B.M., 816 m. $\frac{13}{156}$.

[4] In 1670 the English government had imposed taxation on sugar in favour of the English colonies (*Dom. St. P. Cal.*, 541); but this policy

In spite of this discouragement, however, as late or later than 1690, about 2,000 chests of the *best* Brazil sugar, costing from £3 to £3, 10s. per cwt., were said to be annually sold in England.

Nor was the Anglo-Portuguese trade in sugars confined to sugar brought to England; about one-fourth of the whole amount purchased by the English from Portugal was said to be re-exported by them through the Straits and elsewhere[1]. Altogether, the trade was of sufficient value to provoke considerable jealousy among the English sugar refiners, on whose behalf it was suggested that none but muscovado sugar should be imported; while the English sugar growers also demanded protection, on account of the great cheapness of production of Brazil sugar. A tax was proposed, ranging from a farthing per lb. on muscovados, to three halfpence per lb. on Brazil sugars; and, when the Portuguese merchants objected, the smallness of their sugar trade was brought forward to show that their interests could not be very greatly affected[2]. The traders to Portugal, however, had some reason to object to anything that was likely further to injure their trade. The Dutch practically monopolised the salt trade. The French were proving rivals, and, according to the English account, favoured rivals in the general trade with Portugal. In 1683, Maynard complained loudly on this subject, maintaining that,

was not steadily pursued. In 1685 a tax of 2s. 4d. per cwt. was levied on muscovados, and 7s. on refined sugar. A glut of plantation sugar arose from the working of the Navigation Act, which compelled all colonial sugar to be sold in England, thereby lowering the price from £5 or £6 the cwt. to 45s. On the other hand, a Portuguese tax of 25 per cent. on refined sugars was thought to be some protection to the English produce. (Case of His Majesty's Sugar Plantations, B.M., 816 m. $\frac{13}{137}$, and Case of the Sugar Refiners, B.M., 816 m. $\frac{13}{166}$).

[1] Case of the Sugar Plantations in America, B.M., 816 m. $\frac{13}{156}$.

[2] Case of the Sugar Refiners, B.M., 816 m. $\frac{13}{166}$.

as a matter of fact, the English trade was far more profitable to Portuguese than the French. The English send necessaries like cloth, stuffs, bays, worsted stockings, and fish to Portugal, and took Portuguese produce, such as salt, wine, oranges, lemons, oils, and "wonderful quantities of suggers" in exchange. The French brought only "superfluous" goods, such as silks, cloth of gold, periwigs, etc., and took but little Portuguese produce in exchange. Yet the Portuguese showed far more amity to them than to the English. Maynard was very indignant[1].

In fact, the excessive privileges of the English joined with the mercantile beliefs of the time to prejudice the Portuguese against the foreign trader. Scarburgh, the English envoy, wrote in 1688 that "they look upon our merchants as the only men who will ruin Portugal[2]." An unlucky event in 1682-84 at once served to deepen the Portuguese hostility to England, and to show the difficulties under which trade laboured. A considerable number of English merchants and factors in Portugal were arrested on the charge of exporting bullion to England. The bullion was found on board two English ships, and the confessions of some of the merchants showed the truth of the accusation; but the arrests had been arbitrary, and without reference to the Conservador, and the offence, according to Maynard, was common — which, indeed, seems probable. Hence, the action of the Portuguese government evoked numerous protests from England, and, eventually, the English prisoners were released, and their goods, with the exception, of course, of the bullion in question, restored. From Maynard's letters, it is, however, apparent that the members of the English factory at Lisbon made a practice

[1] Maynard, July $\frac{20}{30}$, 1683. *For. St. P. Portugal*, 15.

[2] *For. St. P. Portugal*, 16.

of smuggling out bullion, whenever they found an opportunity. He declared that other nations, particularly the French, pursued the same custom to an even greater extent. But the English appear to have been considered the chief offenders; and the Portuguese government, or at any rate the Portuguese officials, seem to have regarded with sullen dislike the privileged strangers, who were thus draining away the sorely-needed wealth of the country[1].

The English Revolution added political dislike to economic jealousy: the Portuguese had had a strong leaning towards the Stuarts, and, as a nation of Catholics, they could not but feel some indignation at this Protestant victory[2].

This feeling of hostility lent unpleasant significance to the Acts by which the Portuguese government tried to revive its vanished industries. In 1677 a Pragmatic had been issued, prohibiting the Portuguese from wearing any foreign-made cloth, belts, hats, etc.[3]. This, however, did not affect the bulk of the English woollen trade, which consisted mainly in the new draperies, bayes, sayes, and so forth, rather than in cloth technically so called. The demand for these goods, indeed, continued in such force that the English wool trade increased by more than one-half between 1668 and 1697; but the English were not satisfied, complaining that the increase would have been even more marked, save for the recently founded wool manufactures in France, Holland, Portugal, and elsewhere[4].

In fact, the Portuguese did make considerable efforts to supply themselves. In 1682 Englishmen

[1] *For. St. P. Portugal*, 15. Maynard's Letters, 7th and 20th January, etc., 1682-83. Fanshawe's *Letters*, 16th and 30th March, etc., 1683.

[2] For evidence of Portuguese Jacobite sympathy, see Santarem, *Quadro Elementar, etc.*, XVIII. 183-84.

[3] *Collecção de legislação antiga e moderna do reino de Portugal.*

[4] *Board of Trade Com. MS. Trade Report*, Series II. Vol. DCXLII.

from Colchester and other places were brought to Portugal to give instruction in the art of making bayes and other favourite draperies[1]. Maynard seems to have dreaded greatly lest these fabrics also should be included in the prohibition of foreign goods. In 1686 English sole leather was prohibited, and, in 1688, all foreign druggets[2]. The same spirit is visible in the Portuguese dependencies. Madeira declined English goods in exchange for its wines, preferring to obtain such commodities as were wanted from Lisbon. The English protested vehemently against these prohibitions, but in vain. The Portuguese government conceived it had granted quite enough favours to its aggressive ally. The Portuguese ambassador in England was instructed, if the point was raised, to reply by asking what Portugal would gain by revoking these prohibitions.

These restrictions, however, do not appear to have lessened the Anglo-Portuguese trade. Bayes, perpetuanos, black cloth, stockings, and rugs were sent to Portugal[3]. Between 1662 and 1699-1700 the imports from Portugal were almost doubled, and the exports thither had increased nearly one and a half times[4]. There was a slight decline during the two following years, but the average increase was so great as to make the lamentations of the traders seem ludicrous; yet there can be no doubt of the alarm occasioned by the Portuguese attitude.

Whilst the commercial relations of the two countries had thus reached a stage at which some concession appeared to be demanded from England, the political situation also rendered it desirable that she should propitiate Portugal. The long threatened rupture with France had become an accomplished fact soon after the accession of William III. From

[1] *For. St. P. Portugal*, No. 15.
[2] *Collecção, etc., Leis Extravagantes, etc.*, II. 197.
[3] *Board of Trade Com. MS.*, Series I. Vol. XXVII. T. 103, 1729.
[4] *Board of Trade Com. Trade Report*, Series II. Vol. DCXLIII.

1692 to 1698 the English sought every occasion to draw Portugal into the struggle against Louis XIV.[1], and thereby to deprive France of its most convenient market. This attempt, however, was unsuccessful. Portugal showed a definite preference for neutrality[2]; and this attitude she still maintained, when in 1700-1 the near probability of a union of France and Spain rendered the Portuguese alliance of the utmost value to all who dreaded the House of Bourbon.

The same events, however, which enhanced the importance to England of the political alliance of Portugal, served to indicate more emphatically the method by which the commercial connection between the two countries might be strengthened. Colonial produce, first spices, then sugar, had for more than a hundred years superseded the native commodities of Portugal as the principal articles of her commerce; but, as has been shown, a certain trade in wine had long existed.

Portuguese wines had, however, never rivalled those of France. Spanish wines, first coming into general popularity at the beginning of the seventeenth century, maintained a high place, but the taste for the produce of Portugal remained, comparatively speaking, in abeyance. The freight on Portuguese wines was higher than that on French. In addition to this disadvantage, the tax levied on them was almost prohibitive. Whenever England and France were at war, however, the consumption of Portuguese wines in England increased to an extraordinary degree. From 1675 to 1678 (inclusive) the consumption of French wines averaged over 8,500 tuns, and that of Portugal about 120 tuns. Then came the first threat of war with France; the consumption of French wine instantly sank to almost nothing, while from 1679 to 1685 the average consumption

[1] Letters of John Methuen, 1692-98. *For. St. P. Portugal*, No. 17.
[2] Instructions to Port Ambassador, 1697. Santarem, *Quadro Elementar, etc.*, XVIII. 190-202.

of Portuguese wines seems to have been 7,000 tuns. It sank for the five years from 1685 to 1690, although remaining considerably above its old level. Then it sprang up again in 1690 (the year after war commenced), and continued at an average of about 6,000 tons through the ensuing ten years[1].

The result was a better balance of trade. In 1699-1700 the English exports to Portugal were worth £336,598, about double what they had been thirty years previously; but the imports from Portugal were worth £279,156, or more than quadruple what they had been in 1668-69[2]. In other words, the imports from Portugal at the latter date were somewhat above three-fourths of the exports to that country, instead of being little more than one-third, as in 1668-69; and though this high proportion was not maintained, yet, in the four years, 1699-1703, the imports to England from Portugal averaged one-half of the exports to that country[3].

This result sprang almost entirely from the increasing import of Portuguese wines consequent on the war which made it impossible to procure those of France; nor was this the only advantage which the Portuguese drew from the tremendous struggle which, towards the close of the seventeenth century, involved almost every European country except herself. As the one neutral, she attracted trade from all other countries, and Lisbon momentarily regained a shadow of its old position as a world mart. As early as 1693 the English envoy, John Methuen, wrote of the probability of Portugal's "trading for all the other nations." The Portuguese "goe really great shares in all sorts of trade . . . which is quite new and never known before[4]." English

[1] *Egerton MSS.* 921, p. 49.
[2] *Board of Trade Com. MSS. Customs Account*, Series I. F. 62.
[3] *Board of Trade Com. MSS.*, Series I. F. 62.
[4] *For. St. P. Portugal*, XVII. John Methuen, $\frac{25}{15}$ July 1693.

politicians frowned on this revival, as confirming Portugal in that attitude of neutrality, which they disliked; but English economists saw in the rising Portuguese wine trade a possible means of compensation for the lost commerce with France, and were eager to point out its advantages. The wines of France had to be bought with money; those of Portugal might be exchanged for goods, and should this market be open to the English, it might serve to check the recently established Portuguese cloth manufacture, and English might again send cloth to Portugal, as she now sent bays, and serges, and other worsted goods. The cloth trade, strictly so called, had indeed almost disappeared from Portugal at the end of the seventeenth century; only a few hundred pieces were sent between 1698 and 1702[1]. Many merchants, however, thought that the removal of the restrictions which had stifled the trade might be secured by diplomacy. Certain prominent English traders in Lisbon wrote in 1697 that they believed this could be done, if a strong complaint was made of the treatment of the English themselves, who were forbidden to wear their own cloth, and fined for so doing. "Ye Portuguese gentlemen," they declared, "will never bear to see us wearing fine cloth, and they be denied it." Therefore, if redress on this point was stoutly demanded, the Portuguese government might admit English cloth freely again rather than grant a fresh privilege to the English residents in Portugal[2].

The argument was a curious one; but the event showed that the prohibition of cloth was not irrevocable, and the desire for its repeal, coupled with the wish to guard against any further restrictions,

[1] The general wool trade, however, continued to flourish; 15,937 double bays were exported to Portugal in 1701-2, as well as perpetuanos, serges, and stuffs; and numerous hats were sent (probably smuggled) despite the prohibition (*Egerton MSS.*, 921, pp. 47 *et seq.*).

[2] *Board of Trade Com. MSS.*, Series I. B. 55.

formed the economic justification for the Methuen Treaty. The political justification was obvious enough. Portugal was wavering between France and the allies. In 1701 she had guaranteed the family compact[1], and the change which forty years had wrought in her relations with England appeared in the conditions of the agreement by which Spain promised to uphold Portugal in the struggle about the Bombay dependencies which was still continuing. As a result of this agreement, war between England and Portugal was thought to be so near, that many English families left Portugal, and more were preparing to withdraw[2]. But England was not disposed to let her old ally slip away from her. She perceived the necessity of outbidding the Spaniard, and cast about for some attraction sufficiently potent to win Portugal from her alliance with the House of Bourbon; but for some time no conclusion was arrived at. There were numerous small additional causes of friction between England and Portugal. The debts created by Rupert's aggressions remained unsettled. In 1701 Rooke went to Lisbon to enforce the payment of debts incurred in Cromwell's time, causing great panic. Portugal, in 1702, actually made a treaty with France and Spain, which, however, she assured England was only intended to keep Philip V. on the Spanish throne[3]. Much anxiety was excited in England, and the rumour that the Portuguese harbours were to be closed to the English and Dutch caused considerable dismay. The English threatened the Portuguese coast[4]; but open war averted, and the necessities of the time drove the English to make offers, which bore, at least, the appearance of reciprocity. In 1702, therefore, Paul Methuen, the English

[1] Koch and Schoell, *Histoire Abrégée des Traités de Paix*, II. 19.
[2] *For. St. P. Portugal*, No 18. Methuen's *Letter*.
[3] Santarem, *Quadro Elementar, etc.*, XVIII. 208, 211, etc.
[4] Luttrell, N., *A Brief Historical Relation of State Affairs*, V. 179-99.

envoy, who in the previous year had almost despaired of winning Portugal to the English alliance, was again sent to Lisbon to arrange some compromise with the government. For some time the negotiations hung fire, but eventually two treaties, one largely political, the other strictly commercial, were concluded.

The first was in the main a defensive alliance between England, Holland, and Portugal; but it contained two Articles of economic and colonial interest. Article 15 stipulated for freedom of trade between Great Britain and Portugal, and mutual commercial privileges in both countries. By Article 16, any breach of the Bombay Treaty was to be settled in. "the spirit of the treaty."

The second, the famous Methuen Treaty, was concluded on 6th May 1703. This compact has been described as a bribe to Portugal[1], but though, politically speaking, there is considerable justification for that view, yet economically it was a bribe of considerable benefit to the offerer. It had the double advantage of improving English commerce, and inflicting a considerable blow on France. Pithy and brief to a degree unprecedented among treaties, it declared that English woollen goods should be freely admitted to Portugal on condition that port wines should be brought into England at a duty one-third less than that imposed on French wines[2]. The acceptance of these conditions was carried *nem. con.* by the English House of Commons; and the Portuguese gave practical effect to them in the following year by a decree allowing the use of English cloth or any other English woollen manufacture[3].

[1] Hewins, W. A. S., *English Trade and Finance*, 129.

[2] Chalmers' *Collection of Treaties*, II. 305. The treaty was signed by John Methuen; the negotiations appear to have been carried on both by him and by his son.

[3] *Collecção, etc., Leis Extravagantes*, II. 344.

The result of the treaty, apart from its political bearing, appears in the account of the wine and wool trade for the ensuing two years. During the twenty-one years, from 1675 to 1696, the amount of Portuguese wine consumed had about equalled that of the wines of French growth, and been considerably less than the total of that imported from Spain. From 1696 to 1712 ten times as much Portuguese as French wine was imported; and the excess of Portuguese over Spanish wines was about a third[1]. The contrast is remarkable, remembering that if almost the whole of the second period was a time of war, so was about one-third of the first. On the other hand, the export of cloth to Portugal was said to have quadrupled subsequently to the treaty[2], and the coloured cloths, duroys, cloth druggets, stuffs, hats, etc., formerly excluded, were now admitted[3].

Certainly the whole volume of exports to Portugal greatly increased. For the three years ending 1702 they varied from about £250,000 to about £450,000. The imports averaged over £200,000[4]. In 1709-10 the imports appear to have been worth only £192,113; but the exports had leaped up to £614,635. Five years later, the imports had increased considerably to £333,385, and the exports slightly to £625,381[5].

The increase of exports, however, continued in subsequent years in a much more marked manner than that of the imports, reaching eventually something over £1,000,000, while the maximum of the imports was little more than £400,000[6].

The whole of the increase could by no means be attributed to the Methuen Treaty; much was due to the great development of the Brazil trade which

[1] *Egerton MSS.*, p. 921, p. 49.
[2] Anderson, *Historical Deductions, etc.*, III. 19-20.
[3] *Board of Trade Com. MSS.*, Series I. Vol. XXVII. T. 103.
[4] Ibid. Series I. F. 62.
[5] Anderson, *Historical Deductions, etc.*, IV. 34-43.
[6] Ibid.

marked the early years of the eighteenth century. But the treaty probably gave a considerable impulse to Anglo-Portuguese commerce; and the so-called bribe continued to be lauded as a great stroke of economic policy during the major part of the eighteenth century.

CHAPTER V

THE ENGLISH FACTORIES IN PORTUGAL AND THE BRAZIL TRADE

(1660-1756)

Establishment of the English factories by the Treaty of 1654—Hostility of the Portuguese officials — Question of the English Conservador—The Religious Question—Powers of the English consul — Internal difficulties of the factories—Their constitution—Relations of the consuls of Lisbon, Oporto, and Madeira — The duties of the factories—Their superintendence of general trade—The development of trade — Exports to Portugal — Cloth, provisions—Colonial trade—The Newfoundland fish trade—Its difficulties—Returns from Portugal — The Brazil trade—English privileges—Discovery of the Brazil gold mines—Portuguese jealousy—Rivalry of Dutch, English, and French—Export of bullion—The slave trade — Its connection with Brazil — Rising trade in wine—Oporto factory concerned in export of wine — Difficulties of English trade — Complaints — Growing irritation in Portugal against the English factories.

THE Treaty of 1654, as has been said, marked the increasing importance of the English settlements or factories in Portugal; and, during the remaining part of the seventeenth century, these settlements continued to develop and expand. Not only in Lisbon, but at Oporto, and, as time went on, at Aveiro, Viana, and other coast towns did the English merchants and agents become an important part of the commercial population. Their opportunities were all the greater, as their chief rivals were the Portuguese Jews, who, being subject to the fearful power of the Inquisition, competed on very unequal terms with the privileged English.

These very privileges, however, to some extent hampered the latter by the jealousy which they excited among the Portuguese. Such a case, for example, as that in 1661 when the English alone were exempted from an immensely heavy poll-tax[1], was calculated to stimulate the hostility of all who were suffering under this burden; and a similar effect was perhaps produced by the secret decree of 1656[2], exempting the English from paying "decima" on stock, and from being forced to keep stock. Thus the general feeling in Portugal appears to have been that England had taken unfair advantage of her strength to wring concessions from her ally; and, from the highest official to the lowest, this feeling probably stimulated continual exactions until, in 1682, Fanshaw declared that a fresh treaty was becoming necessary, since the English were forced to spend half their time and money in lawsuits[3].

Religious fervour, too, played its part in fanning the national hostility. It was alleged to be a common practice to discredit English testimony in the law courts on the ground that the oath of a heretic was not to be trusted[4], and the Inquisition was ever the most determined opponent of the English alliance.

This hatred of the English, however, appears to have been the feeling rather of the populace at large, and of the members of the Portuguese civil service, than of the king or the central government of Portugal. To the king the English generally looked for redress, and occasionally obtained it, since from

[1] *For. St. P. Portugal*, 5.
[2] *Os Privilegios, etc.*
[3] *For. St. P. Portugal*, 17.
[4] The king on one occasion severely punished an advocate who used this argument.

his point of view they were the representatives not of a commercial rival, but of a political ally.

That the English privileges were maintained in all their integrity during the second part of the seventeenth century was perhaps due in part to the character of Consul Maynard, who filled the office of consul-general from 1658, or a little earlier, till the Revolution. He seems to have been a man of strong will, and peremptory temper; qualities ill-adapted to make matters run smoothly between the two nations, but calculated, on the other hand, to maintain every point of the English privileges. The two cardinal articles of Maynard's faith appear to have been a hatred of "popery," and devotion to the Treaty of 1654; beliefs which peculiarly fitted him for the struggle he had to maintain.

Of the various privileges granted to the English, the most important, perhaps, was that of being judged only by their own Conservadors. But during the first years of Charles II.'s reign, the English frequently complained that they were forced to sue in other courts than those of their own judges, and that imprisonment or seizure of goods took place without the Conservador's warrant. In 1665 a petition of the English in Portugal was answered by an "alvara," declaring that, save in matters touching the Exchequer, the English need only plead in the court of their Conservador. In 1667 another decree was issued (avowedly because the English privileges were infringed), that neither imprisonment nor execution of goods should take place without the Conservador's warrant. Despite these orders, however, the authority of the Conservador was by no means always admitted, nor was his action always pleasing to the English who desired that his appointment might rest in their hands[1], instead of in those of the "Desembargador de Supplicação." In 1700 a petition was presented by the English at Lisbon,

[1] Maynard, *For. St. P. Portugal*, 15, 1660.

and supported by Paul Methuen, the English envoy, for the removal of the Conservador, Lopez de Oliviera. He was accused not only of specific acts of injustice, but of denying the existence of their privileges, on the ground that by treaty they were to be on the same footing as the native Portuguese. The charges were denied by the Portuguese ambassador, who further maintained that the Conservador had been appointed in 1680 at the express wish of the English merchants, and could not be removed except for malversation, which was not charged against him[1].

Throughout the eighteenth century the question of the Conservador's jurisdiction remained as a point of difficulty. From Oporto and Braga, in particular, complaints were frequent. There was a disposition on the part of the Portuguese to extend the definition of matters concerning the king's revenue, so as to cover as many cases as possible. Points affected by the great sumptuary ordinance of 1749, for instance, were outside the jurisdiction of the Conservador. The right of appeal to the "Relação" also tended to diminish the Conservador's powers, so that, in 1756, the English merchants declared that debtors were in the habit of playing off one court against the other[2]. But with all its drawbacks the English continued to cling to this privilege as their greatest safeguard.

Another difficulty which beset the English factories was the religious question. By the Articles of 1654 and 1661 the English in Portugal were allowed freedom of conscience, and freedom of worship in their own houses. As far as Lisbon was concerned, whenever there was an English envoy resident in the city, the English met for worship in his house. This privilege was never interfered with, but when, in the absence of such an official, the consul claimed the

[1] *For. St. P. Portugal*, Nos. 16 and 17. *Petition of English Merchants*, and Paul Methuen's *Letters*.

[2] *Board of Trade Com. MS.*, Series I. No. 15, Vol. XLV.

same right, it was strongly disputed; much to the disgust of Maynard, who declared that as English trade depended on the regular living of English merchants, the maintenance of religion was essential to the well-being of commerce[1]. With this view he upheld the English privileges steadily. In 1683 he could boast that a chaplain had ministered in his—the consul's not the envoy's—house for twenty-two years. Possibly, the Catholic bias displayed about this time by the English government may have encouraged the Portuguese officials in their aggressive policy. At any rate, despite Maynard's protests, the English preacher at Lisbon was silenced until the arrival of the envoy, Scarburgh, in 1686[2], at whose house the English were at length permitted to attend service till his retirement in 1690[3].

In Oporto the difficulties were still greater. The factory in this town appears to have first risen into prominence towards the end of the seventeenth century, possibly in connection with the increasing wine trade. The merchants here had no such traditions of privileges and immunities as belonged to those in Lisbon, nor had they the advantage of the presence of the English ambassador. Hence it was to be expected that, when in 1682-83 there was an outburst of energy on the part of the Inquisition, the heaviest blow should fall on the Oporto factory. Their minister was not only silenced, but forced to leave the country[4], and the remonstrances of the factory were met by the reply that the king himself could not control the Inquisition[5]. In vain Maynard protested that preaching had been allowed for years at Oporto; in vain another minister was despatched to Oporto. The Portuguese maintained that freedom

[1] *For. St. P. Portugal*, 16. Maynard, November 1686.
[2] Ibid. 19, 11th March 1686-87.
[3] *For. St. P. Portugal*, 16.
[4] Ibid. 15. Maynard, 17th December 1682.
[5] Ibid. Fanshawe, 29th December 1682.

of worship did not include the services of a minister of religion. They even professed to disbelieve that Protestants considered such services as in any way essential[1]. The government was helpless, the Inquisition obdurate, and the dispute lasted into the eighteenth century[2]. By 1718, however, public worship was again established, and from that time onwards the services were held at each house in the factory in rotation[3].

Attacks and encroachments from the Portuguese were not the only perplexities that the English settlements had to face at this time. The questions of the position of the consul at Lisbon, of his power over the factory at Lisbon, and of his relations with the factories in other parts of the Portuguese dominions, also raised considerable difficulties.

The factory had become a tolerably definite body, with definite functions, such as the supervision of the affairs of deceased members, the relief of distressed fellow-countrymen—especially of shipwrecked seamen—the maintenance of English privileges, the support, as we have seen, of religious observances. The consul-general at Lisbon, who was practically the executive officer of the Lisbon factory, had, by patent, the right to levy "consulage" for the general purposes of the factory, to raise another small impost for the distress fund, and to appoint deputy-consuls for Oporto, Madeira, and other commercial centres. It was his duty, too, to summon the factory, and to arrange for the election of other officers, such as the treasurer of the distress fund[4]. Finally, he was the representative of the factory in its relations with the Portuguese government—a position in which it was difficult to avoid offending his own countrymen. Thus, about 1665 the merchants brought forward as

[1] *For. St. P. Portugal*, 15. Maynard, 1683.
[2] *Board of Trade Com. MS.*, Series I. Vol. XV. N. 50.
[3] Ibid. Series II. Vol. DLXIII. N. 2.
[4] *For. St. P. Portugal*, 4. Maynard's patent.

a complaint against Maynard that he had informed the Portuguese government of frauds committed by members of the factory upon the revenue[1]; and when, in 1682-83, various English merchants were imprisoned for illegal transport of bullion, the discovery that the informer was the Lisbon vice-consul was followed by his immediate dismissal.

Apart from complications with the Portuguese government, the internal life of the factories themselves was by no means always peaceful. The political and religious struggles in England were reflected, albeit faintly, in these settlements. In 1638-40 one Thomas Kendall refused to pay consulage on the ground that it was a tax imposed by the king, without the consent of those on whom it was levied. On Charles II.'s restoration, petitions were presented against Maynard as an opponent of the Royalists—an accusation he indignantly denied; and his final dismissal, in 1689, appears to have been partly due to a charge of Jacobitism, preferred by one of the members of the factory[2].

The constitution of the factories themselves also presented difficulties. Its weakness lay in the fact that the consul had no means of enforcing either his own authority, or that of the majority of the merchants themselves. Thus, when in 1715 a merchant chosen as treasurer by the majority of the factory declined to act, thereby hindering the collection of "consulage," and running the factory deeply into debt, the only penalty that could be inflicted on him was the withdrawal of the factory's protection[3].

The question of "consulage" exhibited the same difficulty. Maynard declared that, on the understanding that he was to pay £50 a year to a chaplain,

[1] *For. St. P. Portugal*, 16 (paper undated).

[2] Ibid.

[3] *Board of Trade Com. MS.*, Series I. Vol. XVII. O. 19.; Series II. Vol. DCL. 277-301.

the merchants had unanimously granted to him double the consulage previously raised[1]. This amounted to one-half per cent. on all British goods imported, raised on their valuation at the Portuguese Custom House, and four crowns on every English ship coming into harbour. It seems to have been inadequate, for Maynard petitioned for the right to exact consulage on goods, like beef or corn, which were untaxed by Portugal. By Consul Milner's Patent (1703-11) the levy of consulage was further organised. Twelve milreis were laid on every English ship bringing English goods, save on such as brought necessaries, and took back fruit and salt; these only paid 9 milreis. Out of this sum, 3 milreis on every ship went to the vice-consul, and the consul had to pay 300 milreis a year to the chaplain. In addition, 4 milreis were levied for charitable purposes on all goods belonging to English merchants in the Lisbon Custom House; and also on corn, butter, etc., which paid no dues to Portugal[2].

But the consulage and charitable dues, however levied, were by no means always easy to obtain. At one time nearly the whole factory at Lisbon declined to pay[3]. This refusal was only temporary; but there were frequently a few recalcitrant members of the factory who declined to take their share of the common burdens. Among the British inhabitants of Lisbon the Irish Roman Catholics, of whom there were several, refused to contribute, resisting especially the payment of money for charitable purposes, and remained obdurate on this point till well into the eighteenth century. An attempt to exact the "consulage" by process of law resulted in an appeal

[1] August $\frac{10}{20}$ 1661. *For. St. P. Portugal*, 5.

[2] *Board of Trade Com. MS.*, Series I. M. 13, No. 58. See Appendix II, 4.

[3] *For. St. P. Portugal*, 16. Maynard's *Petition*.

by the Irish from the Conservador's court to the superior jurisdiction of the Relação[1], thereby bringing English disputes under Portuguese cognisance. The consul at this time, John Milner, desired that the English government should obtain permission from the administration of Portugal for the Conservador to imprison the unruly factors without appeal; but it is not probable that this application succeeded.

Evasion of payment was rendered easier by the method of collecting consulage. It was collected from the receivers of English goods consigned to Portugal[2], and it was a perpetual complaint of the English residents in Portugal that they thus paid a larger impost than did the Portuguese or other non-English receivers of English commodities, who contributed nothing to the English factory. In 1711 at least half the goods sent to Portugal were said to be consigned to foreign merchants, and so could be sold at a lower price than those imported by English traders[3].

The scheme most favoured for solving these various difficulties was that the impost should be paid by all English ships conveying English goods to Portugal, whether the consigners were English or not. That the money might be duly levied, each captain was to be compelled to show his bill of lading to the consul, nor was he to receive the consul's bill of clearance till he could show a receipt from the treasurer of the factory in proof that the consulage had been duly paid. From 1711 to 1720 this scheme was frequently propounded[4], and in 1722 the question was settled as far as the money for charitable purposes was concerned. An Act was passed, by which the factory was empowered to levy 200 reis per ton on all

[1] *Board of Trade Com. MS.*, Series I. Vol. XIX. P. 72.
[2] Ibid. Series II., Vol. DCLI. 480-82.
[3] Ibid. Series I. M. 14, No. 12.
[4] Ibid. Series II., Vol. DCLVI. 186 *et seq.* Series I. Vol. XIX. B. 72, and Vol. XXI. O. 46 and 47.

tonnage goods (save grain and timber which paid 100 reis) and 15 per cent. on all other goods. The said sums were to be raised on goods brought in British ships from British dominions, and the proceeds were to be applied not only to charitable purposes, but to the payment of the chaplain of the factory at Lisbon[1].

A difficulty, which for the time loomed even greater than that of the consulage, was the question of the relations of the various factories to each other. The patent of the consul at Lisbon made him consul-general of all the English in Portugal, with power to appoint deputy-consuls at Oporto and elsewhere. These deputy-consuls usually managed the affairs of the different factories, but in times of exceptional difficulty, when they were forced to approach the Portuguese government, recourse to the consulate at Lisbon was generally necessary. This system, however, was not established without some resistance on the part of the subordinate factories. At Oporto, for instance, a serious revolt against the power of the consul-general arose out of the religious difficulty[2].

The question of the expulsion of the English chaplain already alluded to, was, according to Maynard, much complicated by the recent conversion of the Vice-Consul Murcott to Catholicism. Maynard therefore wished that Murcott should be dismissed, but the consul-general's commands were vigorously resisted by the factory on the plea that, since the vice-consul was paid by a share of the "consulage" levied at Oporto, the members of the factory who paid the tax had a right to a voice in the appoint-

[1] Geo. I. 8, cap. 17.

[2] *For. St. P. Portugal*, 15. Maynard's *Letters*, $\frac{6}{16}$ February, 6th March 1682-83, April $\frac{2}{12}$, 1683, August $\frac{6}{16}$, 1683. *For. St. P. Portugal*, 16, 21st January 1684, July $\frac{15}{25}$, 1684, etc.

ment of the vice-consul. If Maynard made the appointment without consulting them, Maynard might pay the salary. Maynard pointed out that his own income was only 850 milreis, of which he had to pay 100 to the minister at Lisbon; that Murcott's salary was 50 milreis, and, therefore, if each of the sixteen vice-consuls made the same demand, he should be left penniless[1].

This controversy, which had no definite result, may possibly have been ended by the death or withdrawal of Murcott. At any rate, the succeeding deputy-consuls continued to be appointed by the consul at Lisbon, and paid by the merchants at Oporto.

In the case of Madeira, the consulship was actually separated from that of Lisbon for some years before 1708. The commercial connection of Madeira with the Portuguese capital was apparently slight[2]. It was asserted that only one or two ships went thence annually to Lisbon. The trade between England and Madeira may be estimated by the fact that between 1710 and 1714, 196 ships went from England to the island; but a large part of the trade[3] done at this time by the English in Madeira was with Newfoundland, New England, and Virginia, which colonies sent fish in return for wine from the island. The English in Madeira, therefore, had comparatively little in common with the traders in Lisbon, and might reasonably desire an independent representative. Another circumstance was alternately urged for and against their independence, to wit, their exceedingly unsatisfactory relations with the Portuguese governor. Possibly, the fact that in Madeira he was beyond the influence of the central government, may have had some effect on this

[1] *For. St. P. Portugal*, 15. Maynard's *Letters*, August $\frac{6}{16}$, 1683.

[2] *Board of Trade Com. MS.*, Series I. N. 16, No. 271.

[3] Ibid. Series I. O. 17, No. 19.

functionary's conduct. At any rate, arbitrary imprisonment, arrest of goods, detention of ships, seizure of cargoes, were declared by English merchants to be matters of frequent occurrence[1]. From 1704 to 1708 Madeira had an independent consul, one Benjamin Heming, whose great achievement was that he procured the removal of an additional tax on the export of wine (400 reis per pipe) imposed by the Madeira governor[2]. He could not, however, save himself or the principal members of the factory from imprisonment[3], and, in 1708, his consulate was again merged in that of Lisbon. Petitions for the re-establishment of the independent consulate were sent up in 1715 and 1718, not only from traders in Madeira, but from their English correspondents in Bristol[4]. It was urged that an independent consul at Madeira, employing an agent at Lisbon, would be able to exact better terms from the governor of the island, than a deputy-consul who was looked on as being only a servant to another man[5]. The petitions, however, were disregarded, and the only concession recommended by the Board of Trade was that the pay of the deputy-consul should be raised from one-third to one-half of the consulage levied in the island[6]; and though by 1789 the two consulates had long been independent, the separation did not take place till after the period at present under discussion.

Despite the frequent disputes with the Portuguese officials—disputes which recur again and again with wearisome reiteration—the connection between the English and Portuguese was on the whole strengthened during the early years of the eighteenth century. While the War of the Spanish Succession hampered

1 *Board of Trade Com. MS.*, Series I. P. Vol. XIX. No. 143.
2 Ibid. Series II. Vol. DCXLIV. 36.
3 Ibid. 197.
4 Ibid. Series I. O. Vol. XVII. 2, 3, 4, 5.
5 Ibid. P. Vol. XIX. No. 143.
6 Ibid. Series II. Vol. DCXLIX. 259-62.

trade in some ways, on the other hand, it largely increased the English exports to Portugal. Arms, military accoutrements, powder, provisions, clothing for the troops, both English and Portuguese, all poured in from the richer country[1]; and the importance of the political interests, which united the two countries, caused the establishment for the first time of direct postal communication between them, by means of packet boats sailing from Falmouth to Lisbon[2].

In these various activities the English factories, of course, took their share. Previous to 1692 John Methuen declared that the English merchants had had the whole trade of Portugal in their hands; and though the two ensuing wars somewhat depressed their position, yet, all through the earlier part of the eighteenth century, their influence on Anglo-Portuguese trade was very great. The number of these merchants must have been considerable. In 1717, there were ninety merchants in the Lisbon factory only[3]. In their hands, and in those of their fellows in Oporto rested the management of trade, the protection of external traders to Portugal, the preservation of the stipulated duties on English goods, and of the privileges and exemptions of English ships.

The task grew more difficult as trade increased. In 1716, when the advice of the Portugal merchants was required by the government, their business was declared to be too complicated to be discussed by traders engaged in only one branch of commerce. Not only woollen goods, but gold lace, copper, iron, coal, lead, tin, timber, leather, arms and ammunition, are all mentioned at one time or another as exports to Portugal[4].

[1] Luttrell, N., *A Brief Historical Relation of State Affairs*, V. 507.
[2] *Cal. Treasury P.*, CLI. No. 24.
[3] *Board of Trade Com. MS.*, Series I. O. 18, No. 194.
[4] Ibid. Q. 21, No. 160.

Moreover, as time went on the Portuguese displayed a certain discontent with regard to a trade, the balance of which so decidedly dipped in favour of the English. In 1704, immediately after the Methuen Treaty, English exports to Portugal amounted to £780,664, and the imports from that country to £330,689. In 1714 after the Treaty of Utrecht, the imports sank to £281,268, while the exports rose slightly to £793,623. In the next ten years the average of the imports rose to more than £350,000. From 1714 to 1718 the English exports sank a little, it was said owing to the revival of the French trade after the Treaty of Utrecht, but in 1719 they went up suddenly to £816,367, and from this time onwards they were nearly always double, and sometimes even treble and quadruple the exports[1].

Unsatisfactory as this was to the Portuguese government, no special action was taken, save in the grant of patents to various Portuguese companies, giving them an exclusive right to deal in such English goods, as coal, leather, and pipe staves; thereby, as the English complained, narrowing the market[2]. With this exception, the factory reports are mainly concerned with the ill-behaviour of subordinate officials.

Of these reports many refer to the woollen trade. This trade was said to have increased by two-thirds in thirty years. Fifteen thousand four hundred and ninety-two pieces of woollen goods of all sorts were sent to Portugal in 1713 and 1714, and Portugal was now the most important of England's customers for cloth, except Holland and Turkey[3].

The increase of this trade was stated by Consul Poyntz to be largely due to the development of

[1] For example, in 1726, and for the greater part of the decade, 1730 to 1740 (*Board of Trade Com. MSS.*, Series II. Vol. DLXII. No. 7).

[2] *Board of Trade Com. MS.*, Series I. P. Vol. XIX. 72.

[3] Ibid. Series II. Vol. DCXLIX. 401-17.

the Brazil trade ; but a list of the Articles let in by the Methuen Treaty suggest that, but for this treaty, much of the commerce could not have openly existed at all. Coloured cloths, duroys, cloth druggets, stuffs are mentioned in a paper of 1729 as being admitted only by the Methuen Treaty[1]. English opinion, though divided, was on the whole favourable to Portugal, and recognised that the reduction of duty on Portuguese wines promised by the treaty was essential to the cloth trade with that country[2]. Further, England's inclination to show favour to Portugal was heightened by the fear of French rivalry. French competition in the lighter woollen fabrics was the dread of English cloth makers; moreover, France was ready to take Portuguese sugar, for which, as has been shown, there was little market in England. Hence the peace of 1713 was considered dangerous to Anglo-Portuguese commerce; and a subsequent decrease in the export of cloth excited some alarm[3]. For this decrease, however, there might be other reasons than French rivalry. The Dutch were also competitors with the English; and competitors, whose fabrics were more carefully and honestly manufactured. As early as 1707 the factory at Lisbon had complained of the bad workmanship of English cloth[4], and in 1715 their complaints were renewed with especial reference to the bad making of Colchester bays[5].

Nor was outside competition the only hindrance to the English woollen trade. The old complaint of the over-valuation and consequent over-taxation of English goods in the Portuguese Custom House

[1] *Board of Trade Com. MS.*, Series I. T. Vol. XXVII. 103.

[2] The increase was not only in cloth : the more favourable state of Anglo-Portuguese commerce in general appeared in the augmented export of lead, tin, and corn. (*Portugal Merchants and French Wines*, 1709.)

[3] Anderson, III. 52-3.

[4] *Board of Trade Com. MS. Report*, Series II. No. 643.

[5] Ibid. Series I. P. Vol. XIX. No. 72.

was revived. In the commercial treaty with Portugal, planned in 1713 by Bolingbroke, an Article was to be inserted, stipulating that the duties on English woollen goods were never to be raised above those levied in 1710 upon a valuation made by agreement between England and Portugal[1]. The treaty, however, never came into being, and the complaints continued. In 1715 Poyntz complained of an extra 12 per cent. duty ("variagem") on kerseys and friezes, as well as on other textiles, such as silks and Dutch and Hamburg linens; and of the extravagant valuation of crapes and durances, and other light woollens. Of the goods admitted by the Methuen treaty, duroys and cloth druggets were also said to be over-valued[2].

In 1756 petitions from Lisbon reiterated these earlier statements. A comparison of the taxation on English goods with that on the commodities of France and Germany was made, showing that the average effect of the arbitrary system of valuation was that English goods paid 19 per cent., French 11 per cent., and Hamburg 9 per cent.[3] On textiles, exported by both English and French traders, the latter paid about 1 per cent. less than the former, and it was declared that French crapes had absolutely driven out the English[4]. These excessive valuations were said to encourage the smuggling which took place, and for which the packets from Falmouth, established during the war of the Spanish Succession, offered special facilities (1715)[5]. Despite all these disadvantages, however, the trade in woollens was considered as the most profitable of all English trade with Portugal; and the continually-increasing volume of exports to that country would seem to

[1] *Board of Trade Com. MS.*, Series II. 648.
[2] Ibid. Series I. P. 19, No. 72.
[3] Ibid. Series I. Vol. XXVII. 103.
[4] Ibid. Series I. F. 16, No. 45.
[5] Ibid. P. 19, No. 72.

show that none of the drawbacks enumerated affected it seriously.

The same peculiarities might be observed in other branches of trade; in all, the merchants complained of undue taxation, and all flourished in spite of it. In Poyntz's Report of 1715 he complains of an additional 12 per cent. duty on the import of iron, lead, and tin; coals, pipe-staves, and timber paid 13 per cent. in kind, and 9 per cent. in money, on the valuation of the whole amount of goods imported, including that already taken for the duty; a method of taxation said to bring the sum levied to considerably above 23 per cent.[1].

The trade in provisions also continued, and convoys for corn-ships from England, Ireland, and America, were much needed during the war[2]. But here also the tendency of the Portuguese officials towards interference appeared, as is shown in the complaint (1715), that the English were forced to sell their corn, not at their own houses, but in the Lisbon market where a price was set on it[3]. Meat also was exported to Portugal, but the trade suffered from the additional duty of 41 reis ("uzual") imposed at Lisbon[4]. Similar complaints were also made in 1718[5]. Whether on these points redress was granted does not appear; but there is a curious cessation of remonstrances for many years.

As regards the colonial trade with Portugal, this also was on the increase. Carolina rice was early sent to Portugal, but competition from Italy at first prevented its sale. In 1730, however, it was no

[1] *Board of Trade Com. MS.*, Series I. P. Vol. XXIX. No. 72, Poyntz's Report.

[2] Ibid. M. 14, No. 123.

[3] Ibid. P. 19, No. 72.

[4] This tax Poyntz declared equalled 30 per cent. of the sale price; but its imposition seems doubtful, as in the same year the English merchants at Oporto declared that provisions were admitted to Lisbon duty free, while they had to pay 13 per cent. on butter, and 14 per cent. on beef. *Board of Trade Com. MS.*, Series I. P. 19, No. 72.

[5] *Board of Trade Com. MS.*, Series II. Vol. DCL. 493, 506.

longer required to come through England, paying the English duties, but was allowed to be sent direct from America to Portugal, thereby enabling the colonial produce to supersede the Italian[1]. Manufactured articles, too, began to come from the colonies, such, for instance, as hats; and that, to a sufficient extent to provoke complaint from the English hat-makers in 1732[2].

The Newfoundland trade was of older growth and more value. In 1707 £130,000 was stated to be the value of the fish brought from Newfoundland to Spain and Portugal[3]. From 1700 to 1760 the value of fish sent to Spain, Portugal, and Italy was said to average £400,000 yearly[4]. The returns were made in wine, brandy, salt, oil, and linen; these the Newfoundland fishers took back with them, and sold to traders from New England for tobacco and sugar, and the New England traders in their turn carried on a contraband trade in these southern commodities with southern ports (1707)[5]. During the war, the factories were urgent in requesting that convoys might be sent twice a year to escort the fishing vessels, which were frequently seized by the French[6].

Even in time of peace, however, the method by which the trade was carried on made the assistance of the English in Portugal peculiarly necessary. The salted cod was brought in comparatively small vessels, the captains of which were usually owners of both boat and cargo; and these traders brought their fish, not with a view to any special merchant or company in Portugal, but with the idea of hunting about for the best market, and there disposing

[1] Anderson, *Historical Deduction, etc.*, III. 163-64, and Geo. II. 3, cap. 28.
[2] Ibid. 193.
[3] *Board of Trade Com. MS.*, Series II. Vol. DCXLIII.
[4] Anderson, *Historical Deduction, etc.*
[5] *Board of Trade Com. MS.*, Series II. Vol. DCXLIII. 486-87.
[6] Ibid. Vol. DCXLIII. 111-12.

of their cargoes. Such proceedings as these were opposed to all Portuguese regulations. The officials demanded to see a Charter party, or bill of lading, which the captains, who were also owners and merchants, of course, did not possess[1]. The officials also objected to a ship putting into port, and sailing again without unloading, if the market proved bad; or again, if a ship did unload, the Portuguese officials, whose presence was necessary during the process, were apt to prolong the business beyond the fifteen days allowed by treaty. They demanded, besides the duty on fish, so many fish out of every quintal as a fee for themselves—a fee, first given as a bribe, and afterwards required as a right[2]. The import duty on fish, instead of being 23 per cent. on the custom-house valuation, was 22 per cent. in kind; *i.e.*, 22 quintals of fish out of every hundred were taken, whereby the actual tax levied equalled at least 27 per cent., besides the waste caused by the unpacking and handling of the fish previous to the selection of the 22 quintals[3]. Finally, at Oporto in 1718, fish and other provisions had to be sold in the market at fixed prices, despite all treaty stipulations to the contrary[4]. On all these points the consuls at Lisbon and Oporto defended the cause of the Newfoundland fishermen[5]. They also took up the defence of the inland fish trade, which was much hampered by duties and restrictions. The English fish trade with Spain was partly carried on through Portugal, and extra duties were imposed at the "Portos Seccos" (or Portuguese towns on the Spanish frontier), to

[1] *Board of Trade Com. MS.*, Series I. 11, K. 27 and 19, P. 7.
[2] Ibid. Series II. Vol. DCXLIV. Oporto Report, 128.
[3] Ibid. Series I. Oporto Report, 1718, No. 19, P. 97.
[4] Ibid. Series II. Vol. DCL. 493, etc.
[5] They also appear to have assumed some supervision over the fish trade. In 1718 Consul Poyntz complained roundly of the bad drying and salting of the cod, which caused the Portuguese to prefer fish from France.

the indignation of the English at Oporto, who were largely concerned in this trade[1].

Other quarrels raged about the denial of "franquia," or the right to remain in harbour, and store the cargo ashore without either selling it, or paying the 23 per cent. duty exacted on goods actually imported. The question affected more interests than those of the Newfoundland fishermen. Even the traders in woollen goods found cause to complain. It was pointed out that though by treaty England was to have equal privileges with any other nation, yet the French were allowed "franquia" for six months and the Venetians for twelve; whereas the English were limited to three months, and if they remained a day longer, they had to pay the full 23 per cent. import duty, instead of the 4 per cent. tax exacted for goods in "franquia[2]." The point came up again and again, the Oporto factory being specially loud in their complaints[3].

Some idea of the importance of this question to English trade may be gathered from the fact that from 1710-14 eleven hundred and seventy-seven English ships went from England to Portugal and its dependencies—rather more than one-twentieth of all the English merchant ships sailing in that time[4]. No definite settlement, however, was made, and the point recurs throughout the earlier part of the eighteenth century.

The question of the returns for the various exports must have been one of some difficulty. As has been shown, the Portuguese exports to England rarely equalled one-half of the English exports to Portugal. The balance was largely made up by the profits from Brazil. That English trade, especially the woollen trade, rested on the commerce with Brazil

[1] *Board of Trade Com. MS.*, Series I. P. 17, p. 101.
[2] Ibid. P. 19, No. 72.
[3] Ibid. M. 16, No. 234.
[4] Ibid. O. 17, No. 19.

was reiterated again and again by the English merchants[1]. The proportion of English goods sent to Portugal, and thence transported to Brazil, must have been considerable. In 1715 it was asserted that the bulk of the trade between Portugal and its great dependency was done in English commodities[2]. Throughout the earlier part of the eighteenth century this state of things appears to have continued for, in 1756, it was stated that English goods and English capital were essential to the Brazil trade; yet the Portuguese government ungratefully made its profit by enormous duties levied on the English. It was calculated that on every £100 worth of goods passing from England to Brazil, £68 was paid to the Portuguese government before the returns were made to England[3].

The general trade with Brazil was managed by the Portuguese Company, founded in 1648, which had the exclusive right of trade in fish, wine, Brazil wood, oil, and meat[4]. The English merchants in Portugal, who traded with Brazil, were compelled to send their ships and goods in the Brazil Company's fleet. In this they had so considerable a share that in 1715 it was asserted that, but for the French and Dutch commerce, which together only equalled that of England, the whole of the Brazil trade would be in English hands[5]. Thus the safety of the Brazil fleet was a matter of considerable anxiety to the English merchants, who in 1711 readily supported the Portuguese request for an English convoy. They were the more urgent, because those who had sent ventures to Brazil were not paid until the safe return of the fleet[6].

The concession by which four English families

[1] *E.g.*, *Board of Trade Com. MS.*, Series I. P. 19, No. 72.
[2] *Board of Trade Com. MS.*, Series I. O. 127, No. 117.
[3] Ibid. M. 15, No. 145.
[4] Treaty of 1654, Article 11.
[5] *Board of Trade Com. MS.*, Series I. O. 17, No. 108.
[6] Ibid. M. 14, No. 23.

might reside in Bahia, Pernambuco, and Rio de Janeiro was very highly valued by the merchants, who could thus employ English factors to dispose of the English goods sent out; an arrangement preferred, because English factors were not subject to the authority of the Inquisition, as were the Portuguese Jews, otherwise the best substitutes. Moreover, the 10 per cent. commission paid to the factor in Brazil was in this manner preserved to the English nation[1].

The Portuguese, however, looked with extreme jealousy on these privileges. The exclusive colonial policy, universal at the period, was at this time strengthened in Portugal by the discovery of gold in Brazil. The first mines were opened in the late seventeenth century. In 1700 the rich workings of Villa Rica were discovered, and still more mines were found in the early years of the eighteenth century. For some years from this date the industries of Portugal, especially the sugar industry, were said to have diminished[2]. The attention of the Portuguese was wholly centred on the gold fields; and these, which by the middle of the eighteenth century were said to produce from £3,000,000 to £4,000,000 of gold, were regarded as the chief support of Portuguese commerce. Under the circumstances, the vigilance with which the Brazil trade was guarded was naturally extreme. Foreign nations, indeed, such as the French and Dutch, might, and did trade with Brazil. Indeed, in 1716, the Portuguese ambassador in England declared that it was a matter of indifference to his master what nations traded to Brazil, since all returns must be made in gold[3]. But as far as the Portuguese government could control trade, all goods for Brazil must pass through Portugal, and all the rich returns must be made to the mother

[1] *Board of Trade Com. MS.*, Series I. O. 17, No. 108.
[2] Ibid. N. 15, No. 73.
[3] Ibid. Series II. Vol. DCL., 8-12.

country; once there, the whole aim of the Portuguese government was to keep this so-called wealth at home. The penalty for the transport of bullion without licence was death, and the law was sometimes so stringently enforced that when, during the War of the Spanish Succession, the English in Lisbon desired to forward money for the payment of the Portuguese troops in the English service in Spain, permission was denied them, and the money had to be smuggled out of the country with exceeding difficulty and danger[1].

Such a restriction could not, of course, be uniformly maintained; many payments were of necessity made in money. In 1711 the Oporto factory petitioned for leave to make their returns in bullion[2]. In 1737 the influx of Portuguese gold into Cornwall by the Falmouth packet was such as to engross all the bills of exchange in the country; and it formed the bulk of the gold currency in Ireland[3]. In 1747 "remittance by sea," *i.e.* the sending of specie through England to more distant countries, was an important part of the trade of the English factories in Lisbon, and was considered very profitable to the English, who thus got all the benefit of freight commission and exchange[4]. Practically, bullion seems to have been transported from Portugal without any interference so long as its removal was not too open; but occasionally seizures would take place, usually followed by loud remonstrances from the English, and the return of the money[5]. Such a state of affairs explained the nervous anxiety shown by the English merchants at Lisbon and Oporto, lest attempts at direct trade with Brazil should induce the Portuguese government to prohibit entirely any English trade

[1] *Cal. Treasury Papers*, CLXXX. No. 20.

[2] *Board of Trade Com. MS.*, Series II. Vol. DCXLVI., 290-330.

[3] *Cal. Treasury Papers*, p. 314, No. 73; p. 320, No. 88. See also R. Chalmers' *Colonial Currency*, 53, 396, etc.

[4] *For. St. P. Portugal*, No. 46. February, *Petition for Convoy.*

[5] As in the case of Henry Furnese in 1718, *For. St. P. Portugal*, No. 89.

thither, and thereby, as it was said, ruin the English factories. Early in the eighteenth century there were signs of this possibility. No Brazil trade was allowed to the English merchants at Madeira. Though no division of Brazil had its full complement of four English families, yet no Englishman was allowed to settle there without a licence from the Portuguese king, which was exceedingly hard to obtain; and Portuguese captains were forbidden to carry strangers thither[1]. The English factors in Brazil complained that they dared not leave the country for fear of being forbidden to return. In 1711 an attempt of some English merchants to trade direct to the country provoked a decree, confirming the Portuguese decision that all trade from or to Brazil must pass through Portugal[2]. In face of this, the suggestion in Bolingbroke's proposed Treaty of 1713, that all English ships should be allowed free entrance to Brazil harbours, savours rather of audacity than of statesmanship. The Portuguese were by no means minded to grant fresh facilities to the English. On the contrary, in 1716, they proposed that the latter should give up part of what they already possessed: in short, that they should resign their limited privilege of residing in Brazil[3]. The reason given for this request was that the English conducted all their trade through Portugal, and therefore had no need to reside in Brazil. If they gave up the privilege, the French and Dutch, who only had it because, by treaty, they were to stand on an equal footing with the English, must perforce follow their example. By this concession the English would benefit, as the French, notwithstanding decrees, carried on a direct, though contraband, trade with the Brazil coast, and thereby outstripped the English. The removal of

[1] *Board of Trade Com. MS.*, Series I. O. 17, No. 108.
[2] *Collecção, etc.*, *Leis Extravagantes*, II. 376-78.
[3] *Board of Trade Com. MS.*, Series I. O. 17, No. 108.

the resident families would, it was said, put a stop to this contraband traffic, and give fair traders a chance[1].

The manner in which this question was debated in England, shows the importance of the Lisbon and Oporto factories. Some merchants in England were indifferent; some were hostile; but all were apparently too ignorant to rely on their own judgment: not a wonderful circumstance, considering that they had never been permitted to trade direct with Brazil. The opinion of the English in Portugal, who did so trade, was emphatic and conclusive. On no account would they give up this privilege. For the reasons mentioned above, English factors were essential to the Brazil trade. If they were dismissed, the English might be driven, like the Madeira merchants, to take assumed Portuguese names, and would find this a hindrance to recovering their debts. The English residents in Brazil rather checked than encouraged smuggling. The smuggling was chiefly the work of French merchants, and was carried on among the islands and along the coast. It was a ready money concern, and resident correspondents in Brazil were not needed for it. Besides, what guarantee had England that, if she did resign her privilege, the French and Dutch would follow her example? What was needed for the protection of Anglo-Brazil commerce was the fulfilment of the promises made by treaty, not the remission and nullification of those promises[2]. The project was dropped accordingly, and for the next forty years the trade with Brazil continued apparently with but little disturbance.

Closely connected with the trade to Brazil was the slave trade; first to work in the sugar plantations, and then, increasingly, to work in the mines, the Portuguese needed slaves. The English, Dutch, and

[1] *Board of Trade Com. MS.*, Series II. Vol. DCL., 8-12.
[2] Ibid. 39-50.

French needed slaves also for similar purposes, and between the ships of various nationalities haunting the West Coast of Africa, collisions were not uncommon. In these cases the English not infrequently acted as the protectors of the Portuguese against the Dutch. With the exception of Angola, Cutcheo, and Bisseo, the Portuguese had few settlements on the African coast. They were, therefore, in the habit of trading with the English settlements, such as that at Accra, for slaves, for whom they paid at first in Brazil tobacco (which for some time formed the currency of the coast), afterwards in Brazil gold. The Dutch, however, objected strongly to the Portuguese coming to the Gold Coast. No Portuguese vessel might pass the settlement of Elmina (once Portuguese, now Dutch) without paying a 25 per cent. duty on its cargo[1], and when, as sometimes happened, the Dutch proceeded to violent measures, English mediation and protection were more than once requested by the Portuguese.

In 1708 an agreement was entered into by the Dutch West Indian, and the English African Companies, whereby Portuguese vessels with the African Company's permit were to be allowed to pass without Dutch molestation, and those with Dutch licences were to be unharmed by the English[2]. But this agreement appears from subsequent complaints (1731) to have been violated, and the Portuguese Brazil trade with British Africa was thereby endangered[3].

All Anglo-Portuguese relations were, however, by no means so amiable. More than once, the Portuguese themselves were accused of attacking the English, as in the affrays at Cabinda (1697 and 1721)[4]; and apart from fracas of this kind, the

[1] *Board of Trade Com. MS.*, Series II. Vol. DCXLIV. 150-51.
[2] Ibid. Series I. L. 89.
[3] Ibid. O. 55, No. 57.
[4] Ibid. Vol. XLI.; and Series I. O. 17, No. 27.

rivalry of the two nations in regard to the sugar plantations caused difficulties. The Portuguese traded direct from Brazil to Africa for slaves, whereby they could obtain negroes cheaper than the English planters, and the sale of slaves to them by the English African Company was a subject of considerable complaint[1] (1710); only a part, however, of the Portuguese demand for negroes was supplied by the African Company. The latter alleged that the French, Dutch, and Portuguese rivalry on the coast of Africa injured their trade. Especially was this the case since the discovery of the Brazil gold mines, which, at once increasing the demand for negroes, and supplying the means of paying for them, had raised their price to 5 or 6 ounces of gold per man[2].

The Asiento Clause of the Treaty of Utrecht, of course, facilitated the English slave trade: and the desire to extend it yet further appeared in the clause in Bolingbroke's proposed treaty, that the English should be allowed to send slaves to Brazil. Curiously enough, a little later the King of Portugal was induced, perhaps by increasing dread of the Dutch, to suggest a scheme to the Lisbon factory whereby the English Company should supply his territories with slaves[3]. Nothing came of the suggestion, however, though it was renewed by the African Company in 1737. This Company, when requesting the assistance of the home government, suggested that the English might buy the slaves for manufactured goods, and sell them for Brazil gold[4]. But the enemies of the Company, who were numerous, pointed out that the Portuguese already bought from 6,000 to 10,000 negroes from English and Dutch traders on the African coast,

[1] *Board of Trade Com. MS.*, Series I. S. 24, No. 13.
[2] Ibid. No. 66-67.
[3] Ibid. N. 15, No. 73, 1713-14.
[4] Ibid. Y. 95, No. 36.

paying for them in Brazil tobacco and gold, and that any exclusive privilege would probably damage the trade. The scheme appears therefore to have come to nothing, and the English and Portuguese continued in the mixed relations of rivals, and buyer and seller so far as the slave trade was concerned[1].

Brazil gold, however, whether smuggled, exported under licence, or paid for slaves, was not Portugal's only resource for paying for English commodities. Of her own products the chief now sent to England seem to have been oil, sumach, and wine. The custom called "sacia" was, however, some check on the export trade[2]. If an English ship arrived in port with £1,000 worth of English goods, and departed with £2,000 worth of Portuguese goods, an additional duty of 10 per cent. was levied on the extra £1,000. A remonstrance against this duty by Methuen ended, however, in its remission as far as Lisbon and Oporto were concerned.

During the early eighteenth century the factory of the latter town was rising into prominence with the increase of the wine trade. At the time of the Methuen Treaty, this trade was largely carried on at Viana, but the exertions of the English merchants at Oporto (according to their own statement) before long made the latter city the centre for the rising commerce[3]. As has been shown, however, it was subjected to many more vexations than was the settlement at Lisbon. Moreover, the harbour was a dangerous one: to cross the bar at Oporto was always a matter of difficulty, and during the War of the Spanish Succession there were complaints that English convoys would frequently desert the hapless merchantmen outside the harbour, where they were often snapped up by French vessels of

[1] *Board of Trade Com. MS.*, Series II. Vol. DCXLVIII.
[2] Ibid.
[3] Ibid. Vol. DLXIII. No. 33.

war before they could enter the port[1]. So serious was this difficulty that, in 1707, the factory declared that their cloth trade, formerly nearly as great as that of Lisbon, had diminished to almost one-fourth of its former bulk.

The trade, however, on which the Oporto factory chiefly depended, was that which the French wars had called into existence, and which the Methuen Treaty had firmly established—the trade in wine. The endeavour to nullify the Methuen Treaty and the Treaty of Utrecht was, as has been shown, unsuccessful. Portuguese wines continued to be favoured at the expense of the French: in 1742 the duties on wines imported to London in English ships were, in round figures, £25 per ton for Spanish wines, £31 for German, £52 for French, and only £24 for Portuguese. For the six years from 1736 to 1741 inclusive, the import of wines from Portugal was greater than that from any other country, averaging more than twenty times that from France[2]; and though the trade with Portugal was said ultimately to depend on that of Brazil, it was generally admitted that the trade in wine was the only means by which that in cloth could be preserved.

From the very beginning, however, there was friction about the export of the liquor. Wine came chiefly from Lisbon and Oporto, and as early as 1682 Consul Maynard and other English merchants appear to have been interested in its production. But in the eighteenth century various difficulties were thrown in the way of the English merchants who exported it. In 1715 Consul Poyntz complained that the English were not allowed to keep the wine in their own warehouses ready for shipping; wines were seized and condemned on the ground that they had not been made in the district where

[1] *Board of Trade Com. MS.*, Series II. Vol. DCXLVI. 290-330.
[2] Ibid. Series I. BB. 7 and 8, No 40.

they were found awaiting exportation; declarations were required from the merchants as to the destination of the wine, and checks were put on the employment of Portuguese porters, boatmen, and others[1].

At Oporto, the wine trade was increasing. This city was the port for the most fruitful wine districts, and the English merchants there were eager to employ themselves in the wine trade; but whatever annoyances the factory at Lisbon might suffer were intensified at Oporto. An extra duty of 400 reis per pipe was put on wine exported from this town[2]. Besides this, not only were the prices the English offered for the wines of the Cima d'Ouro refused, but, in 1718, complaints were made of the existence of privileged companies, who claimed the right of seizing the goods of other traders at cost price[3]. In the Tras do Montes region an arbitrary price was fixed[4]. When the wines were actually bought, the carriers, boatmen, porters, and other persons employed by the English to bring down the wine were punished for accepting the work, unless licence had previously been granted them. With the coopers there was a quarrel of long standing. The Coopers' Company had the exclusive right of making barrels, their employers furnishing the timber. The English complained that they exacted unreasonable prices, caused unreasonable delays, and then made the barrels so badly, that a large quantity of wine was lost through leakage. More than once the English obtained leave to employ joiners and coopers directly, and without the intervention of the Company, and more than once the leave was

[1] *Board of Trade Com. MS.*, Series I. D. 72, No. 19.

[2] Additional export duties were also placed on other goods: 1,000 reis per pipe on oil, 2,400 reis on brandy, and 50 reis per arroba on sumach. *Board of Trade Com. MS.*, Series II. Vol. DCXLVI. 290-330.

[3] *Board of Trade Com. MS.*, Series II. Vol. DCL. 493-506.

[4] Ibid. Series I. P. 19, No. 72.

revoked[1]. The general state of hostility to the English is evidenced by the plea of the Oporto merchants for leave to carry arms. This permission was among their general privileges, but the Portuguese administration, following their usual plan of whittling away the concessions they had granted, declined to allow the English to carry pistols[2], and these the Oporto merchants represented were really necessary for their defence amid the rough and lawless population of the wine district[3]. Another point which perhaps shows the peril to the English is the persistence with which, both at Oporto and Lisbon, they pleaded that the consul might undertake the prosecution in cases of murder; by Portuguese law the murderer could only be prosecuted by the relations of the victim, a regulation singularly inconvenient to strangers[4].

The above complaints are frequent and energetic. They reappear in the reports of the factories both of Lisbon and Oporto in 1711, 1714, 1715, and 1718. After 1718 the reports come only at long intervals, and the complaints chiefly concern the over-valuation of goods at the Custom House. The revival, however, about 1756 of complaints nearly resembling those mentioned above, seems to show that no real improvement had taken place during the interval. Thus while the Portuguese government during the early part of the eighteenth century submitted to the control of Portuguese trade by the English factories, the people were by no means satisfied, and the active measures which marked the policy of the Portuguese government from about 1749 onwards, may to some extent have been the outcome of long-continued, national irritation.

[1] *Board of Trade Com. MS.*, Series II. Vol. DCXLIX. 128.
[2] Ibid. Vol. DVI. 493.
[3] Ibid. Vol. DCXLIX. 128.
[4] Ibid. Series I. Vol. XIX. No. 97.

CHAPTER VI

THE COMPANY OF THE WINES OF THE ALTO DOURO

(1756-1787)

Portuguese revolt against English influence — Question of brokers—Revival of Portuguese industry—Effect of the Sumptuary Laws (1749-58) — Ministry of Pombal — His hostility to the English factories—Export of bullion—Establishment of the Junta do Commercio — Decline of power of the English Conservador—Valuation of goods —Additional duties—State of Anglo-Portuguese trade—Establishment of Exclusive companies—Wine trade—Its fluctuations and decay—Constitution, duties, and powers of the Companies of the Wines of the Alto Douro—English complaints—Combination of the English merchants against the Company in 1785—Weakness of the Portuguese government—Increase of the wine trade—Decay of the Oporto factory—Effect of the American war on Anglo-Portuguese trade—Diminution of exports from England—Alienation between England and Portugal—Adam Smith on the Methuen Treaty—The French Commercial Treaty of 1786.

As has been shown in the last chapter, the predominance of the English in Portugal had long been galling to the feelings of the people, and towards the middle of the eighteenth century the government began to take steps to check the intrusive foreigner, and to revive trade and industry among the native population.

The manner in which the question of brokerage had been treated was a sign of the times. About 1718 a decree was promulgated by which a body of twelve brokers was appointed, through whom all goods were, in the first instance, to be sold, or else the price would not be recoverable. Half per cent. on the bargain was the fixed broker's fee. One broker was appointed for exchange and one for insurance[1]. The English merchants complained bitterly. The regulation was a breach of the Treaty of 1654, and of an "alvara" of 1661, which exempted the English from being compelled to use brokers.

Thus there were sound, legal grounds for the English complaints, but trade did not suffer heavily[2]. The most noteworthy point about the affair is that it marked the growing resolve of the Portuguese government to subject the English to the same regulations as those to which its own subjects submitted. A further testimony to this spirit appeared in the decree of 1742, whereby the English in Lisbon were brought under the jurisdiction of the municipal courts in all matters concerning police[3].

The resolution of the government was perhaps strengthened by the tendency towards a revival of Portuguese industries. In 1734, for instance, the English complained that there was no longer an extensive market in Portugal for army accoutrements or other leather manufactures, of which the English had exported large quantities during the War of the Spanish Succession; the Portuguese now preferred to import hides or tanned leather, and produce the finished article for themselves[4]. Later in the century the old native manufacture of cloth, which had been

[1] *Board of Trade Com. MS.*, Series I. P. 19, No. 125.

[2] The most serious practical difficulty seems to have arisen from the appointment of a single broker to manage exchange. This official had a unique opportunity of altering the rate to suit himself, and the English factors at Lisbon were thereby hampered in drawing bills of exchange. As these bills were used in paying the Gibraltar garrison and Minorca fleet, the annoyance of the home government was very great. (*Board of Trade Com. MS.*, Series I. Q. 21, Nos. 129-126.)

[3] *For. St. P. Portugal*, No. 64.

[4] *Board of Trade Com. MS.*, Series I. X. 32, No. 38.

almost killed by the Methuen Treaty, was revived, and in 1764 the Portuguese were said to be largely supplying themselves with hats, which they had previously imported from England and America[1].

The government's somewhat spasmodic care for the national morals incidentally worked in the same direction. The great Sumptuary Law of 1749 was primarily directed towards the suppression of luxury, but the inclusion of foreign-made livery cloth among the prohibited articles was a blow to English traders. Moreover, by the subsequent extensions of the Act in 1752, 1757, and 1758, the list of forbidden articles increased till it included almost all kinds of ready-made goods, besides tanned leather, lawns, silks, mohair, velveteen, etc.[2], thereby proving, if not precisely an incentive to Portuguese industry, at least so great a discouragement to Anglo-Portuguese trade, that in 1759 it was said to be chiefly carried on in wool and gold[3].

Both the jealousy of the English, and the desire of Portugal to become more independent, found a zealous champion in the man who for some years after the death of John V. really governed Portugal—the Marquis de Pombal. A keen patriot, he saw with dismay the bondage to England into which Portugal had fallen, and in some degree discerned its causes. His opinions on the relations of England and Portugal appear strongly in his writings. "The English . . . have conquered it (Portugal) without the inconveniences of a conquest," he declared. "In 1754 Portugal scarcely produced anything for her own support; two-thirds of her physical necessities were supplied by England . . . all the trade of the country was carried on by her (England's) agents. The English monopolised even the commerce of Brazil. . . . These foreigners, after having acquired

[1] *Board of Trade Com. MS.*, Series I. Vol. XLIX. No. 341.
[2] Ibid. A. 17, No. 51, Voucher, B. I.
[3] Santarem, etc., *Quadro Elementar, etc.*, XVIII. 376.

immense fortunes, disappeared, carrying with them the riches of the country." The English cloth trade he thought ruinous to Portugal, and the Brazil gold mines scarcely less so. "Gold and silver are fictitious values . . . the more they are multiplied, the less is their real value[1]."

Holding these views, it was natural that Pombal's measures should be directed to some extent against the English. As has been shown, the latter were in many respects highly favoured. They were exempt from taxes, such as the decima on stock; exempt from the jurisdiction of ordinary courts; and exempt, also, at least nominally, from many commercial regulations to which the natives had to submit. Thus their privileges had enabled them to oust the Portuguese from the control of their own commerce. On these privileges Pombal declared war. He had no apparent desire to treat the English with harshness; but he declared that "Foreigners must be subject to the civil laws of the land in which they live," and this maxim was the keynote of his policy.

In numerous ways the Portuguese government and the English factories came into collision. In 1755 a new scandal arose about the export of bullion. An Englishman, named Humphrey Bunster, was arrested in the streets of Lisbon, carrying two "slings," closely packed with silver bullion, entrusted to him for shipment. The exporters were various members of the English factory, as the consul acknowledged in his homeward letters. The money was confiscated, and Lord Tyrawley was sent from England to arrange the affair, with the expectation that the Portuguese, having asserted their right, would as usual yield to their ally's demand, and reverse the sentence. But the unexpected happened. The court of Portugal maintained its right to uphold its own laws, and the

[1] *Memoirs of the Marquis of Pombal*, by J. A. Smith, 1843, I. 114-16 and 123.

sentence remained in force[1]; so much to the indignation of the English, that in 1773 they were still raising complaints on the subject[2].

In 1756 another cause of offence arose from the establishment by Pombal of the Junta do Commercio. This was a body with special jurisdiction over commercial matters, such as contraband trade, licences for retailers, inspection of shops, recovery of debts, cases of bankruptcy, the inspection of Brazil ships, superintendence of Portuguese manufactures, etc.[3]. A board with such powers was certain to come into conflict with the principal traders of the country. The authority over retailers was thought to be especially aimed at the English, who were the chief shopkeepers in the country, and whom this Board compelled to pay a heavy fine for a licence to trade. But the most serious trouble arose over the question of the jurisdiction of the Conservador of the Junta do Commercio, whose powers were to supersede those of the English Conservador in all cases within the cognisance of the Board. The English protested vehemently. The difficulty they found in collecting their debts in the cases of persons imprisoned by the Court of Exchequer or by the Inquisition was a grievance of old standing, and to this was now added the interference of the Junta do Commercio. This body, it was declared, took the affairs of whomsoever appealed to it under its cognisance; with the result that English creditors were forced to accept any dividend which the Junta might assign to them from the bankrupt's estate, and, further, that the delay in settling what this dividend should be became almost intolerable[4].

Apart from the practical difficulties thus created, these regulations were all breaches of the English Con-

[1] *Board of Trade Com. MS.*, Series I. L. 51, No. 19.
[2] Ibid. B. 70, No. 55.
[3] Ibid.
[4] *For. St. P. Portugal*, No. 64.

servadorial privilege. They were the more resented, because in 1752 a heavy blow had been dealt to the power of the English court, by a decree to the effect that a Conservador of the English, who in any way thwarted or hindered the execution of writs or orders issued by other courts, should be displaced[1]. The outcry against all these various encroachments was so vehement, that, in 1763, the Portuguese government seems to have wavered. They were said to have admitted that the Treaty of 1654, by which the English Conservador's powers were established, could not be superseded by subsequent acts of the Portuguese government[2]. But Luiz da Cunha, Pombal's representative, maintained that the first step on the part of any individual desiring to place himself under the Conservador's jurisdiction, must be to prove his nationality in the court to which he was first summoned, and to this the English objected[3].

Another source of annoyance more directly affecting English trade was the old question of valuation, which was again brought forward in the late 'fifties. The earthquake of Lisbon (1755), or the subsequent fires, had destroyed the old tariff lists, in accordance with which goods entering the Lisbon Custom House were valued[4]. The English had already been petitioning for a new valuation, but when the fresh lists were compiled, they were said to be very unfavourable to England; whereon the English merchants changed their attitude and maintained that there was no necessity for these new lists. From the tariff lists of other ports, and from the books of the Lisbon merchants, the former valuations could have been readily recovered; or if new valuations were necessary,

[1] *For. St. P. Portugal*, No. 64.
[2] *Board of Trade Com. MS.*, Series I. Vol. LXX. No. 55.
[3] *For. St. P. Portugal*, No. 64; and *Board of Trade Com. MS.*, Series I. B. 70, No. 55.
[4] *Board of Trade Com. MS.*, Series I. Vol. XLV. No. 15.

they should have been made according to the 1654 treaty. Also, the method of paying the Custom House officers by a 6 per cent. commission on the value of goods was strongly condemned, as leading to over-valuation[1]. Again, however, the Portuguese government stood firm in its resolution to manage its own affairs in its own way; and even the fresh Book of Rates, compiled in 1782, was made without any consultation with the English merchants[2].

Extra duties were also complained of; after the earthquake, the Portuguese in Lisbon offered to submit to an additional levy of 4 per cent. to supply the public losses caused by the earthquake. This offer was accepted; and, in consequence, a tax was imposed on all merchants, Portuguese and foreign. The English again sought exemption. They had not concurred in the offer; they saw no reason why they should pay. Again they appealed to the 1654 treaty, and again the Portuguese government refused to make any distinction between them and its own subjects. The same disputes occurred in regard to other duties, such as the 200 reis per ton for coast lights, levied on all ships coming to Lisbon, or the "donativo," a 2 per cent. tax on imports, levied at Oporto to maintain a convoy for the Brazil fleet. In both cases the English objected to payment; in both cases the government declined to pay any regard to the privilege they claimed. The days of the English predominance seemed to be passing[3].

If, however, the English power within Portugal itself was decreasing, the actual trade between the two countries continued in many ways to expand. In 1720 the list of goods imported by the English merchants in Lisbon included long bays, Colchester bays, stockings (silk, wool and worsted), gold lace, copper, iron, lead, shot, hides, rice, butter, etc.[4]. In

[1] *Board of Trade Com. MS.*, Series I. Vol. LXX. No. 55.
[2] Ibid. Series II. Vol. DLXIII. No. 21 (Consul's Report on Oporto).
[3] Ibid. Series I. Vol. LV. No. 70; and *For. St. P. Portugal*, No. 64.
[4] Ibid. Q. 21, No. 160.

1777 the list in the "Arte e diccionario do Commercio" of goods from England, in addition to woollen stuffs of all sorts, includes clothing, household utensils, spars, cordage, tools of various sorts, and hardware. In fact, sumptuary laws notwithstanding, the finished products seem to have increased in proportion to the raw material.

As regards quantity, the trade had for some years past been almost stationary. There had been a tolerably steady rise until 1730. From 1730 to 1740 trade was fairly maintained; exports to the value of more than a million were sent to Portugal, and over £300,000 worth of goods were brought from that country to England.

The five yearly averages from 1740 to 1760 show first a slight rise, and then a slight but steady fall in imports to England, while the exports thence are fairly maintained: the figures being roughly:—

	Imports from Portugal.	Exports to Portugal.
1740-45 . .	£428,587	£1,115,100
1745-50 . .	323,766	1,114,189
1750-55 . .	272,308	1,098,049
1755-60 . .	256,600	1,300,681[1]

Such a state of the export trade was, of course, a matter of considerable anxiety to the government of Portugal; and it is typical of the state of things, which induced Pombal and his colleagues to endeavour to revive trade by the establishment of the great companies of Brazil, and of the wines of the Alto Douro. These companies were the subject of loud complaints from the English. The companies of Brazil, com-

[1] I have taken out these averages from the list of Exports and Imports given in the *Board of Trade Com. MS.*, Series II. Vol. DLXII. No. 7. In Series II. Vol. DLXIII. the average exports for 1750–55 and 1755 are given as follows:—

1750–55	£1,100,248.
1755–60	£1,299,794.

As will be seen, these figures differ slightly from mine, but the error is not of a nature to effect the general statement above.

prising those of Pernambuco and of Grão Para, chiefly affected the English merchants at Lisbon; that of the Alto Douro those at Oporto.

The immediate cause of the establishment of the Alto Douro Company, which took place in 1756, was alleged to be the excessive adulteration of the wines in the Alto Douro district.

The prices of wines were subject to great variations. There was not only the natural depreciation of value attendant on a full harvest to be considered, but also the fact that a full harvest was usually the result of a wet season. Hence the grapes at such periods were full of water and the wine of an inferior quality; while a scanty harvest frequently supplied good wine. Thus prices fluctuated to such a degree that, whereas the pipe of wine in 1700 cost 10 milreis, in 1731 it had risen to 48 milreis[1].

This high price tempted the owners of farms in the neighbourhood to convert land hitherto used for corn or other crops into vineyards, with the result that the market became overstocked. Further, the era of high prices had led to adulteration, the reputation of the Alto Douro wines was damaged, and prices fell, till a pipe fetched at the most 20 milreis, and at the least 4, 6, or 8 milreis[2].

The above account of the cause of the rise and fall in prices is that given by the English merchants at Oporto, who in 1754 were so impressed by the badness of the wine, and by the fall in prices, that they published a manifesto to exculpate themselves from having in any way caused these results[3].

The Portuguese version differed considerably. A petition, presented to the Portuguese government by the winegrowers of the Alto Douro region in 1756,

[1] *Board of Trade Com. MS.*, Series I. Vol. LI. Da Cunha declared that in good years the wine rose to 72 or 90 milreis. Ibid. No. 10. *Deduction.*

[2] Ibid.

[3] *Board of Trade Com. MS.*, Series I. Vol. LI. No. 51.

does, indeed, acknowledge the fact of the adulteration; but the petitioners declare that the low prices of the wine were due to the action of the English at Oporto. The latter had the whole export of wine in their hands, and they are represented as agreeing together to buy the wine at a price which would not reimburse the cultivators, and otherwise as tyrannising over the unhappy wine-growers[1].

How far this combination or "ring" existed, it is difficult to say. Pombal declared that he had investigated the allegations of the wine-growers on the subject, and found them to be correct; but it is noteworthy that this special accusation does not appear in the various replies and memorials on the question addressed by the Portuguese to the English government. Moreover, the English, though not specifically denying the charge, do definitely declare that they never paid the lowest prices quoted. Their custom was to buy the best wines for exportation at a reasonable price, such as 14 or 20 milreis per pipe. The smaller amounts, they declared, were subsequently given by Portuguese traders for the inferior wines, thus left on the growers' hands[2].

These statements, however, do not preclude the idea of some combination among the English traders. United as they were by race, language, interests, privileges, such a combination may well have taken place, and may have tended to lower the price of wine without being the only, or even the chief, factor in producing this result.

Doubtful, however, as many circumstances of the case may be, two facts emerge clearly from the confusion; the exceeding adulteration of the wine, and the very great distress of the wine-growers. The final blow was the earthquake at Lisbon, the effects of which completely dislocated all the industry and commerce of the country. In the following year

[1] J. A. Smith, *Memoirs of the Marquis of Pombal*, I. chap. vi.
[2] *Board of Trade Com. MS.*, Series I. Vol. LI.

(1756) the vintagers sent the above-mentioned petition to Pombal, giving a terrible account of their plight. In the Beira, Minho, and Tras os Montes districts, the price of wines was so reduced that it was impossible for the growers to make a living; in many places the people were starving; and it was noted as a special sign of poverty, that in one place a priest left his church, no money being forthcoming to pay him[1].

The response to these complaints was the establishment of the famous Company of the Wines of the Alto Douro. Its avowed objects were to secure the purity of the wines, and to steady their price. Not mentioned in the Company's Charter itself, but tolerably clearly stated in the subsequent correspondence, was the desire that the Company should succeed in taking the export of wine out of the hands of the English interlopers. It was, at any rate, provided that they should not gain an overweening influence in the Company itself. Any one, foreigner or native, might take shares in the Company, but the Provedor, deputies, and other members of the governing body, were to be either native-born Portuguese, or foreigners who had taken out letters of naturalisation. Further, a special Conservador was to be appointed for the Company's affairs, whose jurisdiction in all matters touching the Company was to supersede that of all other courts, and from whom no appeal would lie except to the Relação.

The powers of the Company were extensive; it was their business to oversee, classify, test, and approve all wines produced in the Alto Douro district. They were to make an annual survey of the district, to decide which sections or demarcations produced the best wine, and to permit the export of these wines only. They were to separate the best or exportation wines from the inferior or tavern wines, which were consumed in Portugal itself, and

[1] J. A. Smith, *Memoirs of the Marquis of Pombal*, I. chap. vi.

especially in Oporto. In that city, and in the neighbourhood, wholesale trade was to be carried on only on behalf of the Company, which was to allot to all the various dealers, English exporters, tavern keepers, etc., such proportion of the wines as the Company judged fit they should sell[1]. No wines were to be exported from Oporto, save those sent to the city with a "manifest" from the vintagers, addressed to the Company. The Company were to finance the vintagers where necessary, to have a pre-emption on boats and other means of transport, and to regulate the price of wines at the first sale, never permitting it to rise above 30 milreis per pipe for the best, and 25 milreis for the inferior sorts. For its own special profit, the Company had the monopoly of the brandy and vinegar trade to Brazil; but this was the only direct privilege it possessed in respect of the export trade. It might trade wholesale to other European countries, but it might not trade retail. Otherwise, its regulations directly affected only the manufacture and allocation of wines within Portugal itself. In fact, the Company's avowed function was to act as an intermediary between the grower and the exporter, or retailer, in order to preserve the fair dealing of each, and the purity of the article in which they traded[2].

The indignation of the English merchants at Oporto may be readily conceived. Every point in the Company's charter was in their eyes a breach of their privileges. At first they argued that it was an infraction of the general freedom of commerce

[1] This, however, did not imply that the Company bought up all the wines. They merely estimated what the amount of wine would be, and left the English and other traders to buy of whom they pleased in the allotted districts, limited by the allotted amount and price. No wines were to be brought into the Alto Douro district from outside without a certificate of their place of manufacture.

[2] *Collecção, etc., Leis Extravagantes*, III. 486 *et seq.*; and *Board of Trade Com. MS.*, Series I. Vol. LI. No. 24.

guaranteed by every treaty from 1642 onward[1]. Pombal, however, and his colleagues maintained their favourite point, that such a general stipulation could not hinder the Portuguese government from making what particular regulations it thought fit. Moreover, they carried the war into the enemy's country by complaints of the Navigation Act, the Tonnage and Poundage Act, and other English commercial regulations which hindered Portuguese trade[2]. The English government therefore dropped the general plea (not without a snub to the merchants for having taken it up), and proceeded to contest each special point of the Company's charter[3].

The creation of the Conservador, the pre-emption on boats, the exclusive brandy trade to Brazil, were all quoted as breaches of the Treaty of 1654, which they certainly were. But the main attack was on the establishment of the Company at all. It was alleged that practically the Company had a monopoly of the wine trade, and that from the operation of such a monopoly the English merchants were by treaty exempted. The Portuguese sturdily denied that there was any monopoly in the case. The English might join the Company if they chose; they might buy wines of the Company as they chose; the regulation of the price merely fixed a maximum, not a minimum, to which the merchants surely had no reason to object. The Company's object was simply to keep the wines pure, and this would surely be beneficial to the English traders. But the English traders could not be induced to take this view; in respect to their ability to join the Company, they alleged that there was no greater tyranny than to compel a merchant, if he wished to enter a particular trade, to place his capital in a

[1] *Board of Trade Com. MS.*, Series I. Vol. LI. No. 24. (3).

[2] *Deduction, etc.*, presented by Da Cunha. *Board of Trade Com. MS.*, Series I. Vol. LI. No. 10.

[3] *For. St. P. Portugal,* No. 64.

Joint Stock Company, the operations of which he could not control[1]. So they continued to protest with unabated ardour, and to try in all ways to evade the jurisdiction of the Company[2].

In addition to all the objections made on the score of old rights and privileges, many grievances arose from the working of the Company itself. In a report of the Board of Trade in 1767[3], in a reply of the English government in 1773 to Da Cunha's "Deduction," and in various petitions of the Oporto Company, these grievances are stated in full. Curiously enough, there is no mention in these papers of what might be thought to be the most serious grievance of all—the decree by which the bonds of the Company were to pass current in Portugal at a legally fixed value. The difficulty of carrying out this decree appears in a complaint the following year that neither the Custom House, nor the Company itself, would receive the latter's bonds for the payment of duties[4].

If this question was ignored, there were many other complaints. The Company itself is accused of adulterating wines; and of inciting the growers to ask more than the legal price by promising to buy the wines at the full legal maximum, if they could not be otherwise disposed of. The tasters of the Company were charged with being incompetent, and with using their position to gratify their private

[1] *Board of Trade Com. MS.*, Series I. Vol. LI. 70 (No. 55); and *For. St. P. Portugal*, No. 64.

[2] A curious instance of this is quoted in the *Memoirs of the Marquis of Pombal.* The estate of Oeyras belonging to Pombal, produced a kind of wine which, mixed with that of the Alto Douro, gave the liquid a dark colour much admired by connoisseurs. The sum payable by the Company's regulations for the Oeyras wine was 36,000 reis, which was said not to pay the cost of cultivation. Thereon the English exporters are alleged to have secretly offered a very much larger sum, which was declined. J. A. Smith, *Memoirs of the Marquis of Pombal*, I. chap. ii.

[3] *For. St. P. Portugal*, No. 64.

[4] *Board of Trade Com. MS.*, Series I. 52, Nos. 2, 3, and 21.

animosities; and the trade at Oporto was said to be injured by the delay necessary to comply with the Company's regulations[1].

Another grievance was that the prohibition of the export of inferior wines prevented the English merchants at Oporto from supplying the English navy, so that this trade fell into the hands of the Company. In time of peace this was not a very important matter; but from 1775 to 1783, the years of the American War, the sum of wine supplied to the navy increased tenfold, and the bulk came from Oporto. It was natural that the merchants should complain of any attempt to deprive them of so profitable a trade[2].

There were other complaints. The English desired that they might do as they chose with wine, other than that bought from the Company, and that they should not be compelled to submit it to the prescribed tests. The exporters, they argued, who had now to meet the competition of the Company, were not very likely to adulterate the wines[3]. To force them to submit their wines to the approbation of the Company, was to place them in the power of their rivals, who, by declining to approve the wines, could compel them to sell to the Company only, no other market being open[4].

In 1776 the Charter of the Company, which had been granted for twenty years, needed renewal, and, in consequence, the ardour of the English protests increased. That the English had to buy in an allotted district, while the Company bought where they chose, was a subject of grave complaint. The Company's method of buying was objected to. By a decree of 1769 the governor of the embarcation

[1] A series of vouchers from the English in Portugal contain instances of these various annoyances. *Board of Trade Com. MSS.*, Series I. 51, No. 25 (23).

[2] *Board of Trade Com. MS.*, Series II. Vol. DLXIII. No. 13.

[3] Ibid. Series I. 51, No. 25.

[4] *For. St. P. Portugal*, No. 64.

district (the district where the wines might be bought for exportation) was forbidden to sell until the wines had been approved, and the quantity, price, and cost of carriage ascertained by the Company. Then he was forced to sell to the first bidder. When the Company's survey had been made, a proclamation was usually issued, declaring the wine ready for sale; but of late the proclamation had been withheld until the Company had made its own selection—a piece of "sharp practice," as the English considered. Again, the English complained of the difficulty of getting as much wine as they needed. By an edict of 1774, half the produce of the exporting district was assigned for the tavern wines, and, therefore, taken over by the Company at a low price, ranging from 10 to 19 milreis. The consequence of this arrangement was that the English merchants could only obtain about 8,000 pipes of export wine at 30 or 35 milreis. As the annual export to England was about 20,000 pipes, the Company apparently supplied the difference, for which purpose they must have used a considerable quantity of the so-called tavern wines. This caused great indignation among the English, who inveighed against their rivals' ability to undersell them, and declared that complaints had been made in England of the Company's wines[1].

Further, the right granted to the Company of the exclusive manufacture of brandy in Beira, Minho, and Traz os Montes[2], together with the same body's privilege of supplying taverns, made it impossible for the English to find any market for inferior wines. Altogether, the English maintained that the Oporto factory was on the point of ruin[3].

Despite all complaints the Company's Charter was

[1] "Petition of Oporto Factory." *Board of Trade Com. MS.*, Series II. Vol. DLXIII. No. 59.

[2] *Board of Trade Com. MS.*, Series I. Vol. LI. No. 25.

[3] Ibid. Series II. Vol. DLXIII. No. 59.

renewed in 1776 for another twenty years, and the feud with the English continued. In 1785, unable to gain their point by ordinary means, they attempted by combination among themselves to snatch the trade from the Company. The vintage of this year was especially full, and the price and quality of the wine proportionately lowered; circumstances, of course, favourable to the Company. All the merchants in the Oporto factory, save one, agreed together to offer a higher price than that permitted by law to the growers, and thus to buy up a larger quantity of wine than was legally allotted to them. They hoped to reimburse themselves by getting an extension of the demarcation, and obtaining from the Portuguese exporters some of the wines which the latter had bought. Several growers agreed to these illegal bargains, and the wine thus bought was in some cases guarded by men paid for the purpose, who came to blows with the Company's officers when the latter came to seize the wine. Consequently, there was a great disturbance, and the whole matter was brought into the court of the Relação. But Pombal was by this time out of power, and the government was leniently disposed. So the English were allowed to escape with their dear bought wine, the confiscation of which would have greatly injured the trade; and the Portuguese complained bitterly that the rigour of the law fell on them alone[1].

Two years later, when complaint was made of the engrossing of wine by the Company, the government again showed that they were favourably disposed to the foreign traders. The Portuguese engrossers were commanded to give up from one-third to one-half of the wines to make up the quantity the English required. To prevent engrossing in future, no sales were to take place during the

[1] *Board of Trade Com. MS.*, Series II. Vol. DLXIII. Nos. 80, 81, 87.

first three days after the Company had published its "edital" declaring the wine ready for sale; and subsequently all bargains were to be made in open competition. The English were to have half the boats on the Douro used for the transport of wine. In the matter of brandy, too, the government reduced the price in the English interest. The Conservador of the Alto Douro Company, who was thought to be unfavourable to the English, was dismissed. Altogether the English power seemed to be reviving[1].

The export trade in wine seems to have falsified the prophecies of the ill effects which would be produced by the establishment of the Company. It rose steadily from 1761, when 8,163 tuns of Portuguese wine, costing £202,840 were brought to England, till 1771, when the amount reached 11,554 tuns, worth £286,191. The latter quantity (and cost) appears fairly to represent the average English import per annum till 1785[2].

Despite these facts, the Oporto factory certainly declined after the establishment of the Alto Douro Company; but it is hard to say if the factory members were correct in their belief that the decline was entirely due to the baleful influence of that Company. The members of the factory lessened. In 1769 it included thirty-nine mercantile firms; by 1784 these had sunk to twenty-six[3]. Further, the number of ships coming to Oporto after the Company's establishment in 1756 showed considerable decrease; from 1748 to 1755, 1294 ships arrived; from 1756 to 1763 (inclusive) only 757[4]; but as the last period was that of the Seven Years' War, in which Portugal herself was at last involved, the

[1] *Board of Trade Com. MS.*, Series II. Vol. DLXIII. Nos. 80 and 81.

[2] Inspector General's Report. *Board of Trade Com. MSS.*, Series II. Vol. DLXII. No. 4.

[3] *Board of Trade Com. MSS.*, Series II. Vol. DLXIII. No. 2.

[4] *For. St. P. Portugal*, No. 64, p. 133.

evidence is not conclusive as to the ill effects of the Company.

Another external event, probably more injurious to trade than the establishment of the Company, was the revolt of the American colonies. Portugal showed her real desire for England's friendship by closing her ports to the rebels in 1776. But apart from this political demonstration, England, of course, lost the profits of the trade with America, with the exception of the Newfoundland traffic. Thus, the consul at Lisbon reported that American exports to Portugal in 1773 had amounted to more than twice as much as in 1785[1]. The case of the fish trade probably illustrates the extent of the injury. The accounts of this trade show that from 1765 to 1773, an average of about 7,500 quintals of cod was sent annually from the American colonies and Newfoundland to Madeira; from 1773 to 1785 it reached only 1,700 quintals[2].

The English shipping trade must have suffered also. Previous to the war, the Anglo-Portuguese trade had been chiefly carried on in English ships, but during the war Portuguese vessels took their place. In 1781 an Act was passed permitting imports from the Portuguese colonies to be brought to England in Portuguese vessels while the war lasted[3]. After 1784 the old state of things returned; but, for the time being, the loss to the English must have been considerable[4].

Otherwise, the effect of the war on Portuguese trade seems not to have been very serious. It was true that a considerable diminution of English exports to Portugal had taken place; but this had begun

[1] *Board of Trade Com. MS.*, Series II. Vol. DLXIII. No. 61.

[2] Ibid. Vol. DLXII. No. 2, etc.

[3] Anderson, *Historical Deduction, etc.*, IV. 398.

[4] *Board of Trade Com. MS.*, Series II. Vol. DLXIII. No. 2. Pombal had given special attention to Portuguese shipping. After the Seven Years' War, 300 English ship-wrights were brought over to work in the Lisbon dockyards.

previous to the war. The decrease was attributed to the action of the Brazil Company; but another possible reason was the growth of industries in Portugal itself. Pombal used every effort to encourage native manufactures, both by protection and by loans, and his efforts seem to have been so far successful that coarse linen[1], hardware glass, velveteen, cottons, and other manufactures were established in many of the coast towns[2]. The making of cloth also was now revived in Portugal.

From 1772 onwards, there was an increasing manufacture at Portalegre, and Covilhão, but the amount produced was so small, that as late as 1784 the consumption of Portuguese cloths in Lisbon was probably about one-tenth of that of foreign cloths[3].

The effect of these attempts could not, however, have been great; still the exports from England fell steadily. Instead of the average of a million which had been fairly maintained up to about 1765, the average from 1765 to 1770 is stated to be £675,717: from 1770 to 1775, £617,849: from 1775 to 1780, £609,436, and from 1780 to 1785, £621,998[4]; while the imports to England for the same period appear to have remained as a rule at a little over £300,000[5].

The whole volume of trade had thus sunk somewhat since the middle of the century; and this circumstance may have fostered the dislike to the provisions of the Methuen Treaty, which was now increasing in

[1] Anderson, *Historical Deduction, etc.*, IV. 394.

[2] See J. A. Smith, *Memoirs of Pombal*, II. 255, for a list of the industries to which loans had been made by the government. It is noticeable that an Englishman, Stephens, received a loan for the manufacture of glass.

[3] *Board of Trade Com. MS.*, Series II. Vol. DLXIII. Nos. 3 and 81.

[4] Ibid. No. 1. Other accounts (Series II. 424 and 562) would make the average for the latter period not very much above £500,000, but in their account the colonial trade is probably omitted.

[5] *Board of Trade Com. MS.*, II. 424; and *For. St. P. Portugal*, LXIV. 139.

England, as hatred of the Treaty of 1654 had long existed in Portugal.

To some extent, Pombal's measures caused a feeling of alienation among the English traders, not only in Portugal, but also in England. Portugal was thought to be treating England with great ingratitude in her attempt to secure her commerce for herself. Consul Hay declared that, during the Seven Years' War, England's help alone had preserved Portugal from falling a prey to Spain ; and these efforts ought to be requited by the maintenance of English privileges[1]. In 1767 a pamphlet appeared entitled "Occasional Thoughts on the Portuguese Trade," which urged the renunciation of the Portuguese alliance in favour of that of Spain. It was asserted that the balance of the Portuguese trade was by no means so favourable as was generally asserted. £300,000 was said to be the maximum of the bullion now actually imported into England ; an estimate which, if the Custom House accounts of the time are to be trusted, was not very much below the mark. The hindrance to trade caused by the various exclusive companies was energetically denounced.

It is plain that Portuguese commerce was falling from the high place it had long maintained in English esteem. Thus, when in 1776 Adam Smith in the chapter on Commercial Treaties in the "Wealth of Nations," selected the Methuen Treaty as an example of a convention in no way really advantageous to England, he perhaps had the stream of popular prejudice rather with him than against him. Many who might find it hard to grasp the general statement that the increase of the precious metals is not the increase of wealth, would probably be able to perceive its particular application in the case of the Anglo-Portuguese trade.

Hence, when in 1786 Pitt endeavoured to put Adam Smith's principles into practice by the famous

[1] *Board of Trade Com. MSS.*, Series I. Vol. LI. No. 25 (15).

commercial treaty with Portugal's great rival, France, there was no strong popular protest on behalf of England's old ally. As far as the letter of the treaty itself went, Portugal had no ground of complaint. A special clause excepted the Methuen Treaty from any infringement, and though the duties on French wines were to be reduced, a proportionate reduction was also to take place on liquors of Portuguese growth. But, despite this promise (duly carried out in the Consolidated Customs' Act of the following year), the treaty was held to mark a considerable change in England's relations with Portugal. Hitherto, hostility to France had been a ruling factor in England's commercial policy; and hence the products of France, wine, brandy, vinegar, and oil, had little opportunity of rivalling those of Portugal. Now, save in respect of wines, Portugal was no longer protected from the competition (commercial as well as political) of one of the greatest powers in Europe. Such being the case, it was not surprising that the opposition poured forth prophecies of the ruin of the Portuguese trade, and suggested that the alienation of Portugal might mean the loss of English power in the Mediterranean. Their protests were vain, however; and the upheaval of all international relations, consequent on the French Revolution, renders it impossible to guess how much truth there may have been in these forebodings.

CHAPTER VII

THE BRAZIL TRADE

(1786-1807)

Importance of Brazil trade—Rise of trade in cotton—Diminution of English exports to Portugal—Detail of diminution—Decrease attributed to Brazil companies—Establishment of companies of Grão Para and Maranhão, and of Paraiba and Pernambuco—Their constitution—English protests—Effect of companies on trade—Disputes between English and Pombal—Portuguese privileges in England—Complaints of England in Portugal — Consuls' Reports for 1783-85—English influence lessened — Balance of trade between England and Portugal changing—Balance affected by cotton trade—Development of trade—Great demand for cotton in 1791—Effect of cotton trade on commerce with Lisbon—Balance of trade reversed in 1791—Effect on rate of exchange — Effect on Anglo-Portuguese relations — French Revolution—Attitude of Napoleon—Invasion of Portugal—English intervention—Flight of the House of Braganza to Brazil—Anglo-Portuguese convention of 1807 —Conclusion.

FROM 1654 onward an important—according to contemporary opinion, a vitally important — factor in Anglo-Portuguese trade is to be found in the connection of Portugal and Brazil. It was at first, however, an underlying factor only. English merchants did not trade direct to Brazil: the chief product of Brazil was gold, which, though acknowledged to be essential to English trade, yet had frequently to be conveyed to England clandestinely, and with the connivance rather than the permission of the Portuguese government.

From 1760 onward, however, the Brazil trade becomes more and more prominent. First, the exclusion of the English merchants of Lisbon from their share in the trade is indicated as the cause of the diminishing commerce with England, and then the course of Brazilian commerce seemed to lead to the separation of England and Portugal. Then, about 1785, the development of the cotton manufacture in England contemporaneously with the growth of cotton in Brazil, created a fresh bond of interest between England and Portugal at the very time when, by the Treaty of 1786, the English government might appear to have repudiated their old ally. Finally, the French Revolution and the wars of Napoleon made Brazil the refuge of the House of Braganza, and at last induced the latter to consent that the Brazilian ports should be opened to direct English trade.

The diminution of exports from England has already been mentioned as one of the reasons for the acquiescence of English traders in the desertion of Portugal, supposed to be involved in the French treaty. This diminution occurred to a great extent in the most important of English exports, *i.e.*, woollen goods. From 1760-65 the average yearly value of these exports is stated at £622,422; from 1765-70 it falls to £446,815. In both cases it is roughly two-thirds of the total export[1]. This later level and this proportion continued to be maintained with fair regularity for about twenty years. A considerable increase of duties, which took place near the beginning of this period, may have had its share in lessening trade. Thus, in 1756, an additional duty of 4 per cent. was put on cod brought to Oporto, and another 2 per cent. in 1761. On cloth an additional 6 per cent. was first imposed at Oporto, and 4 per

[1] *Board of Trade Com. MS.*, Series II. Vol. DLXIII. No. 1.

cent. at Lisbon, and then an extra 2 per cent.—circumstances highly discouraging to trade[1]. But, in the main, the decrease in trade, and the decrease in the woollen trade in particular, was attributed by the English merchants at Lisbon and Oporto to the establishment of exclusive companies, and especially to the creation of the Companies of Grão Para and of Pernambuco[2] for exclusive trade with Brazil.

The establishment of these Companies took place in 1755 and 1756, nearly ten years before any marked diminution of English exports to Portugal took place; but during several of those years England was at war with France and Austria, and for a short period with Spain. Thus, the importance of the Portuguese market was increased in a way that may have counterbalanced the hindrances arising from the establishment of the Companies.

The constitution of the Companies shows what these hindrances were. The Grão Para and Maranhão Company, established in 1755, resembled the Alto Douro Wine Company, in that its ruling body was to be composed of subjects of the King of Portugal[3] (Section 2), and was to include a Judge Conservador, whose jurisdiction superseded that of all other tribunals in cases connected with the Company's trade (Section 7). No vessel of any sort was to sail to Grão Para or Maranhão, except in the Company's fleet (Section 20), while the Company itself possessed exclusively the whole trade, both export and import, of these two captaincies (Section 22). Privileges were also granted in respect of customs; wood, for instance, exported by the Company to foreign countries was to go free of duty. The Company of Pernambuco and Paraiba[4] was established in 1759 with similar privileges. And

[1] *Board of Trade Com. MS.*, Series II. Vol. DLXIII. No. 66.
[2] Ibid. Series I. 51-2.
[3] *Collecção, etc. Leis Extravagantes*, III. 436-65.
[4] Ibid. IV. 261-93.

thus the English were prevented from controlling the Brazil trade, and even from sharing it, save as members of the Company.

Their protests were vehement. That the establishment of the Company at all was a violation of the privilege of trading to Brazil, granted to the English by Articles 11, 12, and 13, of the Treaties of 1654 and 1661 was, of course, their main contention; to which, equally, of course, the Portuguese government replied by claiming the right to make whatever arrangements appeared best for Portugal[1]. Further, the Portuguese pleaded that the English right of direct trade with Brazil, for which the treaties stipulated, had been so long disused as to become void. The English, however, would by no means admit this, and the Portuguese replies neither prevented them from making the general objection stated above, nor from adding special complaints which serve to show the importance of the Brazil trade to England. Except the Companies, the English could not now find customers for their best goods, as no individual merchant might trade with Brazil[2], and thus the Portuguese traders outside the Company could take fewer foreign commodities. Hitherto, the English merchants had made a profit of 15 to 20 per cent. Henceforth this would be impossible[3]. Moreover, this limitation of trade made it harder for the English to collect their debts. These were usually paid on the arrival of the Brazil fleet. Formerly, individual Portuguese traders dealt with the inland traders in Brazil, but the latter would now be compelled to bargain solely with the Company which had, by Charter, a prior claim to all payment of debts. Thus the private trader would go unpaid, and the security of the English for the goods they supplied

[1] *For. St. P. Portugal*, No. 64.

[2] *Board of Trade Com. MS.*, Series I. Vol. L. No. 25; Series II. Vol. LI. No. 19.

[3] Ibid. Series I. Vol. LI. No. 22.

to them would vanish to the general dislocation of commerce.

Again, the Company was directed to prefer Portuguese goods to English for export, nor would it, being established by the government, export bullion, as was the case with the private traders. The bills of the Companies, too, were a source of trouble. Their payment was said to be delayed, and they were rarely paid *in specie.* Hence creditors, who were in haste, often had to recoup themselves by buying the Brazil Company's goods at public auction —a very unprofitable proceeding[1].

As to the effect of the Companies upon the Brazil trade itself, English statements were diametrically opposed to those of Pombal. According to a report of the Board of Trade, the Companies had resulted in Portugal's losing three-fourths of her Brazil trade. Previous to 1756 fifteen or sixteen ships had been annually employed in this commerce; by 1767 it was alleged that the Company of Grão Para sent out only three or four vessels every year[2]. Pombal retorted that the Brazil trade had increased; twenty vessels were employed in it, and the demand for English goods was greater than ever. Formerly, Brazil had been backward and uncultivated, with but little trade; now its resources were being developed to the advantage of English as well as of Portuguese commerce[3]. About twenty years after these statements, Consul Hort reported in 1787 that the Brazil trade was undoubtedly increasing, but that the English had no direct share in it, though English floating capital was still esteemed necessary for its maintenance[4].

[1] *Board of Trade Com. MS.*, Series I. Vol. LXX. No. 3.

[2] *For. St. P. Portugal,* No. 64.

[3] J. A. Smith, *Memoirs of Pombal,* II. chap. xvi. 56. In proof of the backward state of Brazil commerce, it may be noted that so late as 1791 Brazil merchants were said to be unacquainted with foreign bills of exchange. *Board of Trade Com. MSS.*, Series I. Vol. LXXIII. No. 95.

[4] Ibid. Series II. Vol. DLXIII. No. 2.

Pombal, however, was not content with rebutting the English statements. He maintained that the English themselves violated their engagements in their treatment of Portuguese traders. In 1768 this accusation elicited a report from the London Custom House, pointing out numerous privileges possessed by the Portuguese. They paid lower duties than any other nation. Cochineal and indigo might be sent to England from *their* colonies, while nothing might be received from those of France and the Low Countries. Goods from Asia, Africa, or America might be brought from Portuguese or Spanish ports if carried in English ships. Portuguese ships had the same export privileges as the English vessels, save in respect of trade with the English colonies, and various commodities, such as spices, tobacco, olive oil, etc., might be freely imported from both Spain and Portugal, but from no other country[1]. Such a list of privileges, though the English government made the most of them, looked somewhat scanty beside those claimed by the English in Portugal, and even after Pombal's fall the Portuguese government continued to use this inequality as a weapon wherewith to parry the English demands[2]. The dispute continued vigorously; first Lyttleton, then Walpole, were instructed to enforce the English petitions against the interference, not only of the Conservadors of the Brazil and the Alto Douro Companies, but of the officers of the Senado Board of Commerce, and of the Tobacco, Soap, and Cards Companies[3].

[1] *Board of Trade Com. MSS.*, Series I. Vol. LXX. No. 55.

[2] In 1781, for example, the Portuguese government urged that their subjects in England should be exempted from civil and military service, from all taxes except customs; and that no additional duties should be levied on Portuguese vessels, and that all Acts placing the Portuguese in England at a greater disadvantage than the English in Portugal should be repealed. *Board of Trade Com. MS.*, Series I. Vol. LXIX. No. 49.

[3] Ibid. Vol. LI. No. 25 (22).

The new regulations by which the Portuguese government at this time endeavoured to stimulate native industries were also a source of annoyance. In 1771 an "Aviso" was published prohibiting the introduction of new kinds of woollen fabrics, avowedly with the view of protecting the Portuguese cloth manufacture. Considerable perplexity arose over the definition of the word "new," and the English were energetic in denouncing the whole decree as an infraction of the Methuen Treaty[1]. In 1782 the publication of the new Book of Rates aggravated the dispute. About £23,169 were added by this fresh valuation to the duties annually paid on woollens as Oporto; cloth being estimated at 25 per cent. above its first cost.

On all these points considerable protests were raised, but as time advanced they grew more moderate in tone; and the consul's reports for 1783-85 show clearly that the English influence, not only at Oporto, but throughout Portugal, was still diminishing. At Viana, Caminha, and Figueira, the number of English mercantile houses had decreased. Only one existed at Caminha, three at Figueira, two at Viana. This diminution was said to be caused partly by the American war, and partly by the prohibition of particular goods. At Caminha, formerly the depôt for trade with Spain, all textiles had been prohibited, with the result that English trade with that port was almost annihilated. At Viana and Figueira, woollens were also forbidden, to the injury of English commerce, not only in these commodities, but in all others. In fact, thanks to these rules, English commerce was becoming more and more concentrated at Lisbon and Oporto. One curious result of this state of things was that at Viana, a native manufacture of hardware sprang up, which so increased that considerable quantities were sent from this city

[1] *Board of Trade Com. MS.*, Series II. Vol. DLXIII. No. 64.

to Brazil. The English, however, had no share in the commerce with Brazil, carried on by the smaller towns ; and the consul disavowed all knowledge of any illicit trade.

Of the smaller towns, Faro kept up a considerable trade with Gibraltar, exporting thither fuel, lime, bricks, fruit, etc. The legitimate returns were made in old pipes and iron ; but there was also a large contraband trade in Manchester and Birmingham goods. The salt trade of Setubal was chiefly carried on with Ireland. No ships from this port went direct to England ; but Portuguese traders to Ireland sold salt at a cheaper rate than the English merchants could do. The coasting trade at all these towns was said to have passed almost entirely out of English hands during the war[1].

It has, however, been shown that this diminution in the commerce of the English in Portugal occurred after, not before, the diminution in the direct trade between Portugal and England, which became so marked about 1765. This decrease, however, occurred in imports to Portugal, and not in exports from that country; in other words, according to the theory which made the increase of exports a test of prosperity, Portugal's position was improving, and that of England declining. Shortly after 1785 this process was considerably accelerated again, in consequence of the Portuguese trade with England in Brazilian goods. For several years this trade has been increasing ; gold was no longer the sole article in which the returns for English goods could be made. The export of Brazil wood was somewhat uncertain ; but that of indigo was increasing, and above all that of cotton. Its first export was stated to be in 1767, when about £6 worth was brought to England from Lisbon. For a considerable period this export seems

[1] *Board of Trade Com. MS.*, Series II. Vol. DLXIII. Consul's Report.

to have fluctuated greatly, but in 1769 it rose to £1,121; and in 1781 it had increased to £9,190[1].

Meantime, the demand for it was growing with the development of the cotton manufacture in England, which was so marked a feature of the latter years of the eighteenth century. In 1781 the manufacture of muslin was begun by the help of fine cotton from Brazil[2]. Even before the revolt of the colonies, little or no cotton had been obtained from North America. The West Indian Islands were not capable alone of supplying the increasing demand, though they were, of course, favoured by the English tariffs. By the Consolidated Customs Act of 1787, colonial cotton was imported duty free, while that from Brazil paid a penny per lb.; while in the Act of 1803, colonial cotton paid 8s. 4d. and all other cotton 12s. 6d. on each 100 lb. weight if brought in English ships, and £1, 0s. 10d. if brought in foreign ships[3]. From 1786 onward, the annual import, according to the accounts of the Lisbon factory, was between £150,000 and £200,000.[4] In these figures there may be some exaggeration. The factory accounts for 1786 place both exports and imports at a far higher figure than do the accounts for the same year[5] made up by the Inspector-General of Customs in 1787; but the fact of the increase seems to be undoubted.

In 1791 there was an increased demand for all Brazil produce in consequence of the failure of supplies from the French West Indies. Sugar was in considerable demand, and the price increased. Cotton was in still greater demand. It was calculated

[1] *Board of Trade Com. MS.*, Series II. Vol. DLXII. No. 4.

[2] Anderson, *Historical Deduction, etc.*, IV. 656.

[3] Geo. III., 27, cap. 13; and Geo. III., 43, cap. 68.

[4] *Board of Trade Com. MS.*, Series II. Vol. DLXIII. Nos. 116-21.

[5] This appears to be the case even supposing the Inspector-General's accounts to deal strictly with the Anglo-Portuguese trade, and to exclude entirely that of Ireland and America, Madeira, and the Azores.

that about 50,000 bags of Pernambuco cotton would be required at £10 a bag — the largest quantity yet imported from Lisbon. The price, too, was augmented; formerly cotton had been only 240 reis per lb.; now it reached 380 reis[1]. The year 1791 was probably an exceptional one, but the war with France must have tended to increase the trade with Brazil during the closing years of the century.

This growing Brazilian trade had one marked result. It completed that alteration in the balance of trade between the two countries which had long been slowly approaching. As early as 1773, to judge from the factory reports, the balance in favour of England was said to be due in large part to the exports from British America[2]. After the war, these exports, as has been shown, came chiefly from Newfoundland, and as the returns thither were exceedingly small—chiefly salt—the Newfoundland exports, together with the Irish trade, seem to have preserved the balance (diminished as it was) in favour of England.

An analysis of the accounts, however, shows that even this balance occurred chiefly in the trade with Lisbon. Since the growth of the wine trade, the balance of trade from Oporto had generally been against England. In 1773, if the factory accounts are correct, the balance was over £30,000, and it had increased by 1785[3]. As has been pointed out, the various prohibitions with regard to woollen goods, combined with the American war, had greatly injured English trade with the lesser Portuguese towns; and thus, when the development of Brazilian commerce caused a sudden increase of exports from Lisbon, the balance of trade between the two countries was completely reversed. In 1785 the balance of the

[1] *Board of Trade Com. MS.*, Series I. Vol. LXXIII. No. 55.
[2] Ibid, Consul Hort's Report, Series II. Vol. DLXIII. No. 52.
[3] Ibid. *MS.*, Series II. Vol. DLXII.

whole Portuguese trade, by all accounts, was in favour of England. In 1786 the balance against England of the Lisbon trade was stated in the consul's accounts at £174,240; in 1788-89 an increase in the export of woollens, and a drop in the imports of Brazil goods, reversed the case; in 1790 the balance once more turned to the Portuguese side. In 1791 it was recorded that London was sending gold to Lisbon, and Lisbon to Brazil[1]; and in 1792 the imports from Brazil, of which the bulk were cotton, were stated at £686,842, and the balance in Lisbon's favour was estimated at £255,432[2].

Consequent on this somewhat violent alteration was an increase against England in the rate of exchange. Through the greater part of the eighteenth century the rate of exchange for the milrei had been from 65 to 66 pence. With the increase of the export of goods from Portugal and the decrease in the export of bullion, the rate of exchange naturally rose. From 1786 there was a continuous increase. In 1788 the milrei was reckoned at 66½d., 66¾d. in 1789, 67d. in 1790, and 67½d. in 1792. This last was, however, only the nominal rate, the actual rate being stated at 72½d.[3]. This year, however, seems to have been altogether exceptional. In 1798, it was stated as a noteworthy fact that six years previously (1792) Portuguese coins (thirty-six shilling pieces) were actually returned to Portugal from England. By 1798, the intrinsic exchange value per milrei had returned to 67½d.[4]. But the startling fact that

[1] *Board of Trade Com. MS.*, Series I. Vol. LXXIII, No. 5.

[2] Ibid. Series II. Vol. DLXIII. No. 119. This balance was not entirely due to the Brazil trade. A recent item in the factory account had been the export of East India goods, especially tea. This may have been due to the action of Pombal in encouraging the English East India Company to trade direct with China through the Portuguese settlement at Maçāo, as the Chinese ports were closed against foreigners.

[3] Ibid. Nos. 70, 116, 119, and 124.

[4] 67½d. was the intrinsic value, but the cost of transport, etc., sunk it to 66.01d. Despite the alteration in the balance of trade, the

Portugal was now exporting coined money to Brazil in payment for cotton and sugar shows what a change must have come over the whole commerce of the country as plainly as does the diminishing export of gold to England[1].

Indeed, had the peace of Europe been maintained, it seems possible that Portugal might have reached something approaching commercial equality in her relations with her old ally. The manufactures established by Pombal, insignificant as they were, yet pointed to a certain possibility of independence. Moreover, for the first time in three hundred years one of the main Portuguese exports to England—cotton—was in the nature, not of a luxury, but of a necessary, and the demand for this necessary was so great that Portugal had no longer to rely on the jealously-guarded produce of her wines to pay for the other necessaries which she, in her turn, imported from England. Finally, the much dreaded French Treaty had not apparently caused any serious diminution in the Portuguese wine trade: 24,000 pipes were estimated as the amount of the English and Irish demand in 1790 for wines from Oporto, as contrasted with 22,626 pipes exported in 1785[2]..

Altogether, it was long since Portuguese commerce seemed so flourishing; she was, however, by no means free from her dependence on England. Even before the French Revolution forced her to a renewal of her old alliance, a commercial treaty was being negotiated between Portugal and England. Walpole, the English envoy in Portugal in 1790, reported that Pinto, the Portuguese minister, was favourable to the continuance of the negotiation. On the

smuggling of Portuguese money to England was still carried on in the Falmouth packets. The exceptional goodness of the Portuguese coinage at this time probably encouraged its export. (*Board of Trade Com. MSS.*, Series II. Vol. DXIV. No. 23.)

[1] *Board of Trade Com. MSS.*, Series II. Vol. DXIV. No. 23.

[2] Ibid. *MS.*, Series II. Vol. DLXIII. Nos. 21 and 110.

English side, the old complaint of over-valuation was put forward, coupled with demands for the reform of the Book of Rates, suggesting that a fixed duty should be paid on the value of each cargo, as declared by its invoice. The old English privileges in regard to the consuls and the Conservador were again demanded, and the old complaints brought forward with regard to the exclusive companies. The answers of the Portuguese government show a certain desire to assert their equality. If the privileges of the English had been violated, they should be restored. As to the Conservador[1], in 1791 a decree was issued giving the preference to his jurisdiction in those cases where English creditors were concerned. In the case of the wine trade, on the other hand, Pinto declared that he did not understand that the English merchants desired the abolition of the Wine Company, but only that they themselves should be supplied with as much wine as they needed, which he promised should be done. The Portuguese, on their part, claimed that their country should not be excluded from any favour granted to America (in reference to the Annual Shipping Bill), and that otherwise each country should be on the footing of the most favoured nation, in reference to commodities sent to the other[2].

Such demands on either side show that if the relations of the two countries had not essentially altered, yet the position of Portugal had somewhat improved; but the course of events in France soon made all commercial stipulations futile. Like the other rulers of Europe, the Regent of Portugal was filled with horror at the action of the French revolutionaries. He associated himself with Spain in her declaration of war against the French, and readily joined the system of continental alliance which Pitt was forming. The object of the Treaty

[1] *Board of Trade Com. MS.*, Series II. Vol. DLXIII. No. 121.
[2] Ibid. No. 105.

of London in 1793 was said to be the restoration of public tranquillity. In pursuit of this, Portugal undertook to close her ports to French trade during the war, and England in return promised not to make peace without Portugal[1].

From this time forward Portugal was helplessly involved in the turmoil of European warfare. In 1800 Napoleon compelled her to consent to the abandonment of the English alliance, and to the closing of her ports to England. Thereupon the English seized Madeira, which, however, they evacuated at the Peace of Amiens. On the renewal of the war, Portugal strove hard to maintain her neutrality, and above all, to avoid being forced into Napoleon's continental system — a measure not only harmful to her old ally, but ruinous to her; but Napoleon regarded her as a province of England, and was therefore resolved on her conquest. In 1807 he demanded that the Regent should not only close his ports to English trade, but should arrest the persons and goods of all English subjects in his dominions, and seize all English vessels in his harbours.

To the first demand the Regent unwillingly assented; to the second he demurred; it was contrary, he pleaded, to international morality. It was alleged that he wished to give time for the merchants to save themselves by flight; thus at the crisis of Portugal's fate, the old English factories appear once more upon the scene. The Regent's hesitation on their account gave to Napoleon the pretext he desired. A French army immediately invaded Portugal, with such promptitude that it arrived at Abrantes before its presence was known at Lisbon. Under the advice of Sir Sidney Smith, the commander of the English fleet in the Tagus, the Royal family saved themselves by flight, and leaving Portugal to the protection of

[1] Santarem, *Quadro Elementar*, XVIII. 425-40.

the English, departed to their great colony in Brazil[1].

Before leaving Europe the Regent made one more convention with England—a last attempt to keep up the old commercial alliance. By this, it was stipulated that a commercial treaty between England and the House of Braganza should be framed as soon as the Regent should be settled in Rio de Janeiro, and that the closing of the ports in Portugal should be the signal that those in Brazil should be opened to English trade. In fact, as far as England was concerned, a new Portugal was to be created in America[2].

With this convention the old commercial alliance between England and Portugal may be said to have practically ended. In that alliance Portugal at first had the advantage. Till 1580 she was England's political equal, and her commercial superior. But from the blow inflicted by the Spanish conquest, Portugal never fully recovered. To maintain her place among the powers of Europe she had continually to seek the assistance of her stronger ally. To requite that assistance, she was forced to grant to English traders commercial privileges far above those possessed by the Portuguese themselves. These concessions were the more easily exacted, because while English goods were to some extent necessary to Portugal, Portuguese commodities were merely conveniences to England. Thus year by year, Portugal grew weaker and more dependent, until the development of the Brazil trade improved her position—an improvement destroyed by the Napoleonic wars and by the subsequent civil strife in Portugal itself.

When peace was finally restored, the world was changed, and the character of the connection between

[1] H. M. Stephens, *History of Portugal*, 386-96; Oman, *Peninsular War*, I. chap. i.

[2] Santarem, *Quadro Elementar*, XVIII. 450-52.

the two countries changed with it. The independency of Brazil, the principles of Adam Smith, and the results of the French Revolution, destroyed the tradition of centuries. Hostility there was none; but the relations of England and Portugal as they existed before 1807 had passed away.

APPENDIX I

TRANSCRIPTS FROM UNPUBLISHED DOCUMENTS BEARING ON THE COMMERCIAL RELATIONS BETWEEN ENGLAND AND PORTUGAL IN THE MIDDLE AGES.

1. Royal warrant for the payment of a sum of money to two Portuguese merchants. August, 1258. (*Patent Roll*, 42 Hen. III. m. 3.) See p. 29.

Pro mercatoribus de Portigal. Rex, etc., sciatis quod tenemur Johanni de Godeselme Domyngo et Johanni Johannis, mercatoribus de Portingallia, in 30 marcis 10 solidis 6 denariis et obolo qui eis a retro sunt de 67 marcis 3 solidis 10 denariis pro 3535 libris ceræ ab eis emptis ad opus nostrum per manus, etc. De qua quidem summa pecuniæ assignavimus predictis mercatoribus 70 marcas recipiendas per manum Philippi Thesaurarii nostri de denariis mutuo receptis ad opus nostrum de Adomaro Wintoniensi Episcopo fratre nostro et predictas triginta marcas decem solidos sex denarios et obolum eisdem mercatoribus persolvi faciemus ad Scaccarium nostrum in quindena Sancti Michælis proxima ventura. In cujus, etc.

2. Safe conduct for Portuguese merchants in England. 1258. (*Patent Roll*, 42 Hen. III. m. 13.) See p. 34.

Pro mercatoribus regis de Portugalia. Rex omnibus, etc., sciatis quod suscepimus in protectionem et defensionem nostram . . . Roderigum Roderigi, etc. . . (and 6 others), mercatores illustris regis Portingaliæ, et homines res et omnes mercandisas suas; sicut quod salvo eant et redeant, emant et vendant, per totum regnum nostrum; faciendo justas et debitas consuetudines, mercandisas suas contingentes. Et ideo vobis mandamus quod eos manuteneatis protegatis et defendatis ita ut in litteris de protectione. In cujus etc. . . . duraturas, tam dictis mercatoribus quam aliis mercatoribus dicti regis in regnum nostrum cum mercandisis suis venturis quamdiu bona pax fuerit inter nos et regem prædictum. Teste ut supra. . . .

3. Letter from Diniz, King of Portugal, to Edward II., referring to the friendly treatment of English subjects in Portugal, and asking for similar protection from the English king for his own subjects. November 1308. (*Anc. Corr.*, XXXIV. 158.) See p. 5.

Dionisius, etc. . . . Edwardo, etc. . . . Vestræ regiæ celsitudini latere non credimus qualiter vestros mercatores vicinos de Bayona et alios dominio vestro subjectos cum eos in regna nostra venire contingerit sub nostra protectione defendimus et tenemus ita quod ipsi per terram nostram libere possint ire quo voluerint et redire et stare cum omnibus bonis suis et secure per nostra maria cum suis mercibus navigare. Et placeat vobis ut nostros mercatores et alios nostro dominio subjectos cum eos in terram vestram venire contingerit sub vestra protectione defensos similiter teneretis ita quod inter vestros et nostros pax et concordia servaretur prout hactenus extitit observata. Set . . . de novo plures mercatores et homines de terra nostra nobis graviter sunt conquæsti quod mercatores et vicini de Bayona ipsos interfecerunt et suis mercibus et navibus spoliarunt. Et dicunt quod nuper in portu vestro de Garnesey, nulla legitima causa ostenta, quandam navem suam combusserunt et mercatores suos socios interfecerunt et eos suis pannis et . . . mercibus præ oculis spoliarunt. Et firmiter credimus vos hæc penitus ignorare, nam si ad vos talia pervenissent non dubitamus quod vos velletis talia aborrere, nec pertransire velletis permittere impunita, immo potius exegeretis justitia, etc. . . . Quare vestram regiam celsitudinem attente requirimus et rogamus quod placeat vobis talia orrenda commissa corripere et punire, ita quod de vestro dominio subjecti contra nostros talia committere pertimescant, et faciatis nostris subditis de prædita restituere . . . ut vestris et nostris pacem et concordiam reformare ita quod sic nostri subditi in terra vestra, ita vestri subditi in terra nostra, stare et redire et per maria vestra navigare cum mercibus et rebus suis libere valeant . . . etc.

4. Petition from Piers Garcie and Martin Domynges, merchants of Portugal. c. Ed. II. (*Anc. Pet.*, 11866.) See p. 80.

Piers Garcie et Martyn Domynges marchaunts de Portyngal, qe come ils urent affrete la nef qe est appelle le Nicolas de Jarnemue et charges en le port de Loyre en Normandie de aveyr de peis et des vyns et des autres marchandises, e quant ele fust charge le mestre de la nef, qe ad nom Richard Wadetley, e ses compaignons lour promistrent daler en Flandres a descharger, e la devoient rescevoir £15 sterling pour fret de la nef. Et eux qi avaient bon vent e bon temps daler en Flandres maliciousement il pristrent le chemin vers Jarnemue, e mistrent a Dovre une partie des ditz marchantz a terre, e les autres amenerent ovesques eux contre leur volonte fesantz entendant a eux qe ceo fu le chemyn de Flandres. E quant il furent a Crikerslea pres de Jarnemue le mestre e les mariners sen alerent a terre e laisserent la nef a deux mariners e un garson, donc la nef ove les marchandises se perist par defaute de eux. E les marchantz sauverent partie de lour biens e les menerent a Jarnemue. E vindrent Symon seigneur de la nef e le mestre avant dit e firent arrester les petitz biens qe furent sauvez, cest a savoir le seigneur demandant la value de la nef e le mestre le fret. Le remanent de lour biens qe vient a la terre ce qe furent pris parforce en la nef a la montante de £600 sterling vindrent les gents du pais e empristrent chescun sa part. E vient Richard Cold mestre de la nef qe est appele le Peter de Westminster e ses compaignons e pristrent des biens de ditz marchantz a la montante de £200 sterling.

Par quoi prient les ditz marchantz pour Dieu qe remedie de ceste chose lour soit fet.

5. Petition from a Portuguese shipmaster bringing fruit from Algarve to England for an English merchant, c. 1371[1]? (*Anc. Pet.*, 10812.) See p. 88 n.

Julian Piers maistre de la barge nome la Christofre du port de Portugal, qe come la dite barge ore tarde estoit charge en Algarbe ove ffruyt, la quele ore apartient a William Barbour marchaunt de (Loun) dres pur venir ove ceo al porte de Loundres ou de Sandwicz a sa droite discharge, la quele barge ove les marchaundises susditz ore en sa venue est arrestez en la porte de Dertemuthe par les officers et ministres notre seigneur le roi en mesme la porte. Plest a vos tressages discrecions considerer coment si la dite barge ove les merchandises en icell ne soient plus tot deliveres hors darrest la vende de mesmes marchandises sera passe : la quele tournera graund damage et perde taunt al dit marchaunt come a dit suppliant et ces compaignons qe Dieu defende. Et sur ceo vous plese grauntier brief notre seigneur le Roi directs as tous ces officers et ministres esteantz en la dite porte de Dartmuthe eux comandantz e chargeant a disarrester et faire deliverance des ditz barge et les marchandises en icell saunz delay au fin qe mesme barge ove ceo puisse passer a sa droite discharge, pour Dieu et en service de charite.

6. Order to Philip de Courtney, Admiral of the West, to release certain Portuguese merchant ships, retaining only goods to the value of £232, 11s. 8d., to satisfy the claims of two English merchants. (*French Roll*, 48 Ed. III. m. 19.) See pp. 84, 93.

Rex dilecto et fideli suo Philippo de Courteney Admirallo flotæ navium nostrarum ab ore aquæ Thamisiæ versus

[1] It seems likely that there may be some connection between this petition and the arrest in Dartmouth of several Portuguese ships, for the release of which an order was issued, 6th December 1371. See folio 46 above, and Rymer (Record Ed.), III. 929.

partes occidentales, vel ejus locum tenentibus in portubus London, Suthampton, Dertemouth, Plymouth, et eorum cuilibet, salutem. Licet per consilium nostrum ordinatum existat quod navis Sancti Petri, unde Johannes Damaia est magister, navis Corporis Sancti, unde Johannes Geraldes est magister, navis Sancti Petri, unde Joh. Affonsi est magister, navis Sancti Spiritus unde, etc. . . . (twelve ships in all) . . . de partibus Portugaliæ per vos nuper arrestatæ una cum mercatoribus, magistris, mercandisis, et aliis rebus eorundem in dictis navibus inventis, dearrestentur; et quod iidem mercatores, etc. . . . una cum mercandisis et rebus predictis venire quo voluerint libere permittantur. Pro eo tamen quod Johannes Aubray et Willelmus Barret, mercatores civitatis nostræ Londoniæ, coram consilio nostro postmodum personaliter constituti corporalia prestiterunt sacramenta, quod diversa mercandisæ et bona sua ad valentiam £232, 11s. 8d. infra dictam terram Portugaliæ arestata fuerunt, et sub aresto hujusmodi ibidem adhuc sunt detenta, volentes tam predictis mercatoribus. . . . Portingaliæ quam prefatis mercatoribus nostris Londoniæ in hac parte fieri quod est justum, vobis mandamus quod receptis et retentis in manibus vestris sub aresto £232, et de mercandisis et rebus predictorum mercatorum, magistrorum, et marinariorum in navibus predictis inventis quousque eisdem mercatoribus nostris Londoniæ de dicta summa £232, 11s. 8d. pro mercandisis et bonis suis predictis sic infra dictam terram Portingaliæ arrestatis satisfactum aut aliter inde per dictum consilium nostrum fierit ordinatum, naves predictas dearestari et eas una cum mercandisis et rebus in eisdem inventis predictis mercatoribus, etc. . . . Portingaliæ per supervisum et testimonium dilecti servientis nostri ad arma Jacobi de Lyons liberari faciatis, etc. . . . Provisum quod si contingat dictos mercatores aliquas mercandisas infra regnum nostrum Angliæ vendere seu venditas exponere ipsi inde subsidium pro navigio supra mare juvendo[1] concessum et alia denaria nobis inde debita nobis salvant et si aliqua

[1] This is evidently the subsidy of the time for safeguarding the seas. A fresh grant of the subsidy of wools, etc., was made in 46 Ed. III., to last for two years from Michaelmas. Hall, *Custom Revenue*, I. Appendix, 225.

bona inimicorum nostrorum in dictis navibus inventa fuerint ea ad opus nostrum salvo custodiantur, ut est justum.

7. Appointment of Roger Elmham and Robert Lang to keep watch in Portugal for English merchandise brought over without a royal licence. June 1393. (*French Roll*, 17 Ric II.) See p. 54 n.

De scrutinio faciendo in partibus Portugaliæ. Rex, etc. Quia datum est nobis intelligi quod diversi mercatores regni nostri Angliæ et alii ligei nostri tam aurum et argentum in moneta et massa quam pannos laneos et alias mercandisas de eodem regno nostro usque Portugal ante hæc tempora in navibus eduxerunt absque licentia nostra speciali seu solucione custumæ et subsidii pannorum et mercandisorum predictorum et adhuc educere non desistunt, contra forman statutorum et ordinacionum inde editorum, nos de fidelitate et circumspectione vestris confidentes constituimus vos scrutatores nostros in singulis portubus Portugaliæ ad explorandum naves et alia vasa de regno nostro predicto ibidem venientia, et ad scrutandum[1] omnimodo mercandisas in eisdem venientes, ac litteras nostras de coketto earundem mercandisarum necnon mercatores et alios de eodem regno nostro ibidem cum hujusmodi auro et argento absque licentia nostra speciali venientes et ad Thesaurium et barones de scaccario nostro Angliæ de toto facto vestro in hac parte de tempore in tempus certificandum, etc.

---

[1] This vigilance is very evidently connected with contemporary measures affecting exchange in England. See 5 Ric. II. st. 1. c. 2, where the preamble states that great mischief had been done by the export of gold and silver. To avoid this, no exchange was henceforth to be made without a licence, on receipt of which merchants were to swear not to "send beyond the sea any manner of gold or silver." See also a statute of 1390, 14 Ric. II. c. 2, and a paper by Mr Leadam in *Trans. Roy. Hist. Soc.*, N.S. Vol. XIX. 280-81.

8. Petition from a Portuguese merchant in England complaining of ill-treatment on account of the debts of the Master of Santhiago, c. 1399? (*Anc. Pet.*, 10810.) See p. 88.

John de Lere de Portugale qe come ore tarde sicome le dit suppliant fust venus du dit roialme jusque a Sandewich en une nef nome la Barnabe de Bristoliæ charge des vins et autres marchandises sibien par le dit suppliant come par autres ces compaignons en suite la nief ove les marchandises a lour venue a Sandewich furent arrestus par John Broun pur la dette del maistre de Seint Jake en Portugale et Lourenco John Fogaca par longe tempe passe fait. Apres quel arrest le dit suppliant soi passa a Loundres pursuant de avoir les ditz nef et marchandise disarrestus, et a son venue a Loundres il fust arrestus et mye en prison al suyt du dit John Brown par longe temps, deins quele temps les compaignons du dit suppliant avoient harberges et mys en lostiel de John Stille de Sandwich ore mort (la femme de qi est marie a John Fairhead en Sandwych ore vivantz) certains choses et biens ci ensuiants opertants a dit suppliant cestasavoir 1 shipcheste ove 1 mantel, 1 chaperon a icell, lune moite noir et lautre moite vert en icell, 2 paire de chaux blanc et 2 paire de chaux de noir, et diverses autres choses et biens en icell, et 1 grand barell ferme ove une cerure, et 1 lyt, 1 peire des plates et autres choses en icell, et 1 cote furre d'agnell blanc, 1 paire botes, 1 paire des tablez pur. . . . 1 pair kemysez quex furent en autres chestes de ses compaignons des queux il ad les clefs; les queux biens toutditz sount en l'ostiel susdit des qux le dit suppliant null deliverance ne poet avoir. Par quoi pleist a vos treshautes sieurs graunter les tresgraciouses lettres notre tres redoute seigneur le Roi . . . al capitayn de Dovor . . . lui comandant de faire deliverer toutz les dits biens a dit suppliant sans delay, etc.

9. Proclamation of Henry IV. against unauthorised molestation of Portuguese merchants on account of the debts of the Master of San Thiago. February 1404. (*Trans. fr. For. Records*, Series II. No. 153, fol. 543.) See p. 91.

Henricus universis et singulis admirallis, etc. . . . Sciatis quod pluribus locis regni nostri Angliæ quidam naves, navigia et vasa ac alia bona et mercimonia de regno Portugaliæ pretextu marquæ et represaliæ, occasione quorumdam debitorum infra dictum regnum nostrum inter Magistrum Sancti Jacobi Portugalensis et Laurentum Johannem Fogate carissimi fratris nostri regis Portugaliæ ambassatores et nuncios speciales et nonnullos ligeos nostros ejusdem regni olim contractorum, ausu temerario ipsorum ligeorum nostrorum absque auctoritate et mandatis nostris factarum et captarum temporibus retroactis, arrestata et impignorata fuissent diversæque sentenciæ colore hujusmodi pretensarum marquæ et represaliæ late existant ut accepimus. Nos nolentes hujusmodi marquas seu represalias pretensas absque auctoritate nostra factas si taliter se habeant in regno nostro predicto aliqualiter tollerare vobis mandamus quod omnia et singula naves navigia, et vasa ac alia bona et mercimonia de dicto regno Portugaliæ infra regnum nostrum predictum colore aliquarum marquæ et reprisaliæ absque auctoritate sine mandatis nostris seu alicujus alterius potestatum ad hoc habentis sic factarum et captarum indebite arrestata si quæ fuerint sine dilacione dearrestari faciatis et illis ad quos pertinent restitui et liberari permittatis prout de jure rationabiliter fuerit faciendum . . . etc.

10. Letter from John I. to Henry, King of England, asking that a supply of corn may be exported to Lisbon. July 16th, 1413? (*Brit. Mus. Bibl. Cott. Vespasian*, C. XII. fol. 156.) [*Translated from the original Portuguese.*] See p. 59.

John, King of Portugal and Algarve, to the most high, noble, and excellent prince, our friend and cousin Henry, King of England and France. Most affectionate greeting to our cousin and friend, whom we love faithfully and sincerely, whom we prize above all other princes in the world, and for whom we pray that God may give him health and long life with highest honour. Most powerful prince, our much prized cousin, we hereby make known to you that Don John Vasques d'Almada, of our council, shall inform you of certain things of which we have spoken with him, concerning the great need for bread to be sent from your country to our city of Lisbon. We beg you to hear that which will be said from us on this subject, and to do what will please us very greatly, as we would do for you in a like case as soon as we should receive a letter from you. Most high, noble, and powerful prince, cousin, and friend, may God keep you in His care and safe keeping.

11. Petition for denization from a Portuguese woman who came to England in her childhood, with Beatrice, daughter of John I., Countess of Arundel. *c.* 1440? (*Anc. Pet.*, 4227.) See p. 17.

A tres honorables et tressages comunes de cest present parlement, supplie tres humblement Alianore la femme de John Hill del counte Doxenford. Que plese a vos tressages discrecions de prier et supplier a le haute et trespuissant prince le duc de Gloucestre et a les autres nobles pœrs spirituelx et temporelx du cest present parlement de emprier notre tressoveraigne prince le Roi de grauntier au dit suppliant quele poet estre denizon deinz ceste roialme, pour purchaser par ele mesmes ou par autre et auxi aliener, enheriter et estre endowe, si come un liege nostre sovereigne prince le Roi fait et face deins mesmes le roialme. Grantz consideration tres hounres sires qe la dit votre suppliant est neez en la pais de Portugal el continuelement el este demeurant icy del age de six ans tanques en cea en la compaigne notre dame Darundell, etc.

12. Safe-conduct from Alfonso V. for English merchants in Portugal, containing a clause providing for reprisals if necessary. January 26th, 1443. (*Brit. Mus. Lansdowne*, 190, fol. 6.) [*Translated from the Portuguese, and slightly abbreviated.*] See p. 93.

Alfonso, etc. Through our good friendship and ancient treaty with the King of England, our beloved brother, we secure all English merchants coming to our kingdom to trade, with their ships and the merchandise in them, so that they shall not be seized, nor dragged into lawsuits, nor be made to suffer any other harm or discomfort within our domain. Moreover we order the admiral and head captain of our fleet, and all the shipmasters and people of our kingdom, if they meet the English on sea, coming to trade, not to arrest, rob, or spoil them, nor do them any other harm. Also we command all the judges, justices, etc. . . . of our kingdom, and all others whom it may concern, to keep this charter and cause it to be kept, as is here set forth, by which the English are secured in coming, remaining, and departing, paying us our dues. But if any persons of the domain of the King of England shall do any harm to our subjects, from the first day of this month of January in this present year, it shall be set right as is just from the goods of those aforesaid (English) who come here to trade, if there be any of those parts whence come the said malefactors, etc.

13. Grant of privileges in Portugal to Nicholas Brown, an English merchant. 1448. (*Trans. For. Records*, II. 153). [*Translated from the Portuguese, and slightly abbreviated.*] See p. 67.

Alfonso, etc. . . . Nicholas Brown, an English merchant, living in Lisbon, has showed us letters from Duarte :—"To all judges, etc. . . . Wishing to show favour to Nicholas Brown, an English merchant, bearer of this letter, we privilege and grant unto him that henceforth he shall be exempted from paying any of our special taxes, grants, excises, tallages, imposts, services, and all other charges that may be imposed by us or our council; nor shall he serve by sea or land in any part whatsoever, nor in any labours at walls, bridges, fountains, or pavements, nor shall he keep arms nor a horse for our service, nor be guardian of any persons, nor perform any other offices of the council against his will. . . . Moreover, we forbid that any person shall be lodged in his house, nor take his bread, wine, clothes, straw, wood, hens, cattle, nor his beasts of saddle or pack, nor any other of his possessions, under a penalty of 6 milreis. . . . If any person transgress these commands, he is to be treated severely, as one who neglects to obey the royal mandate (1438)."

Nicholas Brown has now asked us as a favour to confirm these letters, which we hereby do as is set forth, and order all our judges, chief magistrates, and officials to see that our instructions are followed.

14. Safe conduct for an English merchant in Lisbon, with special exemption from reprisals. June, 1458. (*Trans. For. Records*, II. 153). [*Translated from the Portuguese, and slightly abbreviated.*] See p. 98.

Alfonso, etc. . . . Wishing to favour John Alberton, an English merchant, now in our city of Lisbon, for certain services we are receiving of him, and hope to receive, we hold him for ours, and keep him henceforth under our special protection, so that he may henceforth safely come, go, and stay in our kingdom, with the merchandise sent to him by his factors, and his ships bringing freights to this country, with the merchandise in them, and the merchants on board them. We also secure the merchandise which comes to John Alberton from other English merchants, that he may sell it and lay out the proceeds; nor shall any reprisals be made, nor any other damage inflicted, upon his person, goods, gold, silver, money, or jewels, in any part of our kingdom; nor shall he be sued for any wrongdoing, robberies, or deaths already caused, or that may henceforth be caused, to our subjects, by those of the King of England, though such may occur through discord between us and the English. But in whatever way we may have to proceed against the English, it shall not extend to John Alberton, nor his servants, nor ships, etc. . . . ; these shall be free and exempt, as though they belonged to Portugal; so long as they shall do no harm to our subjects, in which case those who do the wrong shall suffer, but not the others. This shall be kept for ten years, and for better surety we order these letters of royal protection to be given to him, to be kept henceforth, etc.

15. Revocation of all exemptions from reprisals hitherto granted to English merchants in Portugal. December, 1471. (*Trans. For. Records*, II. 154). [*Translated from the Portuguese.*] See p. 99.

Alfonso, etc. . . . Though there was peace between Portugal and England, certain English subjects, fearful on account of the harm done to the Portuguese by many English ships, for which they were unable to obtain compensation, asked for special safe-conducts, in order that no reprisals should be made on them, and that their goods should not be seized by those of our subjects who had been harmed. We have now been requested by certain cities, towns, merchants, and many others, that we would be pleased to see the rights of the case, and henceforth give no such securities, and withdraw those already given, because they cause great loss to our subjects; for the English ought only to be secure in our country, and treated as friends when they behave as such, and keep the treaty. We, hearing this request, took counsel upon it, and examined the said treaty, which we in no way wish to neglect, but are all the more in favour of its observance. Nevertheless, we hereby notify to all English subjects who hold our special safe-conduct, that from 1st January 1472 these are revoked as though they had never been issued. But by this withdrawal of particular safe-conducts, it is not our intention to prevent the English from coming to our kingdom, or being treated as friends while they are here, or receiving favours and liberties according to the said treaty. That the English may not be able to allege ignorance, we order these our Letters Patent to be published in their chapel of San Domyngos.

APPENDIX II

I.—TREATY BETWEEN ENGLAND AND PORTUGAL IN 1576[1]

Tractatus abstinentiæ et cessationis ab omnibus arrestis et sequestris atque mutui commercii sive intercursus mercium inter subditos Serenissorum Principum Elizabethæ . . . Angliæ, etc., Reginæ, . . . ac Sebastiani . . . Lusitaniæ ac Algarbiorum Regis, citra ultraque mari in Africa Domini Guineæ et conquestus navigationis commercii Æthiopiæ, Arabiæ, Persiæ et Indiæ, etc, pro termino annorum in infrascriptis articulis specificatorum inter Franciscum Giraldum . . . Serenissimi regis Lusitaniæ Oratorem apud Majestatem suam Serenissimam residentem et Franciscum Walsinganum . . . in privato . . . Consilio ejusdem Serenissimæ Reginæ Angliæ . . . procuratores et Commissarios ex parte dictorum . . . Principum sufficienti authoritate munitos et constitutos.

In primis . . . conclusum est quod erit cessatio et abstinentia ab omnibus arrestis et sequestris subditorum Serenissimi Regis Lusitaniæ vel suorum bonorum ac navium in Regno Angliæ et Hiberniæ per Serenissimam reginam Angliæ et ejus subditos, et quod ejusmodi abstinentia . . . initium cepit a decimo quinto die mensis Novembris proxime sequentis per spatium trium annorum deinceps.

Item, . . . conclusum est quod consimilis abstinentia . . . erit ab omnibus arrestis . . . Serenissimæ

---

[1] *El. St. P. For. MSS.*, CXL. No. 854.

reginæ Angliæ subditorum vel suorum bonorum ac navium in regno Lusitaniæ et Algarbiæ per Serenissimum Regem Lusitaniæ ejusque subditos.

Item . . . conclusum est quod post finem . . . dictorum trium annorum licitum . . . erit per spatium trium mensium prædictos tres annos sequentium subditis utriusque prinicipis discedere . . . cum suis bonis ac navibus a dictis regnis respective, si ante præfatum terminum trium annorum inter dictos principes bona et perpetua . . . pax . . . conclusa non fuerit.

Item . . . conclusum est quod infra sex menses post decimum quintum diem Novembris proxime sequentes fiet mutua liberatio et restitutio omnium bonorum mercium, pecuniarum, debitorum et navium subditorum utriusque partis, quæ ab anno Domini 1568 in utriusvis regnis seu dominiis detenta vel sub arresto et sequestro custodita sunt vel erunt, usque ad decimum quintum diem Novembris dictorum principum authoritatem quæquidem speciam suam conseruant et in alterius istorum principum potestate restant. Quorum uterque princeps quatuor utriusque respective bonos et idoneos qualitate alicujus publicæ viros constituent et deputabunt cum amplissima authoritate et potestate infra tres menses post decimumquintum diem mensis Novembris, proxime sequentis, conueniendi . . . et cum effectu determinandi de prædicta mutua liberatione . . . seu æqua compensatione, et quod illorum bonorum et mercium, quæ vendita vel alienata sunt, justa æstimatio Dominis suis reddatur. Vel æqua compensatione ea bonis utriusque arrestatis satisfiat. Quod si lis ulla de rerum vel mercium venditarum justo pretio oriatur aut de nummorum et monetæ æstimatione aut æris alieni debiti recuperatione res ad dictorum utriusque commissariorum judicium . . . referatur qui si ita illis neccessarium aut commodum videbitur, mutuo suo consensu, peritorum mercatorum consilio et auxilio uti poterunt ut res et rationes cum omni jure et æquitate inspiciant. Proque iis bonis . . . quæ forte suppressa vel quouismodo alienata fuerint per alterius regnis subditos sine . . . mandato alterius principis constituentur ab utraque parte recuperatores et judices qui jus cum omni celeritate dicent et legittime omni rimedio utentur aduersus eos qui contra Jus deliquerint.

Item . . . conclusum est quod si aliqui subditi alterius principis . . . fuerint damnificati non debet propterea per litteras represaliarum mercæ vel contra mercæ, debiti admonitionibus non præcedentibus in bonis vel personis ad petitionem damnificatorum impeti vel arrestari nec guerra ob id moveri, sed per principes unius vel alterius partis attentata ipsa debite reparabuntur. Et si aliter literæ de merca vel contramerca fiant, sint ipso jure nullæ

Item . . . conclusum est quod omnes et singulæ literæ represaliarum mercæ vel contramercæ per Cancellarias vel alias Curias dictorum Principum prius confessæ fuerint non exequentur, sed tenebuntur suspensæ usque ad dictum terminum ad hoc per prædictos Principes specialiter deputatum.

Item . . . conclusum est quod durante dicto termino trium annorum erit bona . . . amicitia inter dictos Serenissimos Principes . . . et quod durante eodem spatio trium annorum erit liberum commercium inter subditos utriusque principis ita quod . . . Reginæ Angliæ subditi possint . . . navigare et commercium exercere in Regno Lusitaniæ et Algarbiæ, et in insulis de Madera et de Azores, ac consimiliter subditi dicti . . . Regis Lusitaniæ possint secure et libere navigare et commercium exercere in regnis Angliæ et Hiberniæ.

Item . . . conclusum est quod neuter dictorum principum, auxilium vel favorem aliquem præstabit alterius principis notoriis rebellibus vel profugis . . . neque recipiet illos in suis regnis.

Item . . . conclusum est quod neuter dictorum principum consentiat ut in portubus suorum regnorum recipiantur Pyratæ et Corsarii qui latrociabuntur aut aliquo modo damnificabunt subditos utriusque principis.

Item . . . conclusum est quod præsens tractatus prædicto decimo quinto die mensis Novembris proxima sequentis debite ac mutuo suprascriptis regnis a prædictis Princibus publicetur.

Item, quia tractatus hic abstinentiæ et cessationis vigesimo nono die octobris in Anglia, jam plene conclusus est cum . . . utriusque conclusum sit a die decimo quinto proxime sequentis Novembris omnium arrestorum tam ex parte regni Lusitaniæ quam Angliæ deinceps fore cessationem et intercursum inter subditos utriusque jam dictorum Principum, dubiumque sit an certa hujus tractatus notitia hic in Anglia ad dictum decimum quintum Novembris publicandum ad dictum . . . regem Lusitaniæ commodum deferri possit, atque ea ratione subditis dicti . . . regis tempore oportuno minus fortasse innotescet. Propterea si ea occasione minister quispiam sive subditus dicti . . . Regis per nescientiam hujus presentis tractatus . . . quicquam attentauerit contra subditos . . . Reginæ Angliæ, qui hujus tractatus notitia et confidenter dicto decimo quinto Novembris publicanda, post dictam publicationem more merchandizæ in regnum Lusitaniæ commercii gratia commeaverunt. Prædictus Franciscus Giraldi . . . convenit quod sic ejusmodi quicquam contra subditos dictæ . . . Reginæ Angliæ attentatum fuerit ut prædicitur post dictum quintum decimum Novembris et ante publicationem dicti tractatus et conventionis in regno Lusitaniæ factam dictum . . . regem sine aliquo juris processu, nuda solum notitia . . . intimata ejusmodi factæ attentationis sive arresti in aliquem . . . subditorum dictæ . . . Reginæ Angliæ sive eorum . . . bona mandaturum ut plena et presens restitutio fiat omnium ejusmodi bonorum sic arrestatorum. Dictusque Franciscus Giraldi præterea conuenit ad majorem securitatem subditorum dictæ . . . Reginæ Angliæ, qui post dictum decimum quintum Novembris . . . in regnum Lusitaniæ se contulerint quod omnes et singuli dicti subditi . . . Reginæ Angliæ in Lusitaniam commeantes et hoc ipsum requirentes habebunt literas dicti oratoris in forma notificationis ut ea ratione magis tuti . . . esse possint.

Item . . . conclusum est quod uterque Principum prædictorum omnia et singula capitula in præsentibus articulis contenta per literas patentes manibus suis subscriptas et magnis sigillis suis sigillatas ratificabunt . . . et confirmabunt ipsasque literas ratificationis . . . in sex menses post datum presentum tradere tradive facient bona fide . . . et cum effectu. . . . Atque etiam omnia et singula præmissa uterque ipsorum fideliter observabit in suorum omnium præmissorum testimorum procuratore et Commissarii prædicti prædictum tractatum manibus suis propriis subscripserunt et sigilla sua eidem apposuerint vicesimo nono die mensis octobris Anno incarnationis Dominicæ millesimoquingentesimos septuagesimo sexto.

(Signed) FRCO. GIRALDEZ.
FRA. WALSYNGHAM.

Et ego Johannes Incent publicus authoritate Regia notarius, quia lectione subscripto et sigillato præsentis tractatus presens personaliter interfui ideo signum Notariatus mei præsentibus apposui dicto vicesimo nono die mensis Octobris Anno domini millesimo quingentesimo septuagesimo sexto in præsentia Magistri Valentini Dale, legum Doctoris unius Magistrorum Libellorum Supplicium supradictæ . . . Reginæ Angliæ, Petri Vaaspink et Matthei Fernandez testium ad præmissa vocatorum et specialiter requisitorum.

J. INCENT NOTARIUS.

II.—CHARTER TO THE MERCHANTS TRADING TO SPAIN AND PORTUGAL.[1]

Pro mercatoribus Hispanie.

Regina universis admirallis, capitaneis, castellanis, customariis, contratotulatoribus collectoribus custumorum et subsidiorum, custodibus portium maris et aliorum locorum maritimorum, Justiciariis, Escætoribus, Coronatoribus, maioribus, prepositis, Balliuis, constabulariis Provisoribus, et aliis Officiariis ministris et fidelibus viris quibuscumque tam infra libertates quam extra, ad quos presentes litteræ pervenerint salutem.

(Here follows a recital of the provisions of the charter granted by Henry VIII. to the merchants trading to Spain and Andalusia. September 1st, 1530.[2]

[1] *El. Patent Rolls*, 19. Part 8.

[2] Hen. VIII. 22, *Patent Rolls*, Part 2.; also see Hen. VIII. *Cal. St. P.*, 1st September, 1530, pp. 29, 98, No. 6654 (grants).

It contains no mention of Portugal. The present charter continues as follows:)

Quoniam prædictæ litteræ patentes . . . sic per prædictum præcharissimum patrem nostrum factæ . . . tam pro imperfectione earundem quam pro eo quod mercatores prædicti pro defectu plene et perfecte incorporationis nullam habuerunt potestatem . . . faciendi actus et ordinationes pro meliore gubernatione eorumdem non sortiebantur tam bonum et commodum effectum ut intendebatus. . . . Nos igitur rem publicam regni nostri Angliæ pari cum . . . progenitoribus nostris zelo . . . prosequentes . . . quod mercatores nostri et eorum successoron dictna regna. . . . Hispaniæ et Portugalliæ . . . pro mercatura frequentantes de cætero favore et gratia nostra speciali augeri et in exercitatione ejusdem mercaturæ deinceps proficere et crescere possint . . . ac pro aliis diversis bonis causis et considerationibus nos ad hoc specialiter moventibus de gratia nostra . . . ordinamus ac pro nobis heredibus et successoribus nostris per presentes . . . ordinamus . . . quod præclarissimus consanguinius et consiliarius noster Robertus Comes Leicestriæ, baro de Denbigh, etc., . . . ac dilecti et fideles consiliarii nostri, Jacobus Crofte miles hospitii nostri contrarotulator, Franciscus Walsingham, armiger, unus primariorum Secretarii nostrorum, Necnon Dilecti et fideles Subditi nostri, Henricus Cottame, Thomas Gresshame, Willielmus Wynter, Willielmus Allen, Leonardus Duckett, Johannes Ryder, Jacobus Hawes, milites, Thomas Blanch, Anthonius Gamag, Edwardus Osborne, Willielmus Kympton, Thomas Pullyson, Georgius Barne, Franciscus Bowyer, Thomas Starkye, cives et Aldermanni civitatis London, Henricus Sackeford, armiger, Thomas Duddley, armiger (and 196 more) de civitate nostra London mercatores, Robertus Shappey, Thomas Chester (and 74 more) mercatores civitatis nostra de Bristol, Johannes Peter, Willielmus Chappell (and 29 more) mercatores civitatis nostræ Exoniæ, Johannes Thornton, Jacobus Clerkeson (and 12 more) mercatores villæ nostræ Kyngestoune super Hull, Oliverus Lison, Humfrius Ryckthorne (and 22 more, including "Buttolphus Holder") mercatores in diversis civitatibus, villis et locis infra Hispaniam et

Members of Company.

Portugaliam residentes, Ac Johannes Crooke, Willielmus Sladeby (and 26 others) mercatores infra villam nostram Southamptom residentes, ac omnes et singule alie persone subditi nostri . . . qui communiter et usitate mercandizabant . . . in dictis Regnis . . . Hispaniæ et Portugalliæ seu eorum alter transportandi in eadem . . . mercimonia seu commoditates regni nostri Angliæ vel inveniendi seu apportandi aliqua mercimonia seu commoditates ex dictis regnis . . . in regnum nostrum Angliæ aut in alias ditiones nostras quascumque aut communiter usitate marchandizaverunt . . . in dictis regnis . . . Hispaniæ, et Portugalliæ . . . ante primum diem Januarii qui fuerit in anno ab Incarnatione Domini millesimo quingentesimo sexagesimo octavo et eorum liberi et apprenticii de cetero sint et erunt una societas communitas et unum corpus corporatum et politiquum de se in re et nomine habeantque successionem perpetuam perpetuis futuris temporibus duraturis per nomen presidentis, assistentium, et societatis mercatorum Hispaniæ et Portugallie et ipsos per nomen Presidentis, etc., et successores suos unum corpus corporatum et pollitiquum . . . per nobis, heredibus et successoribus nostris, incorporamus . . . per presentes. Et quod ipsi per nomen presidentis, etc., sint et erunt perpetuis futuris temporibus personæ habiles et in leges capaces ad habendum, perquirendum, recipiendum et possidendum terras tenementa libertates, privilegia, jurisdictiones, franchesias et hereditamenta cujuscumque generis nature . . . fuerint sibi et successoribus suis in feodo et perpetutate vel aliter ad terminum vite vel annorum. Necnon ad dandum . . . eadem terras tenementa et hereditamenta ac ad omnia . . . alia facta . . . facienda et exequenda per nomen prædictum. Et quod ipsi per nomen presidentis, etc., placitare possint et implacitari . . . valeant . . . in quibuscumque curiis et locis ac coram quibuscumque judicibus . . . ac ab personis et officiariis nostris . . . quibuscumque infra hoc regnum nostrum Angliæ seu alia dominia quecumque in omnibus et singulis accionibus . . . causis . . . et demaundis quibuscumque dictos presidentem, assistentes, etc., seu successores suos vel eorum juria, privilegia, res, terras, tenementa, bona, catalla vel negotia . . . tangentibus . . . cujuscumque sint generis . . . eisdem modo et forma prout alii ligii nostri

Name of Company.

hujus regni nostri Angliæ personæ habiles et in lege capaces placitare et implacitari . . . ac habere perquirere recipere possidere dare . . . valeant. . . . Et quod prædicti presidens, assistentes et societas et successores sui habeant in perpetuum commune sigillum pro causis et negotiis suis quibuscumque . . . agendis servitturum. Et ulterius . . . volumus . . . quod de cetero sint et erunt de Societate prædicta unus Presidens, quadraginta assistentes de eadem societate in forma in his literis nostris patentibus inferius specificata eligendi et constituendi. Et pro meliore executione earundem voluntatis et concessionis nostrarum in hac parte assignavimus . . . ac assignamus . . . dilectum et fidelem nostrum Johannem Mershe armigerum unum Societatis presidentem fore et esse primum et modernum presidentem ejusdem societatis volentes quod idem Johannes Mershe in officio presidentis ejusdem societatis erit . . . a data præsentium usque diem lune proxime ante festum Annunciationis beate Marie virginis quod erit in Anno Domini millesimo quingentesimo septuagesimo octavo et de eodem die quousque alius presidens de societate . . . ad officium illud profectus et juratus fuit juxta ordinationes . . . inferius in presentibus expressæ . . . si idem Johannes Mershe tamdiu vixet. Et insuper . . . per presentes concedimus præfati presidenti ac societati et succesoribus suis quod de cetero in perpetuum sint et erint de societate . . . quadraginta homines de melioribus et probioribus personis ejusdem societatis unde decem eorem ad minus erunt commorantes . . . in civitatibus villis et locis extra civitatem nostram London existentibus qui quidem quadraginta homines . . . vocabuntur assistentes et capitales consiliarii ejusdem societatis pro omnibus rebus . . . societatem . . . ac bonum . . . gubernationem ejusdem tangentibus . . . et quod sunt et erunt de tempore in tempus assistentes dicto presidenti seu ejus deputatis pro tempore existentibus in omnibus causis . . . eandem societatem tangentibus. Et assignavimus . . . ac . . . per presentes assignamus . . . dilectos nobis Jacobus Hawes militem, Edwardum Osborne, Thomam Poolyson, Georgium Barne, Franciscum Bowyer, Thomam Starkye, Aldermannos civitatis nostræ London, Ricardum Saltonstall, Johannem Spence, Thomam Aldersey, Ricardum Reynolds, Blaseum Saunders, Arthurum Dawbeney, Willielmus Wydvall,

Common seal.

Constitution of Company.

First President.

No. of assistants

Ten assistants to come from provinces.

First assistants nominated.

Anthemium Garrat, Willielmum Towerson, Christopherum Hodsdon, Thomam Wylford, Willielmum Hewitt, Johannem Heydon, Willielmum Massam, Willielmum Cokayne, Thomam Branbey, Ricardum Staper, Ricardum Venables, Johannem Hawes, Georgium Homes, Ricardum Goddard, Johannem Watt, Willielmum Salter, Ricardum Roughedd, cives civitatis nostræ London, Thomam Chester, Thomam Aldeworth, et Guillielmum Gyttyns, cives civitatis nostre Bristoll, Eustatium Oliver, civem civitatis nostre Exonie, Johannem Crooke, Willielmum Staveley, mercatores ville nostre Southampton, Johannem Barker, ville nostre Gypswich mercatorem, Johannem Thornton et Johannem Fawether mercatores ville nostre de Kingston super Hull mercatores societatis prædictæ fore et esse primos . . . assistentes . . . societatis prædictæ, sic continuandos in eodem officio quamdiu se bene gesserint in officio illo. Et ulterius . . . concedimus prædicto presidenti, assistentibus, etc., . . . et eorum successoribus quod dictus presidens . . . vel ejus . . . deputati ex assensu . . . prædictorum assistentium vel majoris partis eorundem ad tunc præsentium pro tempore existentium, nominare, elligere et constituere possint . . . ad . . . voluntatem suam de tempore in tempus aliquem vel aliquos in dicta societate esse presidentem vel presidentes suos in partibus Hispanie et Portugallie. Qui quidem presidens . . . sic nominatus et electus . . . una cum sex aliis directorum mercatorum de societate . . . pro tempore ibidem existente, Quos quidem sex mercatores dictus presidens . . . sic electus . . . pro suis assistentibus sibi . . . associabit ut assistentes in loco ubi dictus presidens . . . in partibus prædictis adtunc residebit . . . habebitque . . . plenam potestatem . . . gubernationis in dominiis prædictis infra limites sibi per prædictum presidentem assistentes societatis prædictæ residentes in Anglia præscriptæ . . . sive majorem partem eorundem . . . ac omnes et singulos mercatores subditos nostros . . . tam de societate prædicta, quam alios qui non sunt de eadem societate ac eorum factores, agentes et servientes exercitantes mercaturam in Hispania vel Portugalia et ad ministrandum ipsis . . . plenam . . . et expeditam justiciam in omnibus . . . suis causis . . . inter ipsos inceptis . . . in . . . dominiis Hispaniæ vel Portugalie ac pacificandum . . . et determi-

"Presidents" and assistants in Spain and Portugal.

nandum omnes et omnimodos questiones . . . et lites inter seipsos in aliquo dictorum regnorum Hispanie et Portugalie motas . . . pro meliori gubernatione dictorum mercatorum . . . et ad faciendum et exequendum omnia quæ per presidentem vel ejus deputatum et assistentes societatis prædictæ . . . vel per majorem partem eorundem . . . eis . . . mandabitur secundum statuta . . . dictæ societatis. Et præterea . . . per presentes concedimus præfato presidenti, etc. . . . et successoribus suis quod prædicti assistentes . . . sive major pars eorundem . . . de tempore in tempus perpetuis futuris temporibus potestatem . . . habeant et habebunt annuatim . . . in die lune proxima ante festum ascencionis eligendi . . . unum de se ipsis qui erit presidens societatis prædictæ pro uno anno integro tunc proxime futuro. Quodque ille postquam sic ut præfertur electus . . . fuerit in presidentem societate prædictæ antequam ad officium illud exequendum admittatur sacramentum corporale coram presidenti existenti ultimo prædecessori suo, si adsit in præsentia majoris partis assistentium ac societatis prædictæ . . . ad tunc præsentium ad officium illud bene et fideliter exequendum præstabit et quod post hujusmodi sacramentum sic præstitum officium presidentis societatis . . . pro uno anno integro tunc proxime sequente exequi valeat. . . . Concedimus prædicto presidenti . . . et successoribus suis quod si contigerit presidentem ejusdem societatis aliquo tempore infra unum annum postquam ad officium presidentis . . . ut præfertur præfectus et juratus fuerit, obire vel ab officio suo amoveri quod tunc et totiens bene liceat . . . asistentibus . . . sive majori parti eorundem adtunc presentium alium de seipsis in presidentem societatis prædictæ eligere. . . . Et quod ille sic electus . . . officium illud habeat . . . durante residua ejusdem anni sacramento corporale in forma prædicta prius præstando et sic totiens quotiens casus sic accidit. Et ulterius . . . concedimus præfato presidenti . . . et successoribus suis quod quandocumque contigerit aliquem . . . de prædictis quadraginta assistentibus . . . obire vel a loco suo assistentis absentare . . . quod tunc et totiens bene liceat . . . aliis assistentibus et sociis societatis . . . abtunc superviventibus . . . vel majori parti eorundem ad tunc presentium unum alium vel plures alios de communitate societatis . . . in locum

Election of President.

Oath of office.

Vacancies among assistants.

vel loca ipsius assistentis vel eorum assistentium sic mori . . . vel amoveri contingentis eligere. . . . Quodque ille . . . sic electus . . . præstito prius coram presidente et majore parte aliorum assistentium . . . tunc præsentium sacramento corporale erit . . . de numero prædictorum quadraginta assistentium societatis prædictæ. Et hoc totiens quotiens casus sic acciderit. Et ulterius . . . concedimus predicto presidenti . . . quod de cetero in perpetuum bene liceat . . . dicto presidenti seu ejus . . . deputatis . . . ac assistentibus et societate . . . de tempore in tempus in perpetuum seipsos convocare . . . curias et congregaciones totius dictæ societatis mercatorum tam infra aliquem convenientem locum infra civitatem nostram London vel alibi tam infra regnum Angliæ quam infra . . . regna. . . . Hispanie et Portugalie . . . quotiescunque et quandocunque dicto presidenti aut ejus . . . deputatis . . . pro commodo dictæ societatis . . . expedire videbitur. Et ulterius nos pro meliore gubernatione . . . societatis mercatorum . . . per presentes concedimus eisdem presidenti, etc. . . . quod idem presidens vel ejus . . . deputati et assistentes . . . et successores sui . . . vel major pars eorundem . . . de tempore in tempus deinceps in perpetuum . . . ordinare . . . possint . . . leges, pro bono regimine . . . societatis . . . dummodo eaedem leges et constitutiones non sint contrarie . . . aliquibis tractatibus, federibus, ligis, sive convencionibus inter nos . . . et aliquem principem sive potestatem initis vel ineundis tam pro bono regimine . . . dicti presidentis . . . et suorum successorum quam omnium . . . aliorum subditorum nostrorum . . . se intromittentium vel aliquo modo mercaturam exercentium in regionibus . . . prædictis . . . et hujusmodi . . . leges . . . sic . . . factas . . . revocare . . . de tempore in tempus quotiens illis vel eorum majori parti ad tunc presentium expedire videbitur pro eorum meliore gubernatione tam in personis quam in mutuis commerciis. . . . Et quod prædictus presidens et ejus successores vel ejus . . . deputati et dicti assistentes . . . vel major pars eorundem tunc presentium quotiens necesse fuerit dicto statuta . . . exequi et execucioni demandare possint . . . tam infra hoc regnum nostrum Angliæ quam infra dictas regiones . . . mandantes . . . et firmiter injungentes tam omnibus mercatoribus prædictæ societatis

Meetings of Company.

Ordinances.

. . . quam omnibus aliis personis quæ de dicta societate modo non sunt . . . et partes Hispanie et Portugallie pro mercatura frequentaverunt . . . quod in omnibus et per omnia dictis statutis et ordinationibus sint obnoxii et subjecti quodque erunt sub regimine . . . dicti presidentis et ejus . . . deputati et assistentium prædictorum . . . illisque morigeri et obedientes sint . . . in executione dictorum statutorum . . . sic ut præfertur fiendum.

Power of levying money.

Acetiam . . . per presentes concedimus præfato presidenti assistentibus et societati et successoribus suis quod . . . presidens seu ejus . . . deputati ac assistentes . . . habeant plenam . . . potestatem . . . imponendi et taxandi impositiones et pecuniæ quascumque summas tam super mercandisia in Hispaniam vel Portugaliam vel ad insulas ad dicta regna versus austram vel occidentem spectantes exportandis . . . quam super mercandisis extra dicta regna . . . educendis et super navibus quibuscumque cum dictis marchandizis onustis prout illis videbitur necessare . . . pro communi utilitate et sustentatione stipendiorum et aliorum onerum dictæ societatis. Et ulterius . . . concedimus dicto presidenti, etc. . . . quod si aliquis . . . societatis præmonitus . . . fuerit per officiarium . . . societatis ad . . . comparendum ad aliquam curiam conventus per dictum presidentem vel ejus . . . deputatos deinceps constituendum . . . non . . . comparuerit ad horam et locum constitutum vel si aliquis societatis vel aliquis alius ex hiis qui comerciis . . . in dictis Regnis utentur recusaverint solvere . . . impositiones . . . super marchandisis vel navibus suis . . . impositas vel si aliquis transgressionem aliquam fecerit . . . contra communem utilitatem, privilegia, vel libertatem . . . societatis . . . per presentes dictæ societati concessa vel contra aliquos statuta . . . (per)[1] presidentem vel . . . deputatos at assistentes prædictis vel eorum majorum partem in forma prædicta condita vel imposterum condenda vel sit . . . aliqui quicunque aliquo modo directe vel indirecte vel per modum querele aut aliqua alia quacunque cautela arte vel ingenio seu confederatione sive intelligentia cum aliquo principe potentate, vel magistrato alieno vel cum aliquo alienigeno attemptavere aut attemptare fecerunt . . . violare . . . hac nostra privilegia . . . vel aliquem articu-

---

[1] Omitted in MS.

lum in presentibus contentum dictæ societati etc. . . . concessis sive sit infra hoc regnum nostrum Angliæ vel alibi ubicunque, quod tunc bene licebit dicto presidenti . . . et assistentibus vel majori parti eorundem . . . hujusmodi transgressiones obstinationes (sic) et malefactores incarcerare et cuicumque Gaole . . . comittere et ibidem detinere absque ballia . . . quosque per dictum presidentem, etc . . . dimittetur . . . vel aliter per multam finem seu penam forisfactam secundum quantitatem delicti castigare . . . quemadmodum dicto presidenti etc, . . . ad tunc presenti visum fuerit et adjudicabitur. Et pro eo quod diverse persone subditi nostri in marchandizis . . . minime educatur sed omnino inexperte et ignari tam in ordine et rationibus mercaturæ quam in statutis . . . regnorum Hispaniæ et Portugalliæ ac in consuetudinibus custumis vectigalibus ac monetarum valoribus ponderibus et mensuriis in omnibus aliis que ad mercatorem spectant valde necessariis per eorum imperitiam multa inconvenientia . . . committunt ad offensio nem nostram et carissimorum fratrum nostrorum Regum Hispanie et Portugallie offensionem. Nos prædictis incomodis . . . obviare volentes et peritos, exercitatos et experientes mercatores in eorum legiti imo et honesto comercio juvare et premonere intendentes . . . mandamus pariterque prohibemus per presentes ne quis subditorum nostrorum . . . qui non sit vel fuerit virtute presentium de societate prædicta se aliquatenus intromittat in exercitum mercaturæ vel aliquo modo comercii . . . trafiquam aliquam exerceat in dictis partibus Hispaniæ et Portugalie . . . ab oppido Fontrabie in regno Biskaye per totum littas Hispanie et Portugalie usque ad Bassilonam nec etiam infra quascumque insulas adjacentes vel pertinentes ad eadem regna vel meridiem vel occidentem versus spectantes et qui non observaverint . . . omnes et omnimodas huiusmodi ordinationes . . . ac subditi et quemadmodum ipsi ejusdem societatis erunt vel esse debeant virtute . . . hujus nostre concessiones vel alicujus ordinationis . . . facte vel faciende per dictum presidentem, etc. . . . sub pena non solum incurrendi nostram indignationem seu etiam solvendi tales et hujusmodi penas . . . acetiam subeundi incarcerationem aliasque penas transgrediendi dicta statuta . . . dictæ societati debeas (sic) aliqua lege statuto consuetudine vel

Prohibition of ignorant traders.

Punishment of traders disobedient to Company.

ordinatione in contrarium inde in aliquo non obstante. Et ulterius . . . concedimus prædicto presidenti, etc. . . . et successoribus suis quod idem presidens, etc. . . . omnes et singulos subditos nostros . . . de dicta societate mercatonum Hispanie et Portugalie non existentes qui in dictis dominiis . . . aliquem mercaturam exercere contra unum et tenorum presentium in dictis locis . . . attemptaverint juxta statuta et ordinationes suas per fines mulctas incarcerationes aliasque penas rationabiles juxta eorum arbitrium coercere et ut ab hujusmodi attemptatis desistant cum effectu compellere libere . . . possint. Et quod omnes et singuli foris facta . . . collecta ac colligendum pro violacione seu non observacione alicuius actus . . . per ipsum presidentem seu ejus . . . deputatos facti vel faciendi erunt ad opus et usum dictæ societatis . . . volumus tamen . . . dicto presidenti assistentibus, etc. . . . quod ipsi et successores sui in societatem suam nullatenus admittent alicuius artibus mechanicum professorem vel artificem nec mercium quarum cumque minutatim venditores quos vulgo retalliatores patrie vocabulo nuncupatur minime tamen recusabunt in dictam suam societatem omnes alios mercatores assumere de alia mercatorum societate non existentes qui a dicto primo die Januarii anno domino millesimo quingentesimo sexagesimo octavo transportaverit aliquas merces . . . Angliæ in Hispaniam vel Portugaliam per viam mercaturæ . . . modo illi infra annum post datum presentium litterarum nostrarum patientium petierint . . . se admitti in societatem prædictam et tempore admissionum suarum eidem societati quinque libras legalis monetæ Anglie nomine finis ad usum dictæ societatis pendere voluerint et etiam coram dicto presidente vel deputato suo . . . tale et hujusmodi juramentum præstiterint vel in regno Angliæ vel in partibus Hispanie vel Portugalliæ ubi petenti societatem prædictum pro tempore et loco majus commodum et expediens videbitur de se bene et fideliter gerendo in Societate prædicta quale alii qui imposterum admittentur in dictam societatem ibidem tempore admissionum suarum prestare tenebuntur. Alios etiam quoscunque mercatores subditos nostros . . . exceptis preexceptis in dictam societatem absument et admittent qui istud petierunt et tempore admissionum suarum nomine finis summam decem librarum legalis monetæ Angliæ ad usum dictæ societatis solverint et supra-dictum juramentum . . . subierint et præstiterint (volumus tamen quod exceptione quacumque superposita non obstante alii etiam mercatores subditi nostri . . . de aliqua alia societate vel societatibus existentes in hanc etiam societatem admittentur dummodo id petierunt et tempore admissionum suarum finis seu recognitionis nomine tales et tantas pecuniarum summas realiter ad usum huius societatis solverint quales et quantæ ab admittendis per redempcionem in eam societatem ex qua in hanc transierunt solvi solent vel quovismodo et ex quibus vis ordinationibus solvi debent) subeundum et præstandum suarum admissionum tempore predictum juramentum modo et forma superscripta. Et præterea . . . concedimus prædicto presidenti, etc. . . . quod prædictus presidens, etc. . . . quemlibet dictæ societatis pro delictis . . . vel malo regimine commissis . . . contra aliquem actum . . . dictæ societate . . . factis sive . . . faciendis a dicta societate amovere . . . possint et quod omnes hujusmodi personæ sic amotæ vel exclusæ, extunc deinceps cum societate . . . prædicta cum mercature exercicio aut cum aliqua trafiqua mercandizarum ibidem nullatenus se intromittent. Et ulterius . . . concedimus prædicto presidenti, etc. . . . quod dictus presidens . . . assistentes . . . vel major pars eorundem habeant et habebunt plenam . . . potestatem . . . et ad eorum libitum de tempore in tempus . . . ordinare tot et tales officiarios et ministros tam infra civitatem London et in omnibus aliis locis regni nostri Angliæ vel aliorum dominorum nostrorum quam in dictis regionibus transmarinis . . . quot et quales dicto presidenti, etc. . . . videbitur expedire ad . . . levandum omnes compositiones . . . et amerciamenta de omnibus . . . personis tam de dicta societate existentibus quam de omnibus . . . aliis personis qui in prædictis regnis . . . Hispanie et Portugalie mercaturam exercere attempteabunt quique erunt condempnati et culpabiles inventi ob malum suum regimen vel delictum contra has litteras nostras patentes aut aliquod statutum, etc. . . . per dictum presidentem . . . assistentes . . . factos et editos. . . . Volumus etiam . . . quod quilibet officiarii seu ministri sic electi . . . habeat . . . potestatem pro defectu solutionis vel pro inobedentia si necesse fuerit apprehendere tam corpus vel corpora quam bona et cattalla, talem et huiusmodi trangressorem . . . tam in omnibus et singulis locis infra

Expulsion of Members.

Appointment of Officials.

Punishment of Delinquents.

regnum et dominia nostra quia quantum in nobis est in predictis partibus transmarinis . . . ubicumque invenire poterint vel poterit ea retinere et irrevocabiliter custodire donec ipsi et quilibet eorum satisfecerint vel satisfecerit pro suo delicto . . . vel aliter composuerunt . . . aut composuerit . . . pro eisdem cum prædicto presidente, etc. . . . Et insuper . . . mandamus omnibus . . . majoribis, vicecomitibus, ballivis constabulariis, ac omnibus . . . aliis officiariis . . . nostris . . . supportare . . . dictum Presidentem, etc. . . . et suos successores in exequendo dicta statuta . . . et ad puniendum . . . transgressores . . . quousque eis secundum penas et fines per prædictos statuta . . . constituta . . . seu imposterum constituendam . . . plenarie fuerit satisfactam. Et si contigerit dicto presidenti, etc. . . . aliquem vel aliquos dictæ societatis . . . vel aliquum alium subditum . . . nostrum . . . ad aliquam Gaolam . . . mittere ob aliquod delictum contra dicta statuta . . . commissum tunc . . . concedimus dicto presidenti, assistentibus, etc. . . . quod de tempore in tempus omnes . . . gardeani et custodes omnium hujusmodi Gaolarum . . . recipient in eorum custodiam et prisones omnes . . . personas sic sibi per presidentem, etc., missos et ibidem eos salvo custodient sumptibus . . . dictorum transgredientium . . . donec per dictum presidentem, etc. . . . elargandum . . . assensum dederint . . . et quod nec nos neque heredes vel successores nostri ullos modo remittimus . . . hujusmodi . . . transgressores ex prisona sub fide missione vel manucaptione sine assensu dicti Presidentis vel . . . deputatorum suorum . . . donecque iidem transgressores . . . in omnibus . . . satisfecerint prædicto presidenti, etc. . . . secundum statuta et ordinationes prædicta . . . et solverint tales tantas et hujusmodi fines . . . que et qualia per dictum presidentem, etc. . . . pro hujusmodi transgressione . . . solvere adjudicentur. Que quidem omnia . . . pene . . . erunt collecta . . . ad usum dicti presidentis, etc. . . . in perpetuum. Volumus insuper ac . . . mandamus ministris, ligeis et subditis nostris . . . quibuscumque qui modo sunt et imposterum erunt quod sint deinceps adjuvantes . . . prædicto presidenti, etc. . . . Nec non factores substitutes deputatos et servientes et assignatos suos et eorum quemlibet in exequendo et gaudendo præmissa tam super terram quam super mare de tempore in tempus quandocunque ipsi . . . ad hoc fuerint requisiti adjuvabant . . . Et insuper . . . concedimus et licentiam specialem liberamque et licitam . . . et auctoritatem damus prædicto presidenti, etc. . . . cuivislibet mercatorum societatis prædictæ et successoribus suis habendi et recipiendi et perquirendi eis . . . in perpetuum tam de nobis, heredibus et successoribus nostris quam de quibuscunque subditis . . . nostris aut de aliis personis . . . maneria, mesuagia, terras, tenementa, rectorias, decimas redditus, reverciones, servitia ac alia possessiones reverciones, et hereditamenta quæcumque que de nobis heredibus et successoribus nostris non tenentur in capite nec per servitium militare nec de nobis seu . . . de aliquibus aliis per servitium militare absque speciali licencia nostra . . . sive licencia dominorum . . . et quibus prædicta terræ et hereditamenta tenentur dummodo dictam maneria . . . seu alie possessiones . . . non excedant annum valorem centum marcarum per annum statuto de terris et tenementis ad manum mortuam non ponendis aut aliquo alio statuto . . . aut aliqua alia re causa vel materia quacumque non obstante. Et insuper . . . concedimus prædicto presidenti, etc. . . . et cuilibet mercatorum societatis prædictæ . . . quod hec litteræ nostræ patentes ac omnia . . . concessiones . . . et verba quecumque in eisdem contenta . . . adjudicabuntur . . . tam coram nobis et consilio nostro ac heredibus et successoribus nostrorum in stellata camera quam coram nobis . . . in banco nostro . . . coram Justitiariis nostris . . . de Commune Banco et coram Thesaurario et Baronibus Scaccarii nostri . . . et in quibuscunque curiis nostris . . . ac in omnibus aliis locis tam infra dominia nostra . . . benefice et magis graciose ac in favorem prædictis presidentis, etc. . . . et cuiuslibet ejusdem societatis ac servientium et apprenticiorum eorundem . . . et eorum cujuslibet ac præcipue in eorum maximum commodum et utilitatem et amplissine contra nos . . . aliqua prerogativa preheminentia lege consuetudine seu actu parliamenti seu aliqu alia re . . . quacunque inde incontrarium antehac hic ordinata . . . seu usitata in aliquo non obstante. . . . Volumus etiam ac . . . concedimus prefato presidenti, etc. . . . quod habeant et

Tenure of property.

habebunt hos litteras nostras patentes sub magno sigillo nostro Angliæ debito modo factas et sigillatas absque fine seu feodo aliquo magno vel parvo nobis in hanaperio nostro seu alibi ad usum nostrum proinde quoquo modo reddendo . . . Eo quod expressa mencio et in cujus rei, etc. T.R., apud Westmonasterium octavo die Junii per ipsam Reginam.

III.—PATENTS OF THE CONSULS-GENERAL, ILLUSTRATING THE GROWTH OF THE LISBON FACTORY.

A.—*Patent of John Chandler*, 1631[1].

. . . Charles, etc., greeting. Whereas we are given to understand how convenient and necessary it is for the good of all our subiectes trading with Spayne to haue some persons of judgment and experience that are able to gouerne and assist them in their just and lawfull occasions placed . . . as Consulles within the principall Port Townes of that kingdome and the dominions thereof. And whereas the nomination of the said person doth appertain unto us both de Jure nostro Regio and by the ancient treaties heretofore established between the two countries of England and Spayne. Now KNOWE YEE that wee upon the informacion that hath been given us concerning our trustie and welbeloved John Chandler Esq. that for his experience and sufficiencie he is fit to undertake that charge . . . have nominated . . . and doe by these presents nominate . . . him the same John Chandler to be for and to all our merchants, subiectes and people of England Scotland and Ireland and Strangers residing in any of these our saide kingdomes, their Consull Generall in the Kingdomes and dominions of Portugal from Camina Northward to Castro marin Southward on the Mayne, and the Islands of Azores, Madera, Porto Santo the Algarves,

---

[1] *St. P. For. Portugal*, No. 4.

and the frontier Townes in Barbary in so large and ample a manner and with as much power and authoritie as the Consull of any other nation residing in the said kingdome hath had or hath at these presents. To haue and to hold the said Consullship . . . during our pleasure. AND further know ye that wee . . . doe giue . . . unto the said John Chandler full power and authoritie to gouerne our said Merchants, subiectes and people in the . . . limitts aforesaid and to assist them their factors, Agents, and servants in any just occasions whenever they may have need of his Councell and Direccion as well in furthering their trade and commerce in these parts as by way of interposition to compound . . . all contentions . . . that may arise amongst them and may be conveniently ordered without any futher proceeding to Lawe. And also if any just plaint or grievance be offered to our Subiectes in those parts to endeavour by the seuerall magistrates there to redress . . . the same or else to advertise thereof from time to time both our principall Secretary in England and our Ambassador or other publique minister which shall be residing for us at the Court of Spayne to the end that such further order may be given in that behalf as shalbe requisite according to the weight and qualitie of the Cause. And for the better execution of the said office we doe . . . graunt unto the said John Chandler full power and authoritie to substitute and appoint in all or any of the ports and places within the said dominions of Prtugall . . . such . . . fitt and sufficient persons being our subiectes to be deputie Consulls or Assignes under him to assist him in the execution of the said office either in the place where he himself shall reside or in any other . . . places within the foresaid limitts . . . and also to . . . appoint such able persons being our subiectes to be Interpreters for our said Marchants and subjectes as he shall think fitt. And . . . if in case any of our said Merchants, . . . or other our Subiectes shall happen to dye in any of the Ports or places within the . . . dominions of Portugall . . . intestate, Wee doe hereby give full power . . . to our said Consull or his Assigns to seize . . . all the goods . . . of the said . . . persons so deceasing and the same to retayne in his custodie to the use and behoofe

Consul's powers.

Settlement of Quarrels.

Redress of Grievances.

Appointment of Vice-Consuls

Appointment of Interpreters.

Case of Merchant dying intestate.

of such persons as to whom of right the shall appertain. *Consulage.* And know ye also that for the entertainement and mayntenaunce of the said John Chandler in the execution of that service committed to him . . . wee doe hereby give unto him the said John Chandler full power . . . to leavy . . . in those parts over and besides the ancient allowance of One Duckett upon every shipp one fourth part of one in a hundred of all the goods . . . of what kind soever which shalbe carryed . . . from thenceforth during the continuance of these presents into any of the partes within the limits aboue mencioned by any of our subiectes or by or for any strangers residing in any our dominions in any ships, . . . either appertayning to any of our subiectes or in any other shippes . . . whatsoever, whether the said goods . . . be brought forth of any of our kingdoms . . . or from Newfoundland, France, Flanders, Holland, Italy, Barbary, Turkey, or any other parts whatsoever. . . . And our further will . . . is that the like allowance . . . be made to our said Consull of the fourth part of one in the hundred for all shippes and other vessells belonging to any our Subiects of any our kingdoms . . . that shalbe sould in any of the . . . *Method of raising Consulage.* domynions of Portugall. . . . And to the end that the said John Chandler be not defrauded of the meanes . . . intended to him and to take away all contencions . . . that may growe betweene him and our said subiectes and others residing within any our kingdoms . . . wee doe hereby expressly charge . . . all merchants, masters, owners and Pursers of any the Shippes aforesaid and others whom . . . it may concern that they . . . doe upon request shew forth to the said John Chandler . . . and assignes their books of ladings with the contents, marks, numbers and quantitie and quality of the goods so to be brought into any the Ports within the limitts aforemencioned and the names of the owners or factors to whom they are consigned. And our further will and pleasure is that our said Consull and his substitutes . . . shall . . . levy the said fourth part of one in the hundred according unto such rates as each kind of goods and merchandizes shalbe then valued by the officers in the Custom-house or Alfandigues for receiuing of the king of Spayne's Customes there. And wee do straightly charge . . . all our said subiectes and others residing in our kingdomes . . . that they . . . be obedient . . . according to our will . . . herein signified and that none of them presume either directly or indirectly to oppose . . . the same upon payne of our heavy indignation and such paynes and penalties as by the law of this our kingdom and our royall prerogative may be inflicted upon them. In witness whereof, etc.

Given under our Privie Seale at this our Palace of Westminster Two and Twentieth day of January in the sixt yeare of our raigne.

Patent of John Howe, 1634[1].

This patent contains the following points of difference from that granted to Chandler, which in general it resembles.

Merchants dying intestate.

And . . . if . . . any of our said Merchants their factors seruants or other our subjects shall happen to dye in any of the Ports or places within the . . . dominions of Portugall aforesaid, Wee doe hereby give full power . . . to our said Consull and his Assigns togeather with the Marchantes hereafter mentioned, to seize . . . all the goods of the . . . persons so deceasing calling unto him Two or Three of the sufficient Marchantes resideing in the same place that he with them may prize and make a true Inventory of the same and make true valuation of such goods as are perishable and dispose thereof by sale or otherwise, whereby the most may be made of them for the benefitt of whomsoever the may belong . . . unto and keep the said goods and provenewe of any that is thought fitting to be sould . . . in safe custodie until the said . . . owners shall give orders for the disposing of them. *Execution of Wills.* And if any soe dyeing make theire Will not haueing their heires, executors assignes or factors in the place. The said consul with such Assistants as aforesaid shall take possession of his estate making Inventory of the same . . . and keepe the goodes . . . until his heires . . . doe give orders for the disposing of the same or come in person to take possession of it. *Dishonest Servants, etc.* And alsoe that in case anie factors, Apprentices or Servants in the aforesaid Portes of Portugall

[1] *St. P. For. Portugal*, No. 4.

belonging to anie of our Subjects shall nott behave himself as he ought to doe but take such ill courses by keeping Companie or gameing or otherwise, whereby it may be feared that he will consume the goods in his power or dceiue his Master or whom he hath to deale for; That then . . . We doe also authorize our said Consull to call unto him Twoe, Three, or more Merchants resideing there . . . with whom he shall aduise concerning anie such person soe feared and upon theire approbation ytt shall be lawfull for the said Consul . . . to seize . . . all such goods and chattells as are in the possession of the said partie, making a true Inventorie of the same and shall keepe them in safe custodie untill the righte owners shall giue order for the disposeinge of them And the partie soe offendinge to shipp home for England by the first Convenient Shipp. . . .

Relief of Distress.

And alsoe that in case of our subjects by accident of Shipwracke Men of Warr or anie other disaster happen to arrive in anie of the said Ports of Portugal being destitute of friends and meanes to carry them home. . . . Wee do give full power to our said Consull and Deputies to call unto him a convenient number of the Merchaunts in the place where it shall soe happen and there to make a rate valueing everie one of our subiectes according to theire abilities and businesses wherebie a somme maie be raised to convey such persons for theire owne Cuntreyes. . . .

Thomas Maynard's Patent, 1660[1].

Consul Maynard's patent differs from the foregoing, in that the Consul's jurisdiction is now limited to Englishmen trading with *Portugal*; and the Consul is further described as "Consul at Lisbon and the other chief ports of the Kingdom." In other respects, Maynard's patent resembles that granted to Howe, save that the amount of consulage is increased, and that part of it is to be applied to the maintenance of a minister of religion. The clauses referring to these points run as follows:

Consulage.

". . . We do give . . . unto the said Thomas Maynard

[1] Chas. II. *Patent Rolls*, 12. Part 18.

full power to recover for his salary as Consul four crownes on every shipp either in the place where himself shall reside and in any other place . . . within the limits appointed him . . . And further . . . we grant to our said Consul . . . that it shall be lawfull for him to leavy . . . (. . . beside the said allowance of foure crownes on every shipp) one-half per cent or Ten shillings every hundred pound of all money goodes wages and merchandize of what . . . condition soever that shall be carried . . . during the continuance of this our grant into . . . the limits above mentioned by any of our subjects, or by or for any strangers resident in these our kingdoms in any ships . . . whatsoever. And our further will . . . is that the like allowance be made to our said Consul of one-half per cent. of all the freight made to Brazeele or the East Indies and on all ships belong to our Subiectes of their own kingdom or to any alyen or merchant Strangers within the same that shall be sould within the . . . limits aforesaid. Provided that our said Consull doe out of his said one-half per cent. hereby granted . . . allow to the minister that shalbe from time to time appointed to be resident at Lisbon the summe of three hundred Mil Reis Portugal money for his sallary, dyett and lodgeing which allowance shall commence from the time of the election of the said minister by our merchants residing in London." (The manner of levying consulage is the same as that described in Howe's patent; it is, however, also to be levied on provisions which paid no custom at Lisbon; and in this case, therefore, it was calculated on their market price.)

Appointment of Minister.

Patent of Consul Poyntz, 1715[1].

By 1715 the power of the factory at Lisbon, as opposed to that of the consul, had increased. This appears in the manner in which in patents of this period the consuls are directed to act in cases of intestacy, misdemeanour, and the relief of distress, by the advice of the factory, and

[1] George I. *Patent Rolls*, 1. Part 12.

through the factory's agents. Other changes in the manner of levying and of administering consulage appear in the following clauses, quoted from the patent to Consul Poyntz, which is typical.

Consulage.

"And know Ye also that for the . . . maintenance of the said William Poyntz . . . we do grant unto the said William Poyntz . . . that it may be lawful for him, or any other authorised by him to recover . . . for the duty of Consulage of the Masters and commanders of all ships that shall come into the Kingdom of Portugal . . . to lade or unlade the sum of twelve Mill Reis Portugal Money for each ship, except such ships as shall go thither to lade only Oranges Lemons and Salt, carrying out nothing but Necessaries for lading the same, which said ships shall pay . . . but nine Mill Reis for each ship. And no more to be recovered . . . of the several Masters . . . aforesaid.

Payment of Deputy-Consul.

Out of which Duties of Consulage Our said Consul shal allow and pay to the severall vice-consuls for their respective salaries the sum of three Mill Reis for each ship: And Whereas for many years past the merchants and factory our subjects residing in the City of Lisbon

Election of Treasurer.

have yearly elected one of their number as a Treasurer for Pious Uses to whom they have voluntarily paid three reis per mil upon the valuation of all goods in the Custom House or Alfandiga, for defraying the Charges of the Commerce and for Charitable Uses. And Whereas Three hundred Mill Reis per annum were formerly paid by the

Appointment of Minister.

Consul as a salary for the maintenance of a minister who was to have a Place provided in the said Consul House wherein he was to . . . exercise his Ministerial Function: And also whereas now the said Minister is to be paid as hereafter is provided, it is our Will . . . therefore that our said Consul shall constantly provide in his own house or any other House a fitting place for the said Minister at all times to exercise his Ministerial Function and for that purpose there to call together . . . all our said Merchants,

Collection of money for religious and charitable uses.

Factors, and subjects for the worship of God. We doe therefore alsoo give and grant to our said Consul with the Majority of our Merchants of the City of Lisbon full power and authority by these present to receive . . . from all our said merchants and factors residing there and from all Strangers our Subjects trading thither from our

Dominions as much mony as shall not exceed four reis per Mill upon the valuation of their goods in the Custom House or Alfandiga of Lisbon and for all Corn, Grains, Butter and other goods which pay no custom to the King of Portugal so much not exceeding four Reis per Mill on what they shall be valued at to be paid and recovered by such Treasurers as shall be annually chosen by him, the said Consull and the Majority of the Merchants and Factors in the same manner as the two Reis per Mill for pious uses were formerly collected out of which mony the said Treasurer shall pay yearly to the Minister residing there three hundred Mill Reis per Annum for his maintenance . . . and the remainder of the said Mony . . . he, the said Treasurer shall dispose thereof as he shall receive Directions from time to time from the said Consul with the Majority of the Merchants and Factors and at the end of the Year shall be accountable to the said Consul together with the Majority of the said Merchants and Factors and pay what mony shall be remaining . . . to the next Treasurer, who shall be so chosen to succeed him."

IV.—DOCUMENTS ILLUSTRATING THE TRADE IN WINE.

Table of Import of Wines into London from 1675 *to* 1696.[1]

Years.	French.		Portuguese.		Spanish.		Italian.		Rhenish.	
	Tons.	Galls.	Tons.	Galls.	Tons.	Galls.	Tons.	Galls.	Tons.	Galls.
1675	7,495	88	20	41	4,012	16	30	53	539	50
1676	9,645	11	83	103	5,094	126	15	51	465	112
1677	9,789	80	176	248	5,272	57	103	152	808	33
1678	7,212	2	199	206	5,654	6	129	108	1,451	183
1679	3	173	1,013	224	5,209	146	34	56	3,189	161
1680	1	126	1,003	99	8,420	221	82	138	5,958	209
1681	...	...	1,718	230	5,799	91	89	43	7,072	30
1682	...	...	13,860	201	5,448	193	101	129	1,743	138
1683	...	62	16,772	7	5,601	116	103	49	1,260	192
1684	...	...	1,611	108	11,285	181	71	51	1,302	163
1685	...	...	12,185	140	4,430	100	433	96	1,457	174
1686	12,760	237	289	59	4,193	222	57	26	812	101
1687	15,518	97	327	26	3,562	234	140	40	923	91
1688	14,218	171	540	205	3,251	222	282	104	884	191
1689	11,109	92	579	220	4,650	115	156	249	563	193
1690	755	162	1,115	174	4,605	34	8	103	664	76
1691	15	182	2,963	148	5,128	40	593	106	853	38
1692	...	...	6,052	236	6,625	29	107	141	1,290	40
1693	...	...	8,200	172	6,237	87	242	56	1,024	71
1694	...	...	9,459	18	8,623	247	110	34	880	240
1695	...	...	3,983	14	5,934	248	626	247	713	228
1696	...	...	6,668	168	6,619	176	142	200	448	162
Totals	88,525	226	88,822	23	125,662	137	3,661	216	34,309	93

[1] *Egerton MSS.*, No. 921.

CH. TOWER.
D. COLBI.

16*th May* 1713.

Account of quantities of Wine imported into London and Outports of England in sixteen years and a quarter, from Michaelmas 1696 *to Christmas* 1712[1].

LONDON.

Years.	France.	Portugal.	Spain.	Italy.	Rhenish.
	Tons. H. G.	Tons. H. G.	Tons. H. G.	Tons. H. G.	Tons. H. G.
[2] 1696 1697	184 0 18	4,260 0 61	6,935 0 10	332 0 0	396 2 62
1697 1698	1,439 0 34	3,621 0 29	5,931 2 60	775 0 0	693 0 45
[3] 1698	136 1 43	812 0 49	801 1 33	136 0 40	29 2 55
1699	228 2 15	8,017 1 53	8,233 3 45	2,454 1 41	512 0 52
1700	570 0 23	6,584 0 18	9,788 3 26	2,050 3 34	591 0 61
1701	1,732 2 47	6,372 3 53	8,477 2 34	1,288 2 4	669 1 21
1702	1,297 1 62	5,069 0 55	5,849 1 39	932 1 30	632 1 15
1703	156 0 13	7,425 3 6	334 2 27	1,044 0 37	697 3 21
1704	391 0 27	8,164 1 5	980 1 55	1,931 1 58	590 2 52
1705	679 2 17	6,006 1 31	1,661 0 38	1,255 3 53	399 1 29
1706	186 2 11	3,094 2 28	1,623 0 7	205 3 3	299 1 29
1707	733 0 52	7,072 2 5	1,363 1 5	1,229 2 16	522 1 12
1708	119 3 38	7,515 2 41	1,414 3 36	1,670 2 3	524 1 10
1709	302 2 53	6,168 1 32	2,356 3 38	880 2 6	486 0 35
1710	149 2 40	5,427 1 48	4,664 2 13	2,459 1 50	411 1 43
1711	606 1 18	5,811 1 14	3,487 3 61	1,008 2 15	466 3 44
1712	698 1 36	5,647 2 62	3,625 0 62	827 3 4	433 0 18
Totals	9,613 3 43	97,071 1 22	67,530 0 21	20,484 0 24	8,356 0 37

[1] *Egerton MSS.*, No. 921.
[2] From Michaelmas 1696 to Michaelmas 1697.
[3] From Michaelmas 1698 to Christmas 1698.

Outports.

Years.	France.	Portugal.	Spain.	Italy.	Rhenish.
	Tons. H. G.	Tons. H. G.	Tons. H. G.	Tons. H. G.	Tons. H. G.
[1]1696 } 1697 }	100 2 61	514 3 12	633 1 47	0 0 20	15 3 21
[2]1698	1,703 2 40	430 2 4	28 3 21	20 0 24	100 1 15
1698	31 2 43	3 2 44	286 0 39	2 0 59	5 2 33
1699	62 3 37	686 2 27	1,118 2 53	18 2 54	43 3 51
1700	94 1 17	1,073 1 33	2,492 3 42	32 0 56	121 2 53
1701	319 1 16	1,036 0 4	1,295 2 28	124 1 4	128 3 7
1702	387 3 25	857 3 54	562 3 13	157 0 11	66 2 14
1703	702 0 53	1,842 3 23	11 0 38	48 1 19	50 0 6
1704	905 1 12	1,763 1 46	314 1 40	34 1 49	43 1 4
1705	506 3 50	2,444 1 24	253 1 19	49 3 60	42 1 45
1706	335 3 49	1,543 2 0	273 1 43	70 0 8	30 0 28
1707	453 0 55	1,936 1 39	473 3 61	40 3 22	46 2 38
1708	215 3 22	2,118 1 55	824 3 13	22 1 10	45 2 31
1709	427 1 12	1,498 2 11	725 0 24	29 2 18	58 1 11
1710	263 2 57	1,285 1 33	1,250 0 0	81 2 7	18 1 36
1711	218 3 40	1,744 3 23	693 1 1	137 2 6	34 2 2
1712	308 3 38	1,056 0 49	1,028 0 23	21 3 17	11 2 32
Totals	6,939 1 59	21,836 3 40	12,266 3 44	891 0 3	863 3 49

[1] From Michaelmas 1696 to Michaelmas 1697.
[2] From Michaelmas 1698 to Christmas 1698.

TOTAL IMPORT OF WINE.

France.	Portugal.	Spain.	Italy.	Rhenish.
Tons. H. G.	Tons. H. G.	Tons. H. G.	Tons. H. G.	Tons. H. G.
16,553 1 39	118,908 0 62	79,797 0 2	21,375 0 27	9,220 0 23

PRINTED AT THE EDINBURGH PRESS, 9 AND 11 YOUNG STREET.

INDEX